Richard III

The King in the Car Park

TERRY BREVERTON

AMBERLEY

Many ... ...es of Llanllienan Professor
David ... ...lar for help in transla...ion, and
to Do...tor Edward Conley of Tair Onnen ...d Tony
Willic...mbe of Penarth for their continued su...port.

First published 2013
This edition first published 2015

Amberley Publishing
The Hill, Stroud
Gloucestershire, GL5 4EP

www.amberley-books.com

British Library Cataloguing in Publication Data.
A catalogue record for this book is available from the British Library.

ISBN 978 1 4456 4479 0 (paperback)
ISBN 978 1 4456 2111 1 (ebook)

Typesetting and Origination by Amberley Publishing.
Printed in the UK.

Richard III

'I have always thought the actions of men the best interpreters of their thoughts'

John Locke, *An Essay Concerning Human Understanding* (1689)

Contents

Preface: History is not Exact

There is no history, only fictions of varying degrees of plausibility.

Voltaire (1694–1788)

The bloody Wars of the Roses between the Houses of Lancaster and York virtually ended with the killing of Richard III. With the recent discovery of his skeleton, and the consequent dispute between cathedrals over the final resting place of these medieval relics, it is time to re-examine the life of Richard as a duke and king. Was he the grotesque usurper and murderer of the 'Princes in the Tower' (actually a king and prince), as depicted by Shakespeare just over a hundred years after Richard's heroic death in battle? Or has his name been blackened over the years, as claimed by the Richard III Society? This volume sifts the contemporary evidence, placing Richard in the context of his times, and assesses the likelihood of other candidates put forward to have killed the princes. In particular the life of the other major suspect, Henry VII, is compared to that of Richard.

History is not exact. It is not a science. History is full of uncertainties. Most nations' older histories have been rewritten by their conquerors or by writers responsible to rulers. Facts are blurred because of lack of knowledge, the fear of defying accepted wisdom and individual biases. Even events close to today – the supposed suicide of Dr David Kelly after the invasion of Iraq, the death of Diana, Princess of Wales, in Paris – create uncertainties. The recent death of Mrs Thatcher was generally regretted by those in the south of England, but not in many other parts of the country. She was admired by those who worked in financial services, but not by those in manufacturing. Her role in British history is seen as either a woman who smashed the unions and made Britain great again, or as one who killed off British manufacturing and sold British assets to foreign multinationals as part of a free-market dogma. There will never be a factual biography of Mrs Hilda Margaret Thatcher because our opinions and experience alter both writers and their audiences.

People are thus right to mistrust the accepted version of history. It is never clear-cut. Only in 2013 has the role of the British secret service in the murder of Patrice Lumumba in the Congo come under scrutiny. Only in the last few decades have we learned that Britain pioneered concentration camps in South Africa during the Boer Wars. Bishop Stubbs rewrote British history to give crucial importance to the role of the Germanic invaders, and his version of history is still taught across Britain. Stubbs glamorised the barbarian Angles, Saxons and Jutes in their genocide of the Christian Britons, in order to give legitimacy to the descendants of the fifty-eighth in line to the English crown, a minor princeling from Hanover, a country the size of the Isle of Wight.

England glories in its military history, especially against the old enemy, the so-called 'cheese-eating surrender monkeys' of France. This neglects the fact that over the centuries France has won more wars and battles against England. Anthony Charles Lynton Blair went to war with Iraq based upon so-called facts which have been proved to be demonstrably false. The once proudly independent BBC has over the years devolved into a semi-spokesman for the government of the day in order to protect its funding. Hospitals, schools, universities and the like manipulate facts to achieve targets that allow greater funding. Multinationals manipulate profits via transfer pricing and claimed domicile of head offices to understate profits and avoid taxation. Their facts are disguised and stage-managed for the benefit of the corporation instead of the state. True facts are difficult to establish in the present day, let alone for the past.

Historical facts are interpreted in many ways. A major problem is that historical novelists often stray from fact, to form a hypothesis which will in turn sell more books. Unknowing readers then accept these hypotheses as facts because most of the rest of the book follows the accepted version of events. For instance, one best-selling novelist has Henry VII raping his queen-to-be before their marriage in her latest book. Also, increasingly, non-fiction books are being 'sexed up' in order to sell more copies. When a non-fiction writer resorts to continuous derogatory adjectives and motives describing one king, say Henry VII, while his protagonist Richard III is a heroic warrior, loved in the north of England and who died gloriously in battle, one has to beware. The more adjectives there are in a non-fiction book, the more it usually betrays its author's biases. Pro-Richard writers blame his blackened image upon 'Tudor propaganda', with one non-fiction writer referring to Shakespeare as a Tudor 'spin doctor'. However, anti-Ricardian writing and rumour existed both before and in his two years as king and shortly after his death, not only in Britain but across the Continent. There is more to be unearthed, especially in foreign languages, and even in the former British language, Welsh.

Even with a track record of writing over forty well-received non-fiction books, some translated into Japanese, Polish and the like, it is increasingly difficult for this author to be published. There are fewer publishers, with many household names belonging to the same massive foreign multinationals, and increasingly fewer readers. Reading books has too much competition these days from electronic forms of entertainment, and younger people are happier with input being in short, easily digestible chunks rather than in the traditional format. The genesis of this book was my offering a series of books called *Bad Popes, Bad Kings, Bad Businessmen, Bad Politicians* and the like to the publisher. The commissioning editor knew that I had written upon the Tudors, and in the light of the recent finding of the supposed bones of Richard III in a Leicestershire car park, I was asked to write a biography upon this king. I began my research with hopefully no preconceptions.

Nothing is what it seems, even in the present day. There is a Richard III Society, and little will alter its many members' perception of the king. There has been a squabble about where his bones should be buried. There is being arranged a multi-faith ceremony in Leicester Cathedral for this Catholic king, with a £850,000 visitor centre and a £1 million tomb. Semi-hagiographies have been and are being written upon this last Plantagenet king. The object of this book, by describing the career of Richard, evolved to discover whether the king was a usurper and murderer, worthy of an exalted place in a cathedral. We seem to be returning to medieval times, with tourists (pilgrims) being attracted to pay to see holy relics, thus giving the Church and its environment an additional income stream. Roman Catholicism in Richard's days allowed one to go to Heaven if one confessed to one's sins and endowed the Church with money and/or estates. We know that Richard died bravely in battle, but he would have expected a wonderful afterlife in return for his grants to the Church. His wish for a royal burial has been achieved at long last.

There has been some cynicism about the circumstances of the finding of Richard III's skeleton. This was fuelled by some scepticism about the original scientific research and the lack of peer reviews. Then came the arguments over the entombment of the bones and the type of religious service required. With further research, I wondered if the car park bones deserved such reverence, and began with a *tabula rasa*, a blank canvas upon which to spread contemporary evidence about Richard III. Most modern writers, especially those of fiction, have veered towards the notion that Richard Plantagenet was maligned by his Tudor successors as monarchs of England. There are facts, untruths and allegations running together throughout every country's history, so this author simply tried to extrapolate meaning from facts. This is why it is so important to compare Richard III's career and reign to those of his successor. I find the evidence in the case conclusive about the nature of Richard, and will be attacked by other writers. However, facts are facts and I began this research with no opinion as to whether Richard was a black, white or grey king.

One element that strikes the dispassionate researcher is that Richard III's large army of supporters have tried to place any blame for any misdeeds upon his successor, Henry VII. The so-called 'Tudor propaganda' is said to have blackened Richard's legacy. However, Henry VII also has been treated oddly in history. Penn's latest, award-winning biography, *The Winter King*, makes a damning case against Henry, but it is mainly based upon the last decade of Henry's reign. However, we must remember that Henry was followed by England's most wilful king. Henry VIII had no wish to glorify his father, or remind the people that he was only the second in a new dynasty. In Henry VIII's time, writers concentrated upon the glory of the kingdom, as exemplified by the king himself. His father's achievements were ignored, and the men responsible for handing over a full treasury were immediately executed, to curry favour with the masses and the emasculated noble families. This was his first act as king, ensuring immediate popularity. While Penn decries Henry VII, there is also a case to be made for Henry VII being the wisest and greatest king of England, if we examine the facts dispassionately. Because his reign was sandwiched between two rather more colourful characters, Henry VII's contribution to England's development has come to be largely ignored in recent years.

The Wars of the Roses lasted three decades and were

effectively ended by Richard's death, with his successor establishing a dynasty widely regarded as encompassing the most glorious years of Britain's history. However, the snarled skeins of the familial rivalries of the Wars of the Roses, of the claims to the kingship between and within the great noble houses of York and Lancaster, form the backdrop to an understanding of the events of Richard's life. To surmise upon the balance of probabilities as to who killed the Princes in the Tower, we must examine the life of Henry Tudor as well as Richard of Gloucester. The synopsis of the wars and their participants will be necessarily brief, but hopefully will put Richard III and his vanquisher Henry VII into a factual context of those war-torn times. John Locke wrote, 'The actions of men are the best interpreters of their thoughts', and upon this basis the investigation leads to one conclusion.

Introduction: Fifteenth-Century England & the Background to the Wars of the Roses

This is an incredibly convoluted era of British history, with rapidly changing alliances of royal family members and nobles. It must be briefly addressed to have any understanding of the Plantagenets. War swirled across all of England and Wales for over three decades. Kings, princes and great magnates were killed or murdered, in what was basically a power struggle between the rival Plantagenet descendants of two sons of Edward III. Edward came to the throne aged only fourteen, when his mother Isabella and her lover Roger Mortimer, 1st Earl of March, deposed and disposed of his father Edward II. Aged seventeen, Edward III and a small party of men surprised his guardian Mortimer and executed him. Edward III then reigned from 1327 to 1377 and created the first dukedoms in Britain. However, when the king gave his five sons massive power in the form of their estates and resultant vast incomes, he sowed the seeds of a huge struggle for power between the houses of Lancaster and York – their family emblems being the red rose and the white.

These five sons of Edward III, in seniority, became the first dukes of Cornwall, Clarence, Lancaster, York and Gloucester. Edward III's eldest son, Edward, known as the 'Black Prince' (1330–76), was created the first duke in England, becoming Duke of Cornwall in 1337. Since this time, the title now traditionally goes to the first son of the sovereign, as does the title Prince of Wales. Upon the Black Prince's death in 1376, a year before that of his father, the dukedom passed to his nine-year-old son, who succeeded Edward III as Richard II in 1377. Richard II was murdered upon the orders of the Lancastrian Henry Bolingbroke (who became Henry IV) at Pontefract Castle in 1400. Aged only twenty-three, Richard II left no heirs, leaving the families of the dukes of Lancaster and York to fight for the crown.

In 1362, Edward III's second son, Lionel of Antwerp (1338–68), was created 1st Duke of Clarence. Clarence's first wife, Elizabeth de Burgh, gave him a single child, Philippa. Clarence was rumoured to have been poisoned by the father of his thirteen-year-old second wife Violante Visconti. Clarence's daughter Philippa Plantagenet married Roger Mortimer, 4th Earl of March (1374–98). Their son Edmund Mortimer, 5th Earl of March, became heir presumptive to Richard II, and this was the original line to the succession, albeit by a female line. However, Henry Bolingbroke, also known as Henry of Lancaster, then usurped the throne from Richard II, becoming Henry IV. Another Edmund Mortimer, the uncle of the heir presumptive, allied with Owain Glyndŵr and Henry 'Hotspur' Percy of Northumberland to attempt to put Edmund on the throne, but the rising failed in 1403 at Shrewsbury. In 1405 Edmund and his brother Richard were confined by Henry IV in the Tower.

In 1415, Edmund's brother-in-law, the Earl of Cambridge, conspired to take Edmund Mortimer to Wales and to proclaim him king, but this attempt was foiled. Cambridge himself also had a claim to the throne. Cambridge was executed for his part in what is known as the Southampton Plot, but Cambridge's son Richard of York became the father of Edward IV and Richard III. (Incidentally, Cambridge, the second son of the 1st Duke of York, may well have been the result of an illicit liaison between his mother and the Duke of Exeter, as he was left nothing in his father's will.) Edmund Mortimer, 5th Earl of March and the rightful king, died childless, of plague in Ireland in 1425.

John of Ghent (now known as John of Gaunt, 1340–99) was Edward III's third surviving son, and was created the 2nd Duke of Lancaster in 1362. The founder of the House of Lancaster, John acted as a regent to the young Richard II, and became one of the richest men in history. However, upon his death, his estates were declared forfeit and Richard II exiled Lancaster's son Henry Bolingbroke. Henry Bolingbroke later returned from exile and as Duke of Lancaster took Richard II prisoner, having him murdered and becoming Henry IV, the first Lancastrian king. This happened in the same year as John of Gaunt's death, 1399. Henry IV reigned until 1413, being succeeded by his son Henry V. The Lancastrian claim to the crown came from the male line, but in reality had been harmed by the usurpation of Henry Bolingbroke, Henry IV.

The fourth of Edward III's sons to be made a duke was Edmund of Langley (1341–1402). He was created 1st Duke of York in 1385, becoming the founder of the House of York. His son Edward, the 2nd Duke, died at Agincourt in 1415, and his younger son, Richard of Cambridge, became a Yorkist claimant to the crown, and was executed after taking part in the Southampton Plot. Cambridge was the father of Richard, 3rd Duke of York, and grandfather of Edward IV and Richard III. The Yorkist claim was based upon Philippa Plantagenet being senior to John of Gaunt, Duke of Lancaster. She was the daughter of the Duke of Clarence, Edward III's second son, whereas Lancaster was the third son of the king. However, her claim was weakened through passing through the female line, as Salic (Frankish) law against female inheritance was usually followed in England.

Thomas of Woodstock (1355?–97) was the fifth of the five male heirs of Edward III to survive to adulthood. He was made Duke of Aumale (Normandy) and 1st Duke of Gloucester around 1385, and was also first Earl of Essex and 1st Earl of Buckingham. Gloucester became leader of the Lords Appellant, who tried to wrest power from his nephew Richard II. He was murdered in Calais in 1397 upon the orders of Richard II, making the king extremely unpopular among his nobles. We can see from this cursory examination of the lives of Edward III's five ducal offspring that there would be several different claimants to the English crown.

Richard II, the son of the Black Prince, had become king in 1377. He was just ten years old and the grandson of Edward III. The boy-king's immediate problem was that he had three surviving uncles, the sons of Edward III – the dukes of Lancaster, York and Gloucester. More than any other factor, this was the seed of the Wars of the Roses. In Richard's early years, England was ruled by a series of councils mainly to prevent John of Gaunt becoming too powerful. Richard's reign was unstable, with John of Gaunt, Duke of Lancaster, leaving England because of plots against his person. Another uncle, Thomas of Woodstock, Duke of Gloucester, led a group of nobles including Henry Bolingbroke, the son of Lancaster, protesting against Richard II's coterie of favourites. At the Battle of Radcot Bridge in 1387, Gloucester's men defeated the royalist army of the Earl of Oxford.

Gloucester's followers, called the 'Lords Appellant', now virtually took control of Richard II's council and court, but later Gloucester was imprisoned in Calais, and murdered upon King Richard's orders in 1397. Richard II had thus killed one uncle, and another, John of Gaunt, died in 1399. Richard now took the huge estates of John of Gaunt's exiled heir, Henry of Lancaster (Bolingbroke). Henry Bolingbroke returned to Wales and captured and deposed Richard in 1399. The king was probably starved to death at Pontefract Castle by February 1400, and from 1399 to the early 1450s the House of Lancaster ruled England in relative peace. Most of the new king Henry IV's reign (1399–1413) was spent dealing with Owain Glyndŵr's War of Independence, where he led six unsuccessful invasions into Wales. Glyndŵr was joined by the captured Edmund Mortimer and the war did not end until 1415.

The second king of the House of Lancaster was Henry IV's son, Henry of Monmouth (1413–22). Henry V died of dysentery in France, aged only thirty-five. His son Henry VI (1422–61 and 1470–71) was only a few months old. Henry V's brothers, the dukes of Bedford and Gloucester, thus acted as Henry VI's first regents. Henry VI suffered intermittently from mental and physical inadequacies and had no children, which led to constant intrigue as to the succession.

With relative peace in England under Henry V and in the early years of the young Henry VI's reign, there was a series of arranged marriages consolidating greater and greater estates into fewer noble families. These marriages were often contracted between children, and titles could be passed from the female line to their spouses if there were no male heirs. The Mortimer earls of March, who controlled large swathes of Wales and its borders, were descended from Philippa Plantagenet. They intermarried into the Neville family, the earls of Warwick, who possessed huge landholdings in the Midlands, North and North West. In the east of England, the Duchy of Norfolk had been created by Richard II and its dukes became firm supporters of the royal family in the east of England. The Stanleys came to control large parts of North Wales and the north-west of England. The Percy family, dukes of Northumberland, had supported Glyndŵr's war against Henry IV and Henry V, but still virtually ruled the North East and much of the borderlands with Scotland.

Against this background of the immensely powerful Mortimer, Neville, Norfolk, Stanley and Percy families, Richard, 3rd Duke of York, came to be considered next in line for the throne. His father, the 3rd Earl of Cambridge, had been beheaded by Henry V in 1415 for his part in the Southampton Plot. However, Richard had received the title of his childless uncle, the 2nd Duke of York, who was killed at Agincourt in the same year. He also received the title and huge estates of another childless uncle, Edmund Mortimer, Earl of March, in 1425. Mortimer had been the heir presumptive to Richard II, and the focus of the Tripartite Alliance between his uncle Edmund Mortimer, Owain Glyndŵr and the Percys had been to place him upon the throne instead of the usurping Lancasters. Mortimer, the legitimate king, his brother and sisters were kept in custody for years by Henry IV and Henry V.

Richard Plantagenet, Richard of York (1411–60), had claims to the throne through both uncles, and their estates had made him the wealthiest man in England apart from Henry VI. He was 3rd Duke of York, 6th Earl of March, 4th Earl of Cambridge, and 8th Earl of Ulster. However, the House of York had lost political power under Lancastrian kings. In 1430 York was made Constable of England, and in 1432 he was appointed Guardian of the Coast of Normandy. In 1436 he was made Regent of France, advancing with an army almost to the gates of Paris. In 1437 York was recalled, but in 1440 was appointed regent to Henry VI again, holding office until 1445.

During his years in France, in virtual exile, Richard of York had spent thousands of pounds of his own money paying and feeding the garrison, as Henry VI had failed to support him. The Crown owed Richard around £40,000, or at least £30,000,000 in today's money. The income from his estates was also declining. York had been relieved in France by Henry VI's favourite, the Duke of Somerset, a grandson of John of Gaunt. The Lancastrian Somerset, in marked contrast to York, was advanced tens of thousands of pounds for his services to the Crown in France. York was appointed Lieutenant of Ireland in 1449, and was in relative exile as he watched the less competent Somerset surrender lands that had belonged to England for decades. It is thought that Henry VI wished to keep the more popular Duke of York out of England and France, where he might raise armies of loyal troops. After the fall of Rouen to France, the unpopular Somerset returned to England and was fondly welcomed by Henry VI.

However, popular discontent boiled over because of the French losses. In January 1450 Adam Moleyns, Lord Privy Seal and Bishop of Chichester, was lynched by discontented unpaid soldiers at Portsmouth. The bishop was an active supporter of William de la Pole, 1st Duke of Suffolk, one of the king's favourites and his chief councillor. Suffolk spent most of his time fighting the French and was Lord High Admiral. He had negotiated a marriage contract between Henry VI and Margaret of Anjou in 1444, which in a secret clause gave Maine and Anjou back to France. When this was discovered he became deeply unpopular. After losing most of England's remaining possessions in France, Suffolk was sent into exile in Calais. However, Suffolk was beheaded on a ship on his way to exile, it is thought upon the orders of Richard of York.

The House of Commons demanded that Henry VI returned grants of land and money that he had given to his favourites. In the Jack Cade Revolt, Baron Saye and Sele, Lord High Treasurer, was killed, and in September York landed at Beaumaris Castle, Wales, heading for London. He met with the king, but the violence carried on, with the king's favourite Somerset being put in the Tower for a short time for his own safety. However, Somerset was released in 1451 and made Captain of Calais. York realised that he did not have enough support among the nobility to take power, and retired to Ludlow.

In 1452 York marched with several thousand men to London. At Dartford the road was blocked by the king's army, and York demanded that Somerset be put on trial for his misconduct of the war in France. York also wished to be recognised as Henry's heir apparent. Assured by Henry VI that his wishes would be followed, York disbanded his army, but was arrested for two weeks, after which he swore allegiance to the king at St Paul's Cathedral. In 1453, Henry fined York's tenants who had supported him at Dartford, and York lost his offices including that of Lieutenant of Ireland. It seems that he had lost the power struggle for the succession. Queen Margaret was pregnant, and the marriage of Margaret Beaufort to Edmund Tudor gave another Lancastrian line of succession. At the end of 1452 the king had created his half-brother, Edmund Tudor, Earl of Richmond and endowed him at his expense. Henry VI's other half-brother, Jasper Tudor, had been made Earl of Pembroke earlier that year.

However, in 1453 Henry VI suffered a complete mental breakdown, possibly brought on by the defeat at Castillon, which drove the English forces from France. Also, upon 13 October, his long-awaited son and heir, Edward of Westminster, was born. Because of the circumstances, it was rumoured at the time that Somerset or James Butler, Earl of Wiltshire and Earl of Ormond, was the father of Henry's only child. There may well be truth in the rumour. In this same year, York's relatives the Nevilles had been in bitter dispute with the Percys in the north of England. We have noted that York's rents and income from land were also suffering, as were those of the Nevilles and Percys.

The great agrarian crisis of the late 1430s had affected their great estates in northern England far more than those further south. It led to a permanent fall in rents of up to 15 per cent in the 1440s, and in the early 1450s Richard Neville, Earl of Salisbury, and Henry Percy, Earl of Northumberland, were facing financial losses. Salisbury was in royal favour and managed to keep financially secure by his possession of royal offices and prompt payments from the royal exchequer. However, Northumberland spent proportionally more of his income upon fees to retainers and had great difficulty in securing royal payment for his garrison at the border town of Berwick. Royal favour was necessary for the earls, their sons and their retainers. The Percys began a campaign of violence and disorder against the Nevilles. In 1453 their armies actually faced each other at Sand Hutton before the Archbishop of York mediated.

The Nevilles' alternative to backing York in the power vacuum brought on by the king's illness was York's enemy, Edmund Beaufort, Duke of Somerset, also a kinsman. However, Somerset was in dispute with the Earl of Salisbury's son, Richard Neville, Earl of Warwick, over parts of the immense Beauchamp inheritance. York, with little political power among the nobility, now made a sensible alliance. Over the winter of 1453/54, the Nevilles decided to back Richard, Duke of York, in his bid to be made Protector of the Realm. York was Salisbury's brother-in-law, married to his youngest sister Cecily, and Richard Neville, Earl of Salisbury, wished to remain close to royal favour. The Nevilles stormed into Somerset's Great Council and demanded that the absent York be appointed as Protector of the Realm and Chief Councillor.

York almost immediately had Somerset placed in the Tower, while the Percys suffered at the hands of the Nevilles. Salisbury and Warwick were now committed to York's cause but in grave danger if Henry VI recovered, which he did at Christmas 1454. Somerset was then released and naturally allied himself with the Percys. York, Salisbury and his son Warwick could no longer command the council or court, and Somerset, Exeter and the Percy earls of Northumberland were restored to favour. The Yorkists were dismissed from their royal offices. This is the much simplified background to what we now know as 'The Wars of the Roses'.

In March 1455 York and his Neville allies, the earls of Salisbury and Warwick, fled from London. Richard Neville, 16th Earl of Warwick, proposed to raise an army in the Midlands and Welsh Marches to give the Yorkist faction the crown. In the war that followed, York and the Nevilles would be known as the Yorkists, while King Henry, Somerset, the Tudors and the Percys would be called the Lancastrians. Their respective flags featured the white rose emblem of the House of York and the red rose of the House of Lancaster. The main battles of the Wars of the Roses in the period 1455–71 demonstrate how unstable England and Wales were at this time, with shifting alliances and an increasingly bitter movement from chivalrous behaviour to battlefield executions of captured nobles. Of the seventeen major battles, the Yorkists won twelve, leading to the House of York taking power for fourteen years from 1471 until the unlikely final victory for Lancaster at Bosworth in 1485.

York and Warwick now led a force of about 3,000 on a march towards London. Upon 22 May 1455, the First Battle of St Albans saw a Yorkist victory. Henry VI had moved from London to intercept the Yorkists, halting at the fortified town of St Albans. Alongside him were Edmund Beaufort, Duke of Somerset; Humphrey Stafford, Duke of Buckingham; Jasper Tudor, Earl of Pembroke; Henry Beaufort, Earl of Dorset; Thomas Courtenay, Earl of Devon; William Neville, Lord Fauconberg; Henry Percy, 2nd Earl of Northumberland; Lord Thomas de Clifford and around 2,000 men. The king's army seemed to be expecting a negotiated settlement, as had been achieved at Dartford three years earlier. However, Warwick knew that his future was unsafe if Henry retained power, and made a surprise attack. The Lancastrian dead included Somerset, Northumberland and de Clifford. Dorset was injured and Devon and Fauconberg were captured. Jasper Tudor escaped the field. Warwick had ordered his archers to pick off the men around the king, so that Henry VI was captured unharmed. His queen, Margaret of Anjou, and her two-year-old son, Edward of Westminster, fled. Margaret of Anjou now took command of royalist followers in the north of England. Henry VI was escorted to London with York and Salisbury riding alongside him, and Warwick bearing the royal sword in front. Lord Fauconberg now switched sides to join the Yorkists.

Richard of York took over as Protector, guarding the enfeebled king, who appointed York Constable of England and Warwick as Captain of Calais. It was not in York's interest to kill the king at this time. As long as Edward, the infant Prince of Wales was alive, York would find it difficult to ensure a Yorkist succession to the throne. The king was held prisoner but recovered in February 1456, and York gave up his role of Protector. Salisbury and Warwick acted as councillors, and York went north to deal with a threatened invasion from Scotland. While Henry seemed content with the situation, Margaret of Anjou realised that York in power was a threat to her son's succession, and moved the royal court to Coventry, in the centre of her landholdings. She also gave royal favour to the Percys against the Neville cause in the North. In 1459 a Great Council was called at Coventry, but York, the Nevilles and other Yorkist sympathisers feared charges of treason and arrest. York and Salisbury raised armies, and Warwick returned from Calais, bringing troops to meet them at Worcester.

There had been attempts to agree terms between the rival forces, but Margaret of Anjou needed to finally put an end to Yorkist claims to the throne. She realised that the longer there were two rival factions, the more likely that her son Edward of Westminster, Prince of Wales, would not succeed Henry VI. Equally, Richard of York decided to act before his forces lost momentum. He decided to concentrate his troops around Ludlow Castle and then attack the Lancastrian army. During the march from Middleham Castle in Yorkshire to Ludlow, the Earl of Salisbury (Warwick's father), with 3,000–6,000 Yorkists, was unexpectedly intercepted by 6,000–12,000 Lancastrians under Baron Audley at Blore Heath near Market Drayton, Shropshire. Baron Audley died in the fighting, along with Lord Dudley and perhaps 2,000 Lancastrians. The Battle of Blore Heath was won by the Yorkists upon 23 September 1459.

The tide seemed to turn with a Lancastrian victory upon 12 October 1459 at Ludford Bridge. After Blore Heath, the Yorkist armies had regrouped at Ludford Bridge at the town of Ludlow and advanced towards Worcester. They fell back to the bridge when they encountered a much larger Lancastrian force led by Henry VI. The Lancastrians took up a position opposite the Yorkists across the River Teme, and the Yorkist army seemed disheartened at seeing the king's banner raised against them. They had believed the king to still be ill, and in need of York's support. They now realised that York was fighting against the king, rather than against his advisers. Andrew Trollope, the captain of the Calais contingent, switched sides after accepting the king's pardon, taking his troops with him to join Henry. In the night many Yorkist troops deserted, which led to a full-scale retreat the next morning.

Deserted by their leaders, the Yorkist army submitted to the king. Salisbury, Warwick and York's eldest son, Edward, Earl of March escaped to join Warwick's loyal garrison left behind at Calais. York with his son Edmund, Duke of Rutland, fled to Wales and then to Ireland, where the Parliament of Ireland still backed him. His wife Cecily Neville, and their younger sons George and Richard (the future Richard III) were taken from Ludlow Castle to imprisonment in Coventry. Things looked black for York, but the rapacity of the Lancastrians at court and across the land led to popular support waning.

From Calais, Warwick controlled the English Channel, spreading propaganda that York was loyal to the king, and only wanted his councillors to be punished. In December 1459, York, Warwick and Salisbury suffered attainder, the most extreme punishment for a noble. They were to be executed for treason if caught. Their lands were confiscated and their heirs were not to succeed to their titles or lands. York was in the same situation as had been Henry Bolingbroke, John of Ghent's son, sixty years earlier. He could either hide for the rest of his life, or take the crown on behalf of himself or one of his sons. York was still in Ireland when a Yorkist force under the Earl of Salisbury, his son the Earl of Warwick and Edward, Earl of March (the future Edward IV), sailed from Calais, landing at Sandwich. The men of Kent joined their small band. Warwick controlled the lucrative trade of the London wool merchants through Calais, and London welcomed the invasion.

Warwick next marched north to attack the Lancastrian army, which was marching south from Coventry. The Lancastrians stopped at Northampton to build up a defensive position. When Warwick arrived he spent many hours trying to contact Henry VI and negotiate a settlement, but this was refused by the Duke of Buckingham. Upon 10 July 1460, the 10,000-strong Yorkist army then attacked 5,000 Lancastrians. During the middle of the battle, Lord Grey of Ruthin, who was commanding a wing of the king's army, switched sides to the Yorkists, deciding the outcome of the battle. Warwick and March had secretly arranged before the battle that Grey's troops were not to be attacked, and Grey's men laid down their arms, allowing the Yorkists access to the royal camp. The Lancastrian Duke of Buckingham, the Earl of Shrewsbury, Lord Egremont and Lord Beaumont were killed trying to prevent the king's capture.

Henry VI was now again under Yorkist control. Two months after the battle, upon 9 September, York landed in Chester from Ireland, and made his way to London. He marched under the arms of his wife's great-great-grandfather Lionel, Duke of Clarence. York entered London displaying a banner of the coat of arms of England, signifying his royal descent. In Parliament, he attempted to claim the throne, but was met with silence, as even his allies were not prepared to support such a step. Instead, the House of Lords passed an Act of Accord, by which Henry VI would remain king, but York would again govern the country as Lord Protector. Henry's son Edward of Westminster (also known as Edward of Lancaster) was disinherited, and York or his heirs would become king upon Henry's death. In November 1460, the king was forced to accept that the York and his sons were the rightful heirs to the crown. However, Margaret of Anjou was with Jasper Tudor assembling an army in Wales, in order to continue the fight for her son Edward of Westminster to be king. She was also in contact with James II of Scotland, asking him to invade England.

After Northampton, Queen Margaret and her seven-year-old son Prince Edward had fled from Eccleshall Castle in Warwickshire to Harlech Castle, being joined by Lancastrian nobles including Henry VI's half-brother Jasper Tudor, 1st Earl of Pembroke, and Henry Holland, Duke of Exeter. In the north of England, the Earl of Northumberland, John Neville of Raby, Lord Roos and Lord Clifford also rallied Lancastrian forces. They were joined by the Duke of Somerset and the Earl of Devon, with troops from the West Country. The fathers of Northumberland, Clifford and Somerset had all been killed five years earlier at the First Battle of St Albans.

The Northern Lancastrian forces, perhaps numbering

15,000 men, met near Kingston-upon-Hull and began pillaging York's and Salisbury's estates. York quickly despatched his son Edward to the Welsh Marches to contain Jasper Tudor's Lancastrians in Wales, leaving Warwick in charge in London. York marched north accompanied by his second son Edmund, Earl of Rutland, and Salisbury. His force may have been small, as he intended to raise troops in his Northern heartlands. However, the City of York was by now in Lancastrian control, as was the powerful Pontefract Castle. At Worksop in Nottinghamshire, York's vanguard clashed with a contingent from the West Country moving north to join the Lancastrian army, and was defeated upon 16 December 1460.

York had marched north with Salisbury and just 10,000 troops to meet the threat of the Lancastrian force of 18,000 men assembled near the City of York. The Lancastrians were led by Henry Beaufort, Duke of Somerset; Henry Holland, Duke of Exeter; Henry Percy, Duke of Northumberland; the Earl of Wiltshire, Lord Clifford and Lord Roos. On 21 December, York had reached his stronghold of Sandal Castle near Wakefield. He had sent sorties towards the Lancastrian camp at Pontefract 9 miles east, but these were repulsed. York sent for help to his son Edward who was containing Jasper Tudor, but before any reinforcements could arrive, York left his castle on 30 December. It is unknown why he left its safety before reinforcements arrived, but it may have been a strategy of the veteran Andrew Trollope.

It is said that half the Lancastrian army under Somerset and Clifford advanced openly towards Sandal Castle, while the remainder under Roos were concealed in the woods surrounding the area. York was probably short of provisions and may have taken the chance of attacking an army of similar size to his own. York led his men from the castle on a foraging expedition, and as successive Lancastrian contingents joined in the fighting, York's army was outnumbered and badly defeated. Edward Hall recounted, 'But when he was in the plain ground between his castle and the town of Wakefield, he was environed on every side, like a fish in a net, or a deer in a buckstall; so that he manfully fighting was within half an hour slain and dead, and his whole army discomfited.'

Perhaps 2,000 Yorkists were killed at the Battle of Wakefield, including Richard, Duke of York. His son Rutland attempted to escape over Wakefield Bridge, but was overtaken and killed, possibly by Clifford. Clifford's father had been killed at St Albans, so he did not spare Rutland. Salisbury's fourth son, Sir Thomas Neville, and his son-in-law Lord Harington also died. Salisbury himself escaped the battlefield. However, he was captured during the night, and was taken to the Lancastrian camp and beheaded. Lancastrian nobles might have been prepared to allow Salisbury to ransom himself, but he was dragged out of Pontefract Castle and beheaded by local commoners, to whom he had been a harsh overlord. This was to set a terrible precedent for future battles. The heads of York, Rutland and Salisbury were displayed over Micklegate Bar, the western gate through the city walls of York. York was given a paper crown and a sign saying 'Let York overlook the town of York'.

Just over a month after York's death, there was another turnaround. Upon hearing the news of the great Yorkist defeat at Wakefield, Richard of York's eighteen-year-old son Edward of March, now 4th

Duke of York, decided to deploy his army away from the Welsh Marches. Edward of York had been based at the Mortimer stronghold of Wigmore Castle, and gathered troops from the borders and significant Welsh forces under Sir William Herbert of Raglan. Raglan's supporters included Sir Richard Devereux, Lord Audley, Lord Grey of Wilton, and Humphrey Stafford, the future Earl of Devon. Edward of York needed to link with Warwick and prevent the Lancastrian victors of Wakefield from marching south and taking London.

Owen Tudor, a veteran of Agincourt, was the second husband of Catherine of Valois, widow of Henry V. With his son Jasper Tudor, Earl of Pembroke, he led an army of Welshmen, along with French, Bretons and a group of Irish mercenaries led by James Butler, Earl of Ormond and Earl of Wiltshire. The Lancastrians wished to converge with the main Lancastrian force, which was heading for London. Edward needed to block Pembroke's advance and moved north from Gloucester with around 5,000 troops to Mortimer's Cross. The Lancastrians attacked at the great Battle of Mortimer's Cross, 2 February 1461. Wiltshire's division made inroads on Edward's right wing. Jasper Tudor in the centre met an impasse, but decisively, Owen Tudor tried to encircle the Yorkist left wing and was heavily defeated. His men were routed, and Jasper's centre then also broke. Owen Tudor was captured 17 miles away in Hereford and beheaded on the steps of the cathedral. Richard of York's death had been partially avenged.

Yet there was a Lancastrian victory at the Second Battle of St Albans upon 17 February 1461. The Northern Lancastrian army, the victors of Wakefield, had been reinforced by Scots, owing to Margaret of

Anjou's continuing diplomatic efforts. It marched south towards London. The battle at Mortimer's Cross had prevented Edward's plan of marching to the Midlands to meet with Warwick and block Margaret's Northern army from marching upon London. Warwick, with Henry VI in his train, took up position north of St Albans, covering the main road, Watling Street. The other two commanders of his three 'battles' or battle divisions were his brother, John Neville, and Norfolk. The Lancastrians Somerset, Northumberland and Clifford, with a much larger army, outflanked the Yorkists, driving them from the field and once more taking Henry VI captive. The king had been left by Warwick sitting under a tree and guarded by two knights, who were executed. Margaret of Anjou and her army could now march unopposed on to London, but the Lancastrian army's reputation for pillage caused the Londoners to bar the gates. Margaret hesitated, as she had been alarmed by the news of the Yorkist victory at Mortimer's Cross. For various reasons the Lancastrian army dissolved, losing many Scots and borderers who deserted, returning home with the plunder they had already gathered.

Having lost possession of Henry VI, Warwick could no longer claim to be acting upon his behalf. Warwick and Edward of York entered London on 2 March and two days later Edward was proclaimed Edward IV. Edward gathered a large army and marched north towards the Lancastrian army's position behind the River Aire in Yorkshire. Warwick led the vanguard and forced a crossing at Ferrybridge. He had his men repair the bridge while camp was established on the north side of the river. Early next morning the Yorkists were ambushed by a large party of Lancastrians under

Clifford and John, Lord Neville, a distant kinsman of Warwick. Perhaps 3,000 men perished upon 28 March 1461 including the Yorkist second-in-command Lord Fitzwalter. Warwick was wounded and the bridge was demolished again. Edward arrived with his main army and Warwick sent his uncle, Lord Fauconberg, and the Yorkist cavalry upstream. They crossed the ford at Castleford and pursued Lord Clifford, who was executed in the sight of the main Lancastrian army. Clifford had probably killed Edward's youngest brother five years earlier at Wakefield, so could expect no mercy from Edward IV.

Ferrybridge was followed by another Yorkist victory on the following day at the Battle of Towton, 29 March 1461. Edward IV's Yorkist army, with Warwick and Fauconberg, attacked the Lancastrians in a driving snowstorm, up a sloping hill. Using the snow and the wind direction as an aid, the Yorkist archers were able to shoot further than their adversaries. This battle is renowned for the slaughter of the Lancastrian army by 'arrowstorm', the highly effective use of archers that rained down tens of thousands of arrows in a ten-hour bloodbath. Suffering badly from arrow casualties, the Lancastrians knew their best strategy was to charge. After many hours of intense fighting the Yorkist line was showing signs of buckling. John Mowbray, Duke of Norfolk, arrived with reinforcements and the Yorkist army defeated the Somerset's Lancastrians. There were perhaps 28,000 deaths among the 36,000 Yorkists and 40,000 Lancastrians, and it is thought to be the bloodiest battle fought on British soil. Henry Percy, 3rd Earl of Northumberland, was killed and Sir Andrew Trollope and Lord Dacre were also among the Lancastrian losses. On 1 May, the captured Earl of

Wiltshire was beheaded at Newcastle and his estates forfeited. He had commanded the wing of the army which had killed Richard of York at Wakefield.

Henry VI, Margaret of Anjou and their son Edward of Westminster, Prince of Wales, sailed to Scotland and were given refuge by the young James III. They gained troops and other aid from the queen and regent, Mary of Guelders, in exchange for the surrender of the town and castle of Berwick-upon-Tweed. Upon 28 June 1461 Edward IV was formally crowned king at Westminster.

Three years passed without another major battle, but Hedgeley Moor on 25 April 1464 witnessed a third successive Yorkist victory. On his way to Scotland to meet a group of envoys to discuss peace, John Neville (later Lord Montagu), brother of Warwick, clashed with a Lancastrian force of a similar size, about 5,000 strong, under Somerset. The Lancastrian wings commanded by Lords Hungerford and Roos fled, leaving Sir Ralph Percy with the only holding force. Percy's troops were crushed and he died in battle. Montagu continued north and the Duke of Somerset led the dispirited remnants of the Lancastrian army south to Hexham.

After completing his mission at the border of Scotland, Lord Montagu had marched south and engaged the Lancastrian army at Hexham upon 15 May 1464. His men rapidly charged downhill and crushed the Lancastrians, despite both armies having around 5,000 troops. Thirty leading Lancastrians, including the Duke of Somerset, Lord Hungerford and Lord Roos, were summarily executed upon the evening after the battle. Henry VI was kept safely away from the battle and again escaped from the field. Sir William

Tailboys was captured and executed shortly after as he tried to flee north with £2,000 from Henry's war chest. On the loss of its leadership and funding, Lancastrian resistance in the north of England fell away. Only a few castles remained in their hands.

There followed a mopping-up exercise by the successful Yorkists in the north-east of England. After the Battle of Hexham, the Lancastrians held only the castles of Bamburgh, Dunstanburgh and Alnwick, which had all already changed hands more than once. Warwick and Montagu, now appointed Earl of Northumberland, brought the massive siege pieces of Edward IV to the North, and set out to end this last Lancastrian resistance. On 23 June Alnwick yielded, followed by Dunstanburgh the next day, but Bamburgh refused the summons. Bamburgh was held by Sir Ralph Grey, and he had been exempted from a general pardon. The king's great guns, 'London' and 'Newcastle' (both made of iron) and 'Dijon' (a brass cannon), had been brought especially from Calais. Supported by bombardels, they breached the walls, allowing Warwick to lead an assault, and 30 June 1464 saw the Yorkists take the castle. This was the first castle taken by artillery in England, although the gigantic castles of Aberystwyth and Harlech in Wales had been pounded into submission in 1408 and 1409 in the Glyndŵr War of Independence.

Grey had been seriously wounded by falling masonry, but this did not save him from being dragged before the High Constable, John Tiptoft, the 'Butcher Earl' of Worcester. Worcester made good on his reputation of recognising no law but the axe. The capture of Henry VI by James Harrington and the Talbot family, while he was hiding at Waddington Hall near Clitheroe in

Lancashire, meant the rebellion was effectively over. Henry was taken to the Tower of London with his feet tied to his stirrups.

Only in Wales did the Lancastrian cause marginally survive. After the Towton disaster in 1461, Henry VI's half-brother Jasper Tudor, Earl of Pembroke, placed Lancastrian garrisons in Harlech and various other Welsh castles, in an effort to hold Wales against the Yorkists. Pembroke Castle was taken by Herbert, Essex and Ferrers on 30 September and the Yorkist army headed north. Sir William Herbert, the leading Yorkist in Wales, defeated Pembroke at Twt Hill in October 1461, forcing Exeter and Pembroke to flee, the latter to Ireland. This skirmish ended open warfare in Wales. In 1461, Edward IV had promised a pardon to Harlech's defenders if they surrendered and an attainder if they did not. The garrison ignored the offer, knowing that their defences were virtually impregnable unless Edward IV sent his great cannon there. Denbigh Castle surrendered in January 1462, and the wonderfully sited western fortress of Carreg Cennen capitulated in May.

By the end of 1462, Herbert had captured all the Lancastrian strongholds in Wales except Harlech Castle, which remained in the hands of a garrison commanded by Dafydd ap Ieuan, and included such prominent English Lancastrians as Sir Richard Tunstall. Harlech remained largely unmolested for seven years, but kept North Wales in disorder, its defenders seizing cattle, wheat and other supplies, and proclaiming their allegiance to Henry VI. Harlech became a safe point of entry and exit for Lancastrian agents and a link to Ireland and Scotland. In early 1462, the garrison helped foment a conspiracy to bring Pembroke back to

Wales to coordinate Lancastrian attacks there and in England. The Yorkists discovered the plot and executed two Englishmen implicated in it, John de Vere, Earl of Oxford, and his eldest son Aubrey, making John de Vere, Oxford's second son, and the new Earl of Oxford, an implacable enemy of the Yorkists.

In 1464, Parliament called upon the Harlech garrison to submit, and Edward IV issued a proclamation giving the defenders until 1 January 1465 to surrender. Harlech's defenders again ignored the king. In June 1468, Pembroke returned to Harlech with French reinforcements. After attracting large numbers of Welsh Lancastrians to his banner, the earl launched a campaign of destruction across central Wales, seizing and plundering the town of Denbigh. These disorders convinced Edward IV that Harlech had to be taken, and he ordered Herbert to raise an army in the English border counties.

Dividing his force of 9,000 into two parts, Herbert sent his brother, Richard Herbert, to devastate the coast north of the castle while he advanced on Harlech from the south. After the northern force defeated and scattered Pembroke's men, the two wings of the army reunited and forced the surrender of Harlech on 14 August 1468. The garrison had been disheartened by Pembroke's defeat, and Herbert found letters incriminating Margaret of Anjou in treason. Pembroke once again escaped Wales, but his earldom was awarded to Herbert in September. More than anyone, Jasper Tudor, the Lancastrian Earl of Pembroke and Henry Tudor's uncle, was responsible for the eventual Tudor dynasty. From the age of twenty-four at the First Battle of St Albans in 1455, to Mortimer's Cross in 1461, and to eventual victory at Bosworth in 1485 and Stoke Field in 1487, he spent the whole period of the Wars of the Roses fighting, escaping, raising troops and in exile. His importance in holding together the Lancastrian cause and his role in the demise of Richard III has never been fully recognised.

With the fall of Harlech, all England and Wales were for the first time under Yorkist control. The siege is credited with inspiring the song *Rhyfelgyrch Gwŷr Harlech*, 'The March of the Men of Harlech' (first published in 1794). The military march is traditionally said to describe events during the seven-year siege between 1461 and 1468. Commanded by Constable Dafydd ap Ieuan, the Lancastrian garrison had held out in what is the longest known siege in the history of the British Isles. (The song, however, is associated according to some with the earlier, shorter siege of several months in 1408.)

Despite his ongoing problems in Wales, and with the Earl of Pembroke's machinations in exile, Edward IV was not seriously challenged until Warwick 'the Kingmaker' altered his allegiance from the Yorkist to the Lancastrian cause in 1469. After eight years of rule, Edward IV had begun to alienate many of the nobles, including Warwick, because of his marriage to the 'commoner' Elizabeth Woodville and his alliances with Burgundy. Richard Neville, Earl of Warwick, had been instrumental in the ascent of Edward IV, but became disenchanted as his influence at court steadily waned. The situation had worsened when Edward informed Warwick that he had secretly married Elizabeth Woodville, despite Warwick's difficult diplomatic efforts to secure a French wife for the king. Then Edward IV refused to allow his younger brother, the Duke of Clarence, to marry Warwick's daughter

Isabel. Warwick found an ally in Clarence, who was the heir to the throne until Edward IV had a child. They inspired a series of rebellions in northern England before departing for Calais in July 1469. While there, Clarence married Isabel Neville. Forced to react to the Northern rebellions, Edward began marching north, allowing Clarence and Warwick to land in Kent and build an army.

Edward soon found that the rebel forces in the North outnumbered his own, and he fell back to Nottingham Castle to await reinforcements. Among those moving to help the king were troops led by William Herbert, the new Earl of Pembroke in Jasper's place, and the Earl of Devon. On 12 July, Warwick and Clarence declared their support for the rebels, who were led by 'Robin of Redesdale', probably Sir John Conyers, one of Warwick's retainers. Six days later, Warwick began moving north with a large army to reinforce Redesdale. Learning of Warwick's movements, Redesdale began moving south to join with him, bypassing the king at Nottingham.

The Lancastrian army neared the armies of Pembroke and Devon at Banbury, Oxfordshire. On 25 July 1469, William Herbert, Earl of Pembroke, and Humphrey Stafford, Earl of Devon, entered Banbury and supposedly argued over billets, causing Devon to withdraw with his men. This weakened the Yorkist force, not only in numbers but because Devon possessed most of the army's archers. The following morning, Pembroke moved his men to a strong hilltop position at Edgecote Moor, 6 miles from Banbury. The Lancastrians attacked, with their archers inflicting immense casualties. Lacking archers, the Yorkists were forced to charge down the slope, and there were two to three hours of hand-to-hand fighting. Pembroke's men began to gain the upper hand and Redesdale may have been killed, but the advance elements of Warwick's forces under Sir John Clapham approached.

Believing that Warwick's entire army was about to enter the fray, the Yorkists began to break and flee the field. The chronicler Hall wrote,

> Pembroke behaved himself like a hardy knight and expert captain; but his brother Sir Richard Herbert so valiantly acquitted himself that with his poleaxe in his hand he twice by fine force passed through the battle of his adversaries and returned without mortal wound. When the Welsh were on the point of victory John Clapham, esquire, servant of the earl of Warwick, mounted on the eastern hill with only 500 men and gathered all the rascals of Northampton and other villages about, bearing before them the standard of the Earl of Warwick with the white bear, crying, 'A Warwick! A Warwick!'

Terribly outnumbered, the 18,000-strong Welsh army of the Herberts was defeated. Around 170 Welshmen of note were killed and the Herbert brothers unlawfully executed by the vindictive Warwick. They were summarily beheaded at Northampton after the battle.

H. T. Evans called Herbert 'the first statesman of a new era, and the most redoubtable antagonist of the last and most formidable of the old'. This Lancastrian victory is known as the Battle of Edgecote Moor or the Battle of Banbury. After the crushing defeat, Edward IV's army melted away. Many of the king's closest advisers, including Earl Rivers and John Woodville, were captured and summarily executed. Fleeing south, Devon was also taken and killed. Warwick ordered his brother George Neville, the Archbishop of York, to intercept and capture Edward IV, and the king was taken into 'protection' by Warwick. The king had been trapped at Nottingham and, realising that further fighting was foolish, had dispersed his small army and allowed himself to be captured at Olney.

Warwick briefly regained power and attempted to rule in Edward's name. However, the nobility, many of whom owed their positions to the king, were restive, and it seems Warwick was forced to release Edward from Middleham Castle, or perhaps Edward escaped. The king returned to London to public acclaim in October 1469. Edward IV did not seem to seek to destroy either Warwick or Clarence but instead sought reconciliation among them. However, both men could have felt that their time was limited with Edward's return to power, and continued plotting against the king. If Clarence came to the throne, Warwick's daughter would become queen and Warwick's grandson would in time become king.

After the defeat of his forces at the Battle of Edgecote Moor, Edward IV patiently waited for an opportunity to consolidate his power again. A rebellion arose in Lincolnshire under Lord Welles. Richard, Lord Welles and his son Robert, had taken part in the plots of Warwick and Clarence. In March 1470 Lord Welles attacked the house of Sir Thomas Burgh, the king's Master of the Horse, wrecking it. Edward summoned Welles and his brother-in-law, Sir Thomas Dymock to London. Welles pleaded illness, and instead claimed sanctuary at Westminster. He left sanctuary on promise of a pardon, and Edward made him write to his son, telling him to give up Warwick's cause. Edward threatened Robert Welles with the execution of his father unless he submitted. Robert pulled back his troops, but did not submit to Edward, and the angry king ignored his pledge and beheaded Lord Welles and Dymock at Huntingdon.

Edward then marched north to Stamford and found that the rebels were camped at Horn Field, near Empingham in Rutland, under Sir Robert Welles. He was probably awaiting reinforcements from Warwick and Clarence, so Edward IV attacked immediately. The rebels, in fleeing, 'cast off their country's coats to haste their speed away and hence gave to the place its name of Losecoat Field'. This was the Yorkist victory of Losecote Field, 12 March 1470. Sir Robert Welles was captured and beheaded a week later, after making a confession implicating Warwick and Clarence in the rebellion. Both father and son were attainted in the parliament of 1475 and their lands taken by the Crown. The Welles attainders were reversed in Henry VII's first parliament. It is worth mentioning here that virtually all of the Plantagenet illegal and legal land gains under Edward IV and Richard III were reversed by Henry VII, ensuring support among previously disaffected noble families and their gentry followings.

Warwick and Clarence fled to France to make an alliance with Henry VI's queen-consort Margaret of Anjou and Louis XI, now defecting to the Lancastrian cause instead of trying to make Clarence king. Clarence's wife lost a child giving birth upon the ship to Calais in April 1470. Henry VI rewarded Clarence by making him next in line to the throne after the infant Prince of Wales, Edward of Westminster, justifying the exclusion of Edward IV either by attainder for his treason against Henry or on the grounds of Edward's alleged illegitimacy. Warwick agreed to restore Henry VI in return for French support in an invasion, which took place in late 1470, landing at Dartmouth. Edward IV was forced to flee on 2 October when he learned that Warwick's brother, John Neville, first Marquess of Montagu, had also switched to the Lancastrian side, making the king's military position untenable. Henry VI was briefly restored to the throne upon 3 October 1470, while Edward and his younger brother Richard, Duke of Gloucester, took refuge in Burgundy. Burgundy was ruled by Edward's brother-in-law Charles, Duke of Burgundy, and Edward's sister Margaret of York. At Louis XI's insistence, in return for his support, Warwick now followed the French king's wishes, with England declaring war upon Burgundy.

Charles the Bold of Burgundy had initially been unwilling to help Edward, but this Anglo-French declaration prompted Charles to now aid the exiled king. In this period, of course, England had two kings, both of whom are accorded two official reigns. From Burgundy Edward now raised an army and a fleet to win back his kingdom. When Edward returned to England with a relatively small force on 11 March 1471, he only just avoided capture. York only opened its gates to him after he promised that he had only come to reclaim his dukedom, just as Henry Bolingbroke had promised seventy years earlier in North Wales. As he marched southwards Edward began to gather support.

The devious Clarence now deserted Warwick and reunited with Edward, believing that his fortunes would be better off as brother to a king than under Henry VI. To some extent Clarence realised that his loyalty to his father-in-law had been in error. Warwick now wanted his younger daughter, Anne, married to Edward of Westminster, and a ceremony had taken place in December 1470. As it was unlikely that Warwick would replace Edward IV with Clarence, but instead now favour Prince Edward of Westminster, Clarence had returned to Edward IV's side. Edward entered London unopposed, where he took Henry VI prisoner yet again. The period of Henry VI regaining his crown, the 'Readeption', is from 3 October 1470 to 11 April 1471.

Upon 14 April 1471, a Lancastrian army led by Warwick, the 'Kingmaker', forced a battle near Barnet, north of London. Under cover of darkness, the Yorkists moved close to the Lancastrians, and clashed in thick fog at dawn. With the main armies engaged under Warwick and Edward in battle, the Earl of Oxford routed the Yorkists under Lord Hastings, chasing them as far as Barnet. Upon their return to the battlefield, Oxford's men were mistaken for Yorkists. They were fired upon by his allies commanded by the Marquess of Montagu, Warwick's brother. The Lancastrians lost the battle as cries of treason spread through their line, disrupting morale and causing many to abandon the fight. Montagu was killed, and while retreating, Warwick was killed by Yorkist soldiers.

The final major battle in this main period of the Wars of the Roses was fought upon 4 May 1471 at Tewkesbury. Henry VI had been locked in the Tower of London, and his wife Margaret of Anjou was in France with their son Edward of Westminster. When her son reached eighteen she decided to return to England and reclaim the throne for him. After being delayed by severe storms, she landed at Weymouth upon 14

April 1471, and set off for Wales, where Jasper Tudor waited with reinforcements. Unfortunately, upon that day Warwick had been killed and the main Lancastrian army had been destroyed at Barnet. The defeated Lancastrian forces, led by the Duke of Somerset, then marched toward the Welsh border in order to recruit more troops and also meet up with Jasper Tudor, the former Earl of Pembroke. However, alerted by his agents, Edward IV moved at all speed with his 5,000-strong army towards the Welsh border. He needed to intercept the Lancastrians before the forces led by Margaret and Somerset could meet up with Jasper Tudor's Welsh army.

Gathering supporters as they went, Somerset's force headed for Gloucester to cross the Severn, but the city was locked against them, by Edward's orders. Somerset headed for the next crossing point, Tewkesbury, but found that Edward's army was so close behind he had to stand and fight, rather than cross to meet with Jasper's troops. Somerset was forced to quickly take up a strong defensive position. Edward reached Tewkesbury upon 4 May and immediately engaged the 7,000-strong enemy. Somerset believed he saw a weakness in the Yorkist centre and attacked. The Yorkists under Edward IV and Richard, Duke of Gloucester, held off the attack, then counter-attacked and routed the Lancastrians. Somerset's younger brother the Marquess of Dorset, and the Earl of Devon died on the field.

Edward of Westminster, Prince of Wales, was found wounded in a grove by some of Clarence's men. Hutton tells us that 'by the best accounts ever submitted to the world, there were only four persons in the room with Edward the Fourth, when Sir Richard Crofts brought in the Prince; Clarence; Dorset; Gloucester, and Hastings'. The Prince of Wales was summarily executed, despite pleading for his life to Clarence, who had sworn allegiance to him in France barely a year before. Other versions state that Edward IV killed him, or that Edward, Clarence and Richard of Gloucester, the three brothers, jointly despatched the rightful king. Whatever the case, he was murdered after being found. Many Lancastrian nobles and knights sought sanctuary in Tewkesbury Abbey, but two days after the battle, Somerset and other leaders were dragged out of the abbey, and were ordered by Richard of Gloucester and the Duke of Norfolk to be put to death after perfunctory trials. Among them was another brother of the Earl of Devon. This was the eighteen-year-old Richard of Gloucester's second engagement in the wars. The future Richard III had also fought at Barnet.

There were some last minor engagements in the wars. Lancastrians under Jasper Tudor were still active in Wales, and there was an ineffective rising in the North. Edward went to Coventry to make dispositions against the Northern and Welsh Lancastrians. Thomas, the illegitimate son of Sir William Neville, Baron Fauconberg and Earl of Kent, had taken part in setting Edward IV on the throne in 1461. Known as the 'Bastard of Fauconberg' or more usually as simply 'Thomas the Bastard', in 1471 he served Warwick, and helped him reinstate Henry VI. The Bastard was appointed the captain of Warwick's navy, and cruised the English Channel between Dover and Calais to intercept assistance coming to Edward. Around the time of Tewkesbury, Warwick gave him orders to raise the county of Kent in behalf of Warwick and Henry VI. He marched through Kent and Essex, and collected a large number of men. On 14 May the Bastard appeared at Aldgate and demanded admission to the City of London. This was refused, and the Bastard set fire to the eastern suburbs. The garrison of the Tower of London, led by Earl Rivers, the queen's brother, who had been injured at Barnet, repulsed them. The citizens of London also defended vigorously, and pursued the Bastard and his army as far as Stratford and Blackwall.

The Bastard now made his way west to Kingston-upon-Thames, intending to capture or kill Edward IV. Rivers had held London for Edward, and cleverly sent word to the Bastard that Edward IV was leaving England, inducing the Bastard to return to Blackheath. However, on hearing that Edward's army was approaching, the Fauconberg journeyed with 600 horsemen to Rochester and then returned to his fleet at Sandwich. He there learned that the Lancastrian cause was lost, and Edward sent Richard of Gloucester for Fauconberg's submission and to take custody of his thirteen ships and most of his immediate followers. The Bastard's main captain Spysyng was beheaded and many of the rebels were hung. Edward IV rode into Kent and also had the Mayor of Canterbury, who had helped raise men, beheaded. Edward also fined the counties of Kent and Essex. The Bastard was pardoned upon 10 June, and sent to serve Richard of Gloucester in the North, but upon 22 September 1471 Fauconberg was taken to the castle of Middleham, Yorkshire, and was beheaded upon Gloucester's orders. No reason is known and there was no trial. Henry VI's cause was again lost – only Jasper Tudor in Pembroke Castle in the far west of Wales was now active against Yorkist forces.

Together with exiled Lancastrians and mercenaries

from several countries, Fauconberg's army may have numbered as many as 16,000 men in total. If the Bastard had taken London, he could also have captured Edward's wife Elizabeth and their children and released Henry from the Tower. Edward IV realised that Henry VI could no longer be allowed to live, and within a few days of the rebels' assault on London Henry VI had been murdered. As his son and heir Edward of Westminster had also been murdered, there were no real rivals left in England to pose a threat to the Yorkist king.

On his way to suppress Fauconberg and the Kentish rebels, Edward had passed through London in triumph on 21 May, with the captive Queen Margaret of Anjou beside him in a chariot. She was placed in the Tower of London, and Henry VI died in the Tower that same night, at the hands of, or by the order of, Richard of Gloucester according to several contemporary accounts. Gloucester was Constable of the Tower. The Milanese ambassador in France reported, 'King Edward caused King Henry to be secretly assassinated ... he has, in short, chosen to crush the seed.' It was announced in public that the king had died 'of pure displeasure and melancholy', but few believed this. Hutton and others state that Henry was murdered on Ascension Eve, which is always a Thursday, but 'eve' may indicate that he was killed on the previous day. Others believe that he was killed in the early morning of 22 May. Dafydd Llwyd of Mathafarn and others believed that Henry was killed upon Thursday, 23 May. Henry's body was displayed in its coffin as if he had died naturally but it is said that he was stabbed. Margaret of Anjou remained in the Tower, and then was taken to Windsor and Wallingford, before being returned to her father's estates in Anjou in 1475. From Tewkesbury on 4 May 1471 to the death of Fauconberg upon 22 September, Gloucester was named by contemporary sources as having murdered both the Prince of Wales and Henry VI, and Fauconberg was executed by him without trial or reason.

The House of York now was secure in ruling England and Wales. The king's brother Gloucester later married Anne Neville, the widow of Prince Edward and the younger daughter of Warwick. The Wars of the Roses appeared to be over, and there were to be fourteen years of relative peace. With the deaths of Somerset and his younger brother, the House of Beaufort, who were distant cousins of Henry VI and had a remote claim to succeed him, had been almost exterminated. Only the female line of Somerset's uncle, the 1st Duke of Somerset, remained, represented by Lady Margaret Beaufort and her son Henry Tudor. Henry had escaped from Wales with Jasper Tudor, his paternal uncle, and remained in exile in Brittany for the rest of Edward IV's reign. However, the year after the Battle of Tewkesbury, Henry Tudor's mother Lady Margaret Beaufort married Lord Stanley, one of Edward IV's most powerful supporters. This event probably caused the powerful Stanley family to turn against Edward IV's brother Richard of Gloucester when he became king as Richard III, and was instrumental in giving Henry Tudor the kingship.

2

Richard, Duke of Gloucester 1452–1482

Richard Plantagenet was born upon 2 October 1452, at Fotheringhay Castle in Northamptonshire. He was the twelfth of Cecily Neville's thirteen children and the youngest of the seven who survived infancy. Richard was born as the bloody Wars of the Roses was about to begin, being named after his father, Richard, Duke of York, Henry VI's challenger for the throne. His mother Cecily Neville was a granddaughter of John of Gaunt and the aunt of the 'Kingmaker' Richard Neville, Earl of Warwick. Richard Plantagenet was aged only seven in 1459, when his father Richard of York was forced to flee to Ireland and was proclaimed a traitor. Edmund of Rutland went with his father York to Ireland, while Richard's oldest brother Edward of March had escaped to Calais. Richard, his brother George and their mother Cecily Neville were captured in Ludlow Castle. They were handed over by the Lancastrians to Cecily's sister Anne, Duchess of Buckingham, and kept in comfortable captivity in Coventry.

The ageing Archbishop of Canterbury, Thomas Bourchier, apparently had charge of the boys for a time, but Richard was later entrusted to the Earl of Warwick, whose household was said to support 20,000 retainers. Richard would have been trained in arms, hunting, hawking and courtly pursuits, spending most of his time at Warwick's Yorkshire castles of Middleham and Sheriff Hutton. This gave Richard a link with the region, and over the years he formed alliances among leading families in the north of England. Here Richard would have met his future wife, Warwick's younger daughter Anne, while his elder brother George later married her sister, Isabel Neville.

Richard of York returned to England to claim the throne, and was accepted as Henry VI's heir apparent, but in December 1460 was defeated and killed at Wakefield. His son, the seventeen-year-old Edmund, Earl of Rutland, was murdered after the battle, and their severed heads were displayed on the gates of York. Richard of York's head was mockingly topped with a paper crown by the Lancastrians. Edmund's uncle Richard Neville, Earl of Salisbury, was beheaded the day after the battle. Cecily Neville had managed to send George and Richard abroad to the protection of the Duke of Burgundy in the Netherlands.

However, the boys' surviving brother Edward Plantagenet won the great battle at Towton in March 1461, and the exiled brothers returned to see the nineteen-year-old Edward IV's coronation. George was created Duke of Clarence, and also in 1461 Richard was created Duke of Gloucester. In 1462 Richard of

Gloucester received in perpetuity Gloucester Castle and estates across England. He was also named Earl of Richmond (the title had belonged to Henry Tudor's father Edmund, who died in prison in 1456) and was granted in perpetuity castles, manors, lordships, lands, and other possessions in England, Wales and the Welsh Marches forfeited by Robert, Lord Hungerford. Gloucester was named Admiral of England, Ireland, and Aquitaine. In 1463, aged eleven, Gloucester was granted 'during pleasure' the castles, lordships, manors, lands, rents, and services forfeited by Henry Beaufort, the late Duke of Somerset. In the next few years, more properties accrued and in 1469 aged seventeen, Gloucester was appointed Constable of England and Earl of March. Edward IV had previously been Earl of March before taking the kingship.

However, as we have seen in the preceding brief history of the Wars of the Roses, Clarence at this time turned against his brother Edward and was plotting with the disaffected Earl of Warwick. Upon 12 July 1469, Clarence secretly wed Warwick's daughter Isabel Neville at Calais. Warwick had been deeply angered by Edward IV's marriage to the 'commoner' Elizabeth Woodville, and felt that his influence at court was waning. Clarence was next in line to the crown, and Warwick's daughter could become Queen of England. Warwick and Clarence led a rebellion, briefly placing the Neville family in power. Edward IV and Gloucester fled to The Hague. Upon Edward returning and retaking power, Isabel Neville, her sister Anne, Warwick and Clarence fled into exile in France, to ally with Margaret of Anjou, the queen of the dethroned Henry VI.

Upon 25 July 1470, Anne Neville was betrothed in

Angers Cathedral to the Prince of Wales, Edward of Westminster (also known as Edward of Lancaster), the son and heir of Henry VI and Margaret. Supported by Louis XI of France and Queen Margaret, Warwick and Clarence invaded England, leaving Anne in France with her mother and sister. Edward IV fled abroad and Henry VI resumed his throne. Having received papal dispensation, Anne and Edward were married at Amboise on 13 December 1470, aged fourteen and seventeen respectively. Edward and Gloucester returned from exile and took London. Edward IV declared himself king for a second time upon 11 April 1471. The Prince and Princess of Wales were to set sail to England with their mothers Queen Margaret and Elizabeth Neville, but were delayed by poor weather until 14 April 1471. Clarence now reverted to the Yorkist cause, and upon the day of the queen's return, Warwick and his brother the Marquess of Montagu were slain at Barnet, fighting for Henry VI against the army of Edward IV and the eighteen-year-old Gloucester. Warwick, the 'Kingmaker', had fought at the both battles of St Albans, Blore Heath, Ludford Bridge, Northampton, Wakefield, Mortimer's Cross, Ferrybridge, Edgecote Moor, Towton and Barnet over the previous sixteen years.

Warwick's wife Anne Beauchamp took sanctuary at Beaulieu Abbey, but Anne Neville joined the forced march of the defeated Lancastrian army from Barnet to Tewkesbury. Here the Lancastrian army led by Margaret of Anjou was destroyed on 4 May 1471, with Anne's husband, Prince Edward, being killed. Gloucester has been accused of this murder. One account states that Edward was cut down as he fled north after Tewkesbury. Another version is that a small contingent of men under Clarence found Edward near a grove, where he was immediately beheaded on a makeshift block, despite pleas for mercy to his brother-in-law Clarence. The near contemporary *Great Chronicle of London*, Polydore Vergil and Edward Hall all tell us that Edward survived the battle, was taken captive and brought before Edward IV who was with Clarence, Gloucester and Lord Hastings. The king then asked why the Prince of Wales had taken up arms against him. The prince replied, 'I came to recover my father's heritage.' Edward IV then struck the prince across his face with his gauntleted hand and Clarence, Gloucester and the king stabbed Prince Edward to death with their swords. Clarence had sworn allegiance to the prince in France barely a year before. Gloucester was to marry Prince Edward's widow Anne Neville a year later, when she reached the age of sixteen.

The Duke of Somerset, nobles and knights had escaped to what they thought was sanctuary at Tewkesbury Abbey, but were dragged out and killed two days later. Somerset's sixteen-year-old brother John Beaufort, Marquess of Dorset, had died in battle along with the Earl of Devon. Edward IV's troops forced their way into the abbey, and the resulting bloodshed caused the building to be closed for a month until it could be purified and reconsecrated. Somerset, the younger brother of the Earl of Devon and other nobles were now executed upon the orders of Gloucester and the Duke of Norfolk. The Courtenay family of the earls of Devon now had no male head. Also, with the deaths of Somerset and his younger brother, the House of Beaufort, which had a claim to succeed Henry VI, had also been almost exterminated.

Thomas Courtenay, Earl of Devon, had been beheaded after Towton in 1461. The only legitimate brother had been executed after the Battle of Hexham. Only the female line remained, represented by Lady Margaret Beaufort and her son Henry Tudor. Queen Margaret was captured at Tewkesbury by Sir William Stanley. Broken in spirit by the death of her son and the murder of her husband, she was imprisoned by Edward in the Tower. She was later placed in the custody of her former lady-in-waiting the Duchess of Suffolk, where she remained until being ransomed by Louis XI in 1475. She died in 1482, aged only fifty-two.

Gloucester had ordered Somerset and others to be summarily put to death after Tewkesbury, but he has been also accused of the murder of Henry VI in the Tower of London. Henry died during the night of 21/22 May 1471, on the night that Edward IV re-entered London. He had been kept alive so as not to leave the Lancastrian cause with a far stronger leader in Henry's son Edward of Westminster, Prince of Wales. The death of Prince Edward at Tewkesbury on 4 May meant that Henry had outlived his usefulness. *The Historie of the arrival of Edward IV in England and the Finall Recouerye of His Kingdomes from Henry VI. A.D. M.CCCC.LXXI* is a chronicle written by a servant of Edward IV, and tells us that Henry died of 'pure melancholy and displeasure' upon hearing of his son's death. Edward IV was re-crowned the morning after the death, and Sir Thomas More's *History of Richard III* states that Richard of Gloucester killed Henry. Another contemporary source, *Wakefield's Chronicle*, gives the date of Henry's death as 23 May, upon which date Richard is known to have been away from London

The majority of contemporary chroniclers believed Henry had been murdered. Richard Duke of Gloucester was known to be present at the Tower on the night of 21/22, as were others. In *The Death and Burial of Henry VI, A Review of the Facts and Theories, Part I*, W. J. White reveals that the earliest sources recording Henry's death do not name the murderer, although they assume that there was a murder and that Edward IV must have given the order for it. The first to name Richard of Gloucester as the murderer is probably the Frenchman Philippe de Commines, writing around 1490, and John Rous in his *Historia de Regibus Anglie*, written around the same time. The king was buried at Chertsey, and his body was moved to Windsor by Richard III. George V gave permission to exhume the body of Henry VI in 1910. Light-brown hair found matted with blood on the skull confirmed that Henry had died as a result of violence.

During Edward IV's second reign from 1471 to 1483, Richard of Gloucester established himself as the dominant force in the North. In 1471 he was granted in perpetuity the castles, manors and lordships of Middleham, Sheriff Hutton, and Penrith, allowing him to build up a great power base in the North. He was later appointed co-administrator of the principality of Wales, county of Chester and Duchy of Cornwall for the Prince of Wales until he reached the age of fourteen, and was soon granted perpetuity of all lands in Yorkshire and Cumberland held by Richard Neville, late Earl of Warwick. Operating from Middleham in Wensleydale he became warden of the west March, chief steward of the Duchy of Lancaster in the North, keeper of the forests, Sheriff of Cumberland and eventually lieutenant-general of the North, an office created for him as Edward IV went to war with the Scots in 1482.

With his brothers Gloucester and Clarence at his side, it seemed that the Wars of the Roses were over for Edward IV. From 1471 there had been peace in the kingdom. However, there was one last Lancastrian claimant to be disposed of. According to Barnard, in 1472 or 1473 Edward IV despatched envoys to the court of Brittany. Henry Tudor, Earl of Richmond, was the last claimant to the throne of the House of Lancaster. With his uncle Jasper Tudor, Earl of Pembroke, they

> were deprived of power to excite any important insurrection, yet he [Edward] desired to have the young earl in his power; and therefore despatched an embassy to the duke of Brittany, demanding that they should be delivered up; but that prince refused to comply, though he offered Edward that they should never interrupt the tranquillity of his government; in consideration of which promise the king paid a yearly pension, under pretence of granting a maintenance for the two refugees.

After Tewkesbury, Anne Neville had been placed in the custody of her sister the Duchess Isabel and her brother-in-law Clarence. Anne's father and husband, the 'Kingmaker' and the Prince of Wales, had been killed and branded traitors, while her mother was surrounded by an armed guard in Beaulieu sanctuary. The enormous Warwick and Salisbury estates of both her parents were forfeited, and granted to Isabel's husband Clarence. Clarence and her sister had no intention of allowing Anne to marry or receive her share of the Warwick and Salisbury inheritance, but before nine months had passed Gloucester asked for her hand in marriage. This was the marriage that Anne's father Warwick had originally favoured for Anne. Her guardian Clarence, realising that with his brother behind her Anne would be able to fight for her inheritance, refused the offer and sought to conceal her. Gloucester found her and took her to the neutral refuge of St Martin's sanctuary in London. Other Neville lands in the North should have passed to Anne's young cousin George Neville. However, his father, the Marquess of Montagu, had died a traitor at Barnet, with his estates being granted to Gloucester.

Anne Neville agreed to marry Richard and they sent envoys to Rome for a dispensation to cover the affinity between them as the result of Anne's marriage to Prince Edward of Wales, who had been Gloucester's second cousin once removed. In February 1472 Clarence at last also consented to the marriage, under pressure from the king. Clarence agreed to surrender certain estates to Gloucester but again renewed his opposition. Gloucester and Anne were married at some time before the spring of 1473, when Anne was sixteen and Gloucester around nineteen or twenty. This eventually united his Marcher estates with those of the Nevilles in the Midlands, making him the greatest landowner in England, much to the resentment of his brother Clarence. In that summer, Gloucester gained King Edward's permission for Anne's widowed mother Lady Anne de Beauchamp, Countess of Warwick, to be brought from Beaulieu sanctuary to join them at Middleham Castle in Yorkshire. Anne had been surrounded by guards there since Tewkesbury in 1471.

The Countess of Warwick was never restored to her

estates. Both Gloucester and Clarence would have lost lands, and Edward IV did not want her massive wealth going to a great noble if she remarried. Edward tried to settle her estates between Gloucester and Clarence, but the older brother wanted more than seemed equable. By the autumn of 1473 he was in arms against Gloucester. It was reported at this time at the French court, apparently by an English visitor sympathetic to Clarence, that Richard, who 'by force had taken to wife the daughter of the late Earl of Warwick, who had been married to the Prince of Wales, was constantly preparing for war with the Duke of Clarence. The latter, because his brother, King Edward, had promised him Warwick's country, did not want the former to have it by reason of his marriage with the earl's second daughter.' This was noted in the *Calendar of Milanese State Papers*.

Clarence now began objecting that the marriage of Gloucester and Anne was invalid in the eyes of the church, as marriage effected by force and fear was void. It could be argued that Gloucester had abducted Anne from Clarence's guardianship to St Martin's sanctuary. However, a female's own consent, not that of her family, was necessary for the contracting of a valid marriage, and subsequent consensual sexual relations and cohabitation would legitimise a marriage contracted by force. Tiring of Clarence's objections, Edward IV confiscated his estates until he saw reason. In May 1474 the dispute was finally settled by an Act of Parliament, whereby the countess's lands were to be given to her daughters and their husbands 'as though she were naturally dead'. A compromise was reached but the division of the Warwick estates was uneven, with a greater proportion going to Clarence, and Gloucester having to give up the office of Great Chamberlain. Lady Anne de Beauchamp, 16th Countess of Warwick, died in obscurity aged sixty-six in 1492. She survived both her daughters and the sons-in-law who had effectively and illegally disinherited her.

Throughout his short life, Gloucester was disposed to acquiring extra land and supporters, even having been warned by his brother Edward IV. Richard had gone too far when he attempted to recruit John Wedrington, Undersheriff of Northumberland, one of the most senior Percy retainers, and this prompted a complaint to the king. Edward rebuked Gloucester, and told him that he must not stray onto Percy ground. Richard undertook not to trespass on Percy preserves or recruit Percy retainers.

Another example of the pressing need for estates by Clarence and Gloucester is shown in the case of the Earl of Oxford's estates. John de Vere, 13th Earl of Oxford, fought for the Lancastrians at Barnet in 1471, where the Earl of Warwick died and the Yorkists scored a victory. His father, the 12th Earl, had been executed along with Oxford's older brother in 1462. Oxford had fled to Scotland and had continued to plot against the Yorkist government. Edward IV granted the bulk of the Earl of Oxford's estates to Gloucester, in 1471. By 1473, Oxford had turned to piracy but he was captured and imprisoned in Calais in 1474. Ten years later Oxford escaped, joined Henry Tudor and led the Lancastrian centre at Bosworth Field.

In December 1472, Oxford's mother Elizabeth Howard, dowager Countess of Oxford (c. 1410–74) was either confined to, or living voluntarily, in a nunnery at Stratford le Bow, London. The estates of her husband, eldest son and younger son John de Vere had been forfeited as they had been attainted as traitors, but she still had a number of lands across Norfolk, Cambridge and elsewhere of her own inheritance. Gloucester, with an armed entourage, burst into the nunnery and demanded that the countess release her lands to him. The countess, then aged sixty-two, was told that Gloucester had been given custody of her and her lands, and she was made to hand over the keys to her coffers, which were searched by his troops. He then took the countess to Stepney, where his household was staying in the house of Sir Thomas Vaughan. Here, the countess was confined to a room until she agreed to sign over her lands to Gloucester. The countess sent for one of her feoffees (estate-holders), Henry Robson, and told him that if she did not sign over her lands to Gloucester, he would send her to Middleham, a journey she doubted she could survive considering her age and 'the great Cold which then was of Frost and Snow'. She told Robson that she was grateful to have the lands, which now could save her life.

Also the countess's confessor, a Master Baxter, was being threatened by Gloucester's accomplice John Howard. Howard called him a false priest and a hypocrite, because Baxter, another of the countess's feoffees, was dubious about the legality of Gloucester's proposed transactions. The countess was now moved to Walbroke, being placed among Gloucester's servants. Some feoffees, however, would not co-operate in releasing her lands to Gloucester. William Paston was among those threatened by Gloucester, who in 1473 resorted to a suit in chancery against the feoffees. Unsurprisingly, the Lord Chancellor, Robert Stillington (later to achieve notoriety as claiming that Edward IV's children were illegitimate) decided in favour of the king's brother and ordered Paston to make the release. Edward IV dismissed his chancellor shortly after. The countess also now apparently signed the release, having told Robson that 'she was sorry that she for saving her life had disinherited her heirs'. She returned to the nunnery and was dead a year later. Before her death, she asked a former servant to remind her son John, the exiled Earl of Oxford, that she had released her estates out of fear of Gloucester.

In the chancery suit, heard in 1474 after her death, Gloucester stated that the countess had agreed to a release of the lands in return for an annuity of 500 marks (about £330), the payment of £240 in debts, and 'divers benefits, costs, and charges' in aid of the countess, her children, and her grandchildren. There is no record of Gloucester ever carrying out his promises, and the countess died before she could receive her annuity. Gloucester received twenty-eight manors in her Oxford estates, which James Ross reported brought in an income of about £600 per annum. Whenever his disciples rewrite Gloucester's life they seem to omit his venality. As Susan Higginbotham writes,

In his pro-Ricardian book *Royal Blood*, Bertram Fields, a lawyer, attempts to clear his client Richard of the charges of coercion. He argues that Edward IV had already turned over the countess's wealth to Richard, so that in effect Gloucester was doing the countess a service by compensating her for her loss. In fact, the lands Edward IV had turned over to his brother were those of the countess's son, not the countess herself. Richard would have hardly had to go to the trouble of getting the countess and her feoffees to release her lands if they had nothing to release in the first place.

Bishop Stillington, William Tunstall and even Edward IV had reservations about Gloucester's probity in these transactions.

Higginbotham goes on to tell us,

> Richard's supporters have often praised his piety, but it was Elizabeth who was the hapless source of some of the duke's most notable gift-giving. Following Richard III's death at Bosworth, Elizabeth's son Oxford, an ally of Henry VII, succeeded in having Parliament annul the releases made by the countess. In 1495, worried that his title to his mother's lands might someday be impugned, Oxford procured depositions from six witnesses, including William Paston and Henry Robson, who gave their recollection of the events of 1472–73.

The year 1473 saw Gloucester being appointed tutor and councillor of the Prince of Wales, and 1474 had given him almost half of all holdings of Anne, Duchess of Warwick. In 1474 Gloucester signed a treaty with the Earl of Northumberland by which Henry Percy recognised Richard 'the right high and mighty prince' as his 'faithful lord'. Also Ralph Neville, Earl of Westmorland, effectively became Gloucester's man in 1477. It seems that Gloucester had united the Percy and Neville interests in the North after decades of enmity. Along with these great Northern magnates, Gloucester sought loyalty from the higher gentry of Yorkshire, Westmorland, Cumberland and eastern Lancashire. The major land-owning families of the Parrs, Huddlestons, Pilkingtons, Harringtons, Middletons and Dacres, were all related to some degree, and all looked to Gloucester for both security and advancement. As leader of the Council of the North, Gloucester impartially regulated the judicial, financial and administrative offices of a vast area, ensuring personal popularity across the neglected north of England. Unfortunately for Gloucester, nearly omnipresent and omnipotent in the North, he could build up no similarly loyal power base in the South.

An underlying problem for Gloucester was one of his more attractive traits. He was always willing to support his gentry retainers against noble families. For example Gloucester checked the power of Thomas, Lord Stanley in eastern Lancashire by promoting men like the Harringtons and the Pilkingtons into Duchy of Lancaster offices. Edward IV actually had to intervene to prevent Richard from constantly challenging Lord Stanley's power in the North West and supporting Stanley's opponents. Gloucester honourably preferred to respect his obligations to lesser men who had fought beside him and had lost family in the Yorkist cause, rather than surrender to the needs of members of nobility such as Stanley whom he considered to be disloyal. He would need the nobles upon his side, and Gloucester would come to regret his actions towards the Stanleys.

In 1476, Gloucester was given a licence to enter all castles, lordships, honours, alien priories, lands, rents, reversions, services, fisheries, mills, rights, pensions, portions, forests, offices, courts, leets (the jurisdiction of courts), views of frank-pledge (joint-sureties), returns of writs, chaces, advowsons (the right to recommend clergy to benefices), knights' fees, possessions, and heriditaments (anything passed between heirs) that his wife would inherit on the death of her relatives. Would

this have meant those of her sister, Isabel? More and
more wealth accrued from Gloucester's new estates
and fees. Gloucester's marriage to Anne Neville was
thought to have been a fairly happy one at first. The
date of birth of his son, Edward of Middleham, an
only child, is unclear but perhaps as early as 1474 or
as late as 1476.

Gloucester's older brother Clarence had married
Isabel Neville, the elder daughter of Warwick in 1469,
but she died on 22 December 1476, ten weeks after
giving birth to a short-lived son, Richard, who only
lived for another three weeks. She may have died
of childbirth complications, or of consumption, i.e.
tuberculosis. Clarence was convinced that Isabel had
been poisoned. He immediately left the court, retiring
to his country estate. If he had to see Edward IV,
Clarence always refused food and drink, suspecting
that he also would be poisoned. Clarence's sister
Margaret of York was married to Charles the Bold,
Duke of Burgundy. Upon Charles' death in battle
against the Duke of Lorraine at Nancy on 5 January
1477, Margaret proposed that Clarence should marry
her fabulously wealthy step-daughter Mary, Duchess
of Burgundy. Clarence made his proposal and he felt
quite confident about its acceptance. Margaret and
Mary had consulted and agreed upon the marriage.
The new Duchess of Burgundy knew she had to marry
someone powerful enough to keep Louis XI of France
from taking over her country. Clarence's step-niece
was the sole heiress to the massive Burgundian lands
in France and the Low Countries, and known as 'Mary
the Rich'.

Edward IV prevented the marriage, possibly because
he did now wish for his brother to be advanced into

so much power and become a threat to the English crown, as he had been in 1469–71. Clarence in power in Burgundy could also mean war with France and the loss of Edward IV's annual agreed French pension. Earl Rivers was instead proposed as a candidate for marriage with Mary of Burgundy. Although Louis XI wished 'the greatest heiress of her time' to marry the Dauphin, Mary now chose Archduke Maximilian of Austria, which eventually led to two centuries of war between the French and the Hapsburgs. Still maddened by the suspected poisoning of Isabel, Clarence now hardly bothered to attend council, and constantly complained about his brother the king.

Upon investigation, Clarence came to believe that one of his wife's ladies-in-waiting, Ankarette Twynho, had poisoned Isabel. He also accused another member of his household, John Thursby, of poisoning his infant son Richard of Tewkesbury. Clarence had Ankarette paraded around several towns declaring that she had poisoned his wife. Ankarette and John Thursby were brought before the justices at Warwick and in a rigged trial they were found guilty and hanged. Even more importantly than this miscarriage of justice, Clarence was telling everyone that Edward IV's queen, Elizabeth Woodville, was behind the plot to kill his wife, and had also practised black magic and used witchcraft to get Edward IV to marry her. Rumours were also spread possibly by Clarence and others that Edward had already been married before to a lady called Lady Eleanor Butler, who was still alive when he married Elizabeth Woodville. Clarence also expounded that Edward IV was not the true son of the Duke of York, but the son of an archer named Blaybourne. He thus declared that the king's marriage was not legal and his children were illegitimate. The king was obviously incensed and wondered how to proceed against his brother. Clarence had accused his wife and her mother of witchcraft, him of not being the true king and his mother of adultery. We simply do not know if anyone was influencing Clarence towards these claims.

Clarence's trusted retainer Thomas Burdet and two astrologers had supposedly cast the king's horoscope, which, under contemporary law, was treasonable. Thomas Burdet was a loyal member of Clarence's household and he was now arrested under the charge of disseminating treasonable writing and attempting to procure the king's death by necromancy. Burdet was tried before a commission of lords and was condemned to death on 19 May 1477. He passionately pleaded his innocence at the charges and it appeared that an innocent man had been executed on false charges, but basically Edward had wanted to warn and punish Clarence.

However, Clarence insisted upon having his protestations read out at the royal council, directly disagreeing with his king. In early June, Louis XI sent Edward a letter, stating that someone had informed him that Clarence had asked for the hand of Mary of Burgundy three months earlier, only as a means of taking the English throne. Edward summoned Clarence under guard to appear before him at Westminster, and in the presence of the Lord Mayor of London, he accused his brother of subverting the laws of the realm and presuming to take justice into his own hands. Clarence was taken to the Tower. Gloucester's young son Edward was granted Clarence's earldom of Salisbury in July 1477, an indication of things to come.

Clarence's actual treasonable offences of 1469–71 had been pardoned, but he was charged, tried and executed for treason in a parliament specially summoned for this purpose in January 1478. Edward IV led the prosecution, to which Clarence was allowed no defence. The parliament was deliberately packed with servants of the Crown or key courtiers. No divisions were permitted by the king. The Act of Attainder mentions a number of offences, none of them actually treasonable, and Edward failed to convince contemporaries of his brother's guilt. The Croyland Chronicler, who appears to have been present, thought the trial and the verdict unjust. Some historians believe that Elizabeth Woodville was behind the trial. There had been a prophecy that Edward would be succeeded by someone whose name began with G, but this was not George, Duke of Clarence, but Gloucester. The Bill of Attainder passed against Clarence upon 7 February 1478 avoided the scandal of an open trial of the king's brother. Shakespeare blames Gloucester, with Gloucester saying,

> Plots have I laid, inductions dangerous,
> By drunken prophecies, libels and dreams,
> To set my brother Clarence and the king
> In deadly hate the one against the other:
> And if King Edward be as true and just
> As I am subtle, false and treacherous,
> This day should Clarence closely be mew'd up [caged],
> About a prophecy, which says that 'G'
> Of Edward's heirs the murderer shall be.
> Dive, thoughts, down to my soul: here
> Clarence comes.

Upon 7 February sentence of death was passed on Clarence, but Edward stayed his hand until 18 February. The fratricide was carried out privately within the Tower of London, possibly by drowning in his bath. Barnard relates that

> the duke's death brought excited such a clamour among the populace, that the ministry thought proper to conceal the manner of his execution, and gave out that he died suddenly of grief and vexation; and as proof that no violence had been offered to his person, his body was exposed in the cathedral of St Paul; but this trick was so stale, that it served only to confirm the suspicions of the people who without scruple exclaimed against the cruelty of the administration. This was the last transaction of Edward's reign, which was one continued scene of blood, violence, and barbarity.

Hutton believes that Richard

> cautiously improved the quarrel between Edward and Clarence, while he seemed the friend of both. This is in part corroborated by an expression which fell from Edward, while lamenting, when up late, the death of his brother. Intercession having been made for a criminal, he exclaimed between sorrow and anger, 'How many, and urgent, applications are made, to save a wretch who ought to die by the laws of his country, but not one mouth was opened to plead for a brother in distress.'

No one benefited more than Clarence's brother Richard, Duke of Gloucester. Clarence's trial and conviction would have been inconceivable if strongly opposed by the king's only other brother, and his death was a precondition for Gloucester's accession in 1483. Mancini states that Gloucester supported Clarence's fall while pretending otherwise: 'At that time Richard, duke of Gloucester, was so overcome with grief for his brother, that he could not dissimulate [conceal his feelings] so well, but that he was overheard to say that he would one day avenge his brother's death.' Was this play-acting, or a threat to the life of Edward IV? More says that Gloucester opposed it openly, but not so strongly as to put himself in any danger.

Before coming to London for Clarence's trial, Gloucester had sent Edward a letter asking if he could have his own trusted servants to look after him in the Tower. He also asked if he could look after Clarence's two surviving children. Margaret at the time was three years old and Edward eighteen months. Anne Neville took charge of raising their children, her niece and nephew. Dominic Mancini relates that

> following Clarence's death Richard of Gloucester came very rarely to court. He kept himself within his own lands and set out to acquire the loyalty of his people through favours and justice. The good reputation of his private life and public activities powerfully attracted the esteem of strangers. Such was his renown in warfare that, whenever a difficult and dangerous policy had to be undertaken, it would be entrusted to his discretion and his generalship. By these skills Richard acquired the favour of the people and avoided the jealousy of the queen, from whom he lived far separated.

Hutton relates,

> Clarence left two innocent orphans. An act of attainder

was immediately passed, to corrupt their blood, and seize their property. This unjust act could not originate from Edward; he had nothing to fear from younger branches; nay, they might rather be future supports to his family. It could not originate from the two houses [lords and commons]; they were no more than spaniels who fetched and carried at the command of the crown. Richard must have been the author, because no man living could derive the least benefit but himself; besides, it was part of a consistent plan. There were two families between him and a sceptre, those of his two brothers. He had now disposed of one.

The Woodvilles did not profit from any estates of Clarence's, so had no real reason to engineer his downfall. However, a case can be made that Gloucester turned Edward IV against Clarence to such an extent that Edward saw Clarence as a threat to his crown. Clarence's death meant one of two things to Gloucester. Either a chance opened for him to be king, or he might be the next to suffer his brother's wrath. Gloucester stayed away from court as much as possible.

In 1471 Gloucester had become Great Chamberlain of England, which was then given to Clarence as part of Richard's wife's settlement, but restored to Gloucester after Clarence's execution in 1478. Gloucester also took the opportunity to secure the king's consent in 1478 to some revisions in estates in his favour against Clarence's heir, the young Edward, Earl of Warwick. Gloucester also seized lands in Rutland and Lincolnshire by illegal force. War with Scotland was imminent in 1480 and Gloucester was appointed Lieutenant-General of the North as fears of a Scottish invasion grew. Together with the Earl of Northumberland he launched counter-raids, and when the king and council formally declared war in November 1480, Gloucester was granted £10,000 for troops' wages. The king failed to arrive to lead the English army and the result was intermittent skirmishing until early 1482. Northumberland, Stanley, Dorset, Sir Edward Woodville and Gloucester took the walled border town of Berwick-upon-Tweed. In 1483 Gloucester was given a new hereditary palatinate of the counties of Cumberland and Westmorland and any lands he conquered in Scotland.

Gloucester had been granted custody of George Neville, 1st Duke of Bedford during minority, supervising all his landholdings, his wardship and marriage. Bedford was the nephew of the Kingmaker, Warwick, and the son of John Neville, Earl of Northumberland, later to be Marquess of Montagu. His parents' incomes had given him enough income to support a baronetcy, and George also had been heir presumptive to the Neville estates of his uncle the Earl of Warwick, who only had two daughters. He also would be likely to inherit (after his mother and grandmother) a third share of the Tiptoft property held by his childless great-uncle the Earl of Worcester. The inheritances altogether would have yielded around £4,000 pounds a year, compared to the £4,500 annual income of Clarence, and over £5,000 for Gloucester. Bedford's father and uncle had been killed in 1471 at Barnet.

George Neville, born around 1461, was a small boy at the death of his father. He had been sent for safe keeping to Calais, from where he was taken after the Battle of Barnet. A special Act of Parliament in 1475 gave the Neville inheritance in the north of England to

Gloucester. There was a major problem in that neither Neville brother had ever been actually attainted, so the lands should have passed to George. This was solved in 1475 by having Parliament bypass the laws of inheritance. It declared that the Warwick lands would be vested in Richard, Duke of Gloucester, as long as there was any male heir of John Neville alive. George never received any inheritance from his father, uncle or from his maternal ancestors. Instead Gloucester controlled his estates and incomes. There was a reason for restricting his income.

Shortly before he came of age in 1478 Bedford was deprived of his ducal title by, again, a special Act of Parliament, ostensibly for lack of money to maintain the style of a duke. Richard III's defenders laud the charity of the king, for example Kendall noting that 'When [Neville] was stripped of his dukedom... Richard secured his wardship and brought the boy into his household.' The estates of George's dead uncle, Richard Neville, Earl of Warwick, had been entailed in the male line, meaning that in the normal course of affairs, the Warwick lands, including Middleham and Sheriff Hutton, would have gone to George rather than to Warwick's daughters. Warwick's daughters happened to be the wealthy wives of Gloucester and Clarence. Just as the Earl of Warwick's widow, Anne Beauchamp, was illegally deprived of her own estates, George would be deprived of his Warwick lands. These were given by Edward IV to his brother Gloucester and would be the basis for the great influence that Richard was to enjoy in the North.

Gloucester was the sole beneficiary of the 1475 Act vesting George's inheritance in him, and also the sole beneficiary of the 1478 act degrading George. Had

George remained a peer, as an adult he could have used his standing to persuade Parliament to reverse the 1475 Act, as George had been far too young to have been involved in his father's treason. The Dukedom of Bedford was given in 1478 to George Plantagenet, the third son of Edward IV, who died aged just two, a year later.

In 1480 Gloucester obtained George's wardship and marriage, so could profit handsomely from the remaining revenues of his ward's estate. George Neville, even without his Warwick lands, still had a good income, enough to make him a desirable ward. However, he was in Gloucester's custody. And importantly, obtaining George's marriage gave Gloucester the right to choose his bride. For Richard and his heirs to keep George's Warwick land, George Neville needed to have a male heir. His wife must not be too well connected, however, as her family might be able to press for George's restoration to his Warwick lands. However, George Neville died in unexplained circumstances in May 1483, unmarried and childless, and was buried at what should have been his own castle at Sheriff Hutton. Richard's interest in the Warwick lands was thus reduced to a life estate as he had not married George Neville off to a suitable woman.

Several historians have indicated that the George's death meant that Gloucester's hold on his Northern estates was loosened. George died only a month before Richard took the crown. With Edward IV no longer alive to give lands to his surviving brother, Gloucester needed to find a solution. According to A. J. Pollard in *Richard III and the Princes in the Tower*, 'By going all the way and making himself king, even if he did not initially set out with this goal in mind, Richard resolved the question of his title to his Northern estates once and for all.'

In 1481, Edward IV had renewed his alliance with Brittany, and ratified a contract of marriage between his son Edward, Prince of Wales, and Anne, eldest daughter of the Duke of Brittany. After the relative success of Gloucester's campaign against Scotland, Edward IV made preparations to invade France, but was seized with a violent fever, dying upon 9 April 1483 after twenty-three years as king. Edward IV had led a dissolute life with his great friend Hastings, and put on a great deal of weight. He was only forty years old, and his death is still unexplained. He may have been poisoned, as some thought at the time, in which case the main beneficiary would have been Gloucester. If so, Gloucester could have been responsible for the deaths of both his brothers in order to become king. Typhoid and food poisoning have also been suggested. From his lifestyle, a venereal disease or diabetes could not be ruled out. The king had fallen ill in March 1483, after catching a cold on a fishing trip on the Thames at Windsor, which may have developed into pneumonia. Edward left two young sons, Edward, Prince of Wales, and Richard, Duke of York. Of his seven legitimate daughters, Elizabeth of York later married Henry Tudor of Lancaster, Henry VII, and Anne married Thomas Howard, Duke of Norfolk. Gloucester was now left with two male children between him and the crown.

Some Ricardian-leaning modern writers and novelists have blamed his wife's Woodville family for the king's death. Carson even posits that the queen-consort Elizabeth Woodville and/or her brother Anthony Woodville poisoned Edward IV. This is a fairly strange theory, as the Woodvilles virtually controlled Edward IV through his queen, Elizabeth Woodville. However, in *Richard III: The Maligned King*, Carson believes that Elizabeth was no longer attractive to Edward IV, who had a string of mistresses. She believes that Elizabeth could now more easily manipulate her young son than her husband. As proof that the marriage was becoming strained, Carson states that Elizabeth was 'not even mentioned on the list of executors who met to prove the king's will.' She could not have been an executor, however, as she was in sanctuary fearing Gloucester when the will was proven. As we shall see, Anthony Woodville, Earl Rivers, had no motive for any plot. Carson also places the king's closest friend William Hastings as a suspect for Edward IV's death, as Hastings also thought he could more easily manipulate Richard. Hastings was Edward IV's best friend.

Examining contemporary evidence, neither the Woodvilles nor Hastings were ever accused by Richard III of poisoning or murdering Edward IV. Earl Rivers was in Wales, so any poisoning (by aconite?) would have to be carried by an agent, and there is no evidence that Hastings and his drinking and whoring partner Edward IV were on poor terms in 1483. The only realistic suspect for foul play would have been the king's brother Richard, Duke of Gloucester, who had seen his brother George, Duke of Clarence, executed by the king's orders in 1478. Carson, a non-fiction writer, also suggests that Hastings or the Woodvilles could have been involved in the 1483 deaths of George Neville and of the Earl of Essex, who was aged around eighty at the time. Neville was in secure custody at Richard's great base of Middleham Castle, when he died aged just twenty-one. There is no record of his manner of death, which left Richard in secure control of his Neville estates. There seems no apparent motive for the Woodvilles or Hastings to have killed either Essex or Neville, and one wonders why Carson came to these conclusions.

Edward had taken to his bed on 30 March with, apparently, nothing seriously wrong with him. He grew steadily worse and eventually had to accept that he was dying, and he did the best he could in the hours before his agonising death upon 9 April to ensure the safe succession of his son Edward V. There was no opportunity to persuade William, Lord Hastings, and Anthony Woodville, Earl Rivers, to abandon their feud, because Rivers was away at Ludlow Castle with the Prince of Wales. Richard was at Middleham Castle when he received the news of his brother's death, sent by a fast messenger from Henry Stafford, Duke of Buckingham. Gloucester wrote a letter of condolences to Queen Elizabeth, promising to do all that lay within his power to ensure the smooth succession of her son, Edward, Prince of Wales, now King Edward V.

However, Gloucester loathed Thomas Grey, Marquis of Dorset, the queen's elder son by her first marriage, and this feeling was mutual. Gloucester also detested and despised the queen, again with reciprocal feelings. Professor Colin Richmond disagrees with Ricardians that in April 1483 there was in all probability an active Woodville conspiracy against Gloucester, as basically as there was no real need for one. All the queen and her family wanted was the early coronation of the new king – their problems with Richard could be dealt with later. Sir Thomas More related a story heard by his father, and it may have been apocryphal. A lawyer,

Richard Pottyer, did some work for Gloucester. Upon hearing the news of Edward IV's death, he is said to have remarked to the messenger, 'By my troth man, then will my master the Duke of Gloucester be King.' There is better evidence of Richard's intentions in a letter dated 19 April 1483, written by John Gigur, the warden of Tattershall College in Lincolnshire, to its patron, William of Waynflete, Bishop of Winchester: 'I beseech you to remember in what jeopardy your college of Tatteeshall stands in at this day; for now our Sovereign Lord the King is dead we know ... not who shall be our Lord nor who shall have the rule about us.'

Historians state that Edward's will could not be found, but this would relate to a later will than that dated 1475. In this early will, he entrusted the care of his son and heir and his other children to 'our dearest wife the Queen' who was appointed chief executrix. However, upon his deathbed, Edward is said to have realised that the ambition and unpopularity of the queen's family would lead to trouble if the will was allowed to stand. He therefore made a new will which, according to Mancini's informants, gave the custody of the realm and of all Edward's children to Gloucester.

Edward obviously intended that Gloucester should rule as Protector until King Edward V should come of age, and control of the young king would be removed from his present guardian, Anthony Woodville, Earl Rivers, to Gloucester. These details are repeated by Polydore Vergil, and there is a reference to them in the Chancellor's draft of the speech with which he would have opened the first parliament of the new reign. Further confirmation comes from the meeting of the new executors when the queen was hiding in sanctuary, a few days after the king's death. In the days following the king's death, the council met several times. The minutes have not survived, but there were several, including Gloucester himself after he became king, who may have had an interest in destroying them.

3

Gloucester Takes the Throne: The Turbulent Reign of the Last Plantagenet 1483–1485

Treason doth never prosper: what's the reason?
Why, if it prosper, none dare call it treason.
Sir John Harington (1561–1612)

With Edward IV's marriage to Elizabeth Woodville in 1464, the king had begun to provide for her mother, her two sons from a previous marriage, five brothers and seven sisters. They were granted peerages and lands from out of favour nobles, and marriages were arranged to further increase the Woodville family power. Her mother was Jacquetta of Luxembourg, who had lost her first husband John of Lancaster, a son of Henry IV. Jacquetta's second husband, Elizabeth's father, Baron Rivers, was not of the highest rank of nobility, so Elizabeth was scorned as a 'commoner' by the great families of England. The main reason, however, for their dislike was that her family was given major preferments under Edward. Elizabeth Woodville's father had been created Earl Rivers, Constable and Treasurer of England, in 1466 but was executed by Warwick with his eldest son John after the Battle of Edgcote Moor in 1469. Elizabeth's eldest brother, Anthony, Lord Scales became Governor of the Isle of Wight before succeeding Earl Rivers. In fact Rivers and Jacquetta had fourteen children, and all of whom who survived greatly benefited from the marriage, along with other relatives.

Another brother, Richard, succeeded Anthony as the 3rd Earl Rivers. Elizabeth's brother Lionel became Bishop of Salisbury, and yet another brother, twenty-year-old John, was married off to the sixty-five-year-old Dowager Duchess Katherine of Norfolk, gaining massive estates and wealth. The queen's sisters were married off to wealthy heirs, becoming the Duchess of Buckingham, Countess of Pembroke, Countess of Arundel, Viscountess Bourchier, Lady Strange and Lady Grey. Elizabeth's eldest son by her first marriage, Thomas Grey, was made Marquis of Dorset and married the heiress of the Duke of Exeter. The seeds had been sown for upheaval upon Edward's death, if the Woodville family lost their royal protection.

Mancini tells us that Gloucester resented their new wealth, power and influence at court, as did especially Henry Stafford, Duke of Buckingham, and Lord Hastings, Edward IV's chamberlain. Buckingham, with a Lancastrian father and grandfather who had both died fighting at the First Battle of St Albans and Northampton respectively, had never had real influence in Edward IV's Yorkist court. According to Mancini, Buckingham had been forced to marry one of the queen's sisters, whom he 'scorned on account of her humble origin'. In 1464, Edward IV had purchased the wardship of Buckingham from his father, the Earl of Stafford's executors. In 1465, aged ten, Buckingham had been compelled to marry Katherine Woodville, the queen's sister. Buckingham was only too well aware that he descended from a line of kings, and took great exception to his marriage. Buckingham organised Richard III's coronation but did not even invite his own wife. Lord Hastings had endured a violent and long-lasting feud with queen-consort Elizabeth's eldest son, Thomas Grey, Marquess of Dorset.

Kept away from the continuing enmities at court between the Grey/Woodville families and other nobles, Edward IV's twelve-year-old son Edward Plantagenet, Prince of Wales, was based with his household at Ludlow Castle. Prince Edward was under the supervision of his guardian Earl Rivers, the queen's brother, when Edward IV died upon 9 April 1483. Rivers was a noted scholar, and Ludlow was the base from which the principality of Wales was governed. The Prince of Wales's ten-year-old younger brother, Richard of Shrewsbury, 1st Duke of York (in its second creation), and also Duke of Norfolk, Earl of Norfolk, Earl of Nottingham and Earl Marshall, was with his mother in London.

Edward IV died in Westminster and was buried in St. George's Chapel, Windsor, near the tomb of his victim

Henry VI. Dominic Mancini, who was in London until July 1483, described how the king's council assembled in London shortly after Edward IV's funeral upon 20 April. Some lords proposed that Gloucester should govern 'because Edward in his will had so directed'. By codicils added on his deathbed to his will of 1475 Edward IV appears to have named his surviving brother, Gloucester, as Lord Protector, but he probably committed the personal custody of his heir to the prince's maternal kinsmen, headed by Rivers, Dorset, and Sir Richard Grey. There was a heated debate, and the council decided against Gloucester governing the kingdom on behalf of the new king Edward V. Instead, the majority of the lords voted for a ruling council, with Gloucester as chief councillor, because otherwise the duke would have too much power and in Mancini's words 'might easily usurp the sovereignty'. Many of these latter lords were allied to the queen's party in the council, led by Dorset, and obviously feared that they might 'be ejected from their high estate' by Gloucester. Edward IV's councillors thus chose a middle path between those who wanted Richard in control and those who preferred the Woodville family. The council unanimously agreed upon a coronation date of 4 May for the new king Edward V.

Gloucester was at Middleham Castle in the North when informed by Buckingham's messenger of Edward IV's death. The Woodvilles were insistent upon an early coronation, and instructions were sent to Earl Rivers to bring Edward V to London by 1 May at the latest for the coronation on 4 May. In council, a row had broken out over the size of the new king's escort, and Hastings even threatened to withdraw to Calais where he still held command, unless a limit was put on its numbers. The queen asked Rivers to appease the opposition on the king's council to her Woodville family, by having no more than 2,000 men escort the new king into London.

Lord Hastings had fought for Edward IV, and was his most trusted courtier and Lord Chamberlain for the length of his reign. Hastings now sent a messenger to Gloucester to warn him that Edward was to ride to London for an early coronation. The date of his letter is uncertain, but it was in Richard's hands by the date of his brother's funeral, 20 April, and he may even have received it as early as 16 or 17 April. It confirmed Gloucester's view that his retaining power depended upon early action against the Woodvilles. Hastings described the council's refusal to appoint Gloucester as Protector with the full powers of the monarch as an insult. Gloucester wrote to the council that his many years of loyalty and faithful service deserved better treatment than this. At the same time, he followed Hastings' advice to secure the new king before he reached London, and wrote to Hastings and Buckingham to help him achieve this end.

Gloucester also despatched a letter to the queen, saying that a large armed force could be seen as dangerous, and a smaller retinue would do to escort the new king. She naively sent a message to Rivers to just bring a small escort. Gloucester immediately began riding to London with many of his loyal Northern nobility and their armed troops. Simultaneously, the wealthy Duke of Buckingham saw an opportunity of gaining the power he was never given under Edward IV, and moved to join Richard's force. Prince Edward was too young to rule, so Gloucester wished to be in full control of the necessary interim government, instead of the prince's Woodville family. Buckingham saw the opportunity in Edward's death to be more influential at court, and Gloucester and Hastings must have felt that a Woodville king would leave them in the cold, and possibly at risk of reprisals from the Woodvilles.

Gloucester and his allies desperately needed to prevent the coronation happening. Richard II had been crowned at the age of ten and Henry VI at the age of seven, with the very act of coronation giving them greater authority to allow those closest to them to assert their influence. Gloucester somehow had to secure the twelve-year-old Edward V before his coronation, and sent letters to his supporters in the North, trying to build up support to shore his position. Buckingham had been the first of the great nobles to contact Gloucester, and had ridden to York, offering support and a thousand armed men. Gloucester in turn asked Buckingham to bring a smaller force, possibly fearing Buckingham's own claims to the crown. Buckingham's ancestors had included two sons of Edward III. More messages were sent to Gloucester when he arrived at Nottingham with around 500 men, and Buckingham met with Gloucester at Northampton on 29 April, with a smaller force of about around 200 men.

Rivers wished to celebrate St George's Day, 23 April, in Ludlow for which he had made considerable preparations. It was only on 24 April that his party set out in a slow and stately progress. Mancini informs us Gloucester, Buckingham and Earl Rivers agreed to meet somewhere on the way to London, so that the Edward V's entry would be more magnificent before his coronation upon 4 May. This was probably not the idea of Rivers, who could have easily reached

London before Richard or Buckingham. Upon 29 April 1483, the forces of Gloucester and Buckingham met at Northampton. It was only five days before the expected coronation. Rivers escorted the king 14 miles further south to Stony Stratford. Sir Richard Grey, the queen's son by a previous marriage, had been in London for the council deliberations over the coronation, but left the city to meet the new king. There is speculation that he was given a message from the queen urging Rivers to bring the king to London as quickly as possible. Grey, however, was also a member of Edward V's household and possibly he merely wished to accompany his younger half-brother upon his triumphant entry into London.

Leaving the king in lodgings at Stony Stratford, Rivers (and possibly Sir Richard Grey) rode to Northampton to meet Gloucester and Buckingham. Rivers explained that there would not have been lodgings for the king and his small escort in Northampton, and apologised for the change in plans. The nobles spent a convivial evening together, and Rivers stayed in an inn arranged by Richard. The next morning, Mancini tells us that Rivers was locked in, and then arrested in the Northampton lodgings, but the Croyland Chronicler states that Rivers was taken prisoner by Gloucester and Buckingham on his way back to the king at Stony Stratford. The fate of Rivers and Grey, the new king's appointed guardians, was sealed.

On that same morning of 30 April, along with Rivers in Northampton or in Stony Stratford, where Gloucester and Buckingham had ridden to meet the king, Sir Richard Grey was arrested. At Stony Stratford, Edward V's chamberlain, Thomas Vaughan, was also taken and all the king's attendants were either arrested or dismissed. Without leadership, the king's small retinue dispersed in the face of overwhelming force. The king was informed by Gloucester and Buckingham that Rivers, Grey and Vaughan were plotting against him, and that Gloucester was the man best suited to serve as his Protector.

Edward V protested strongly, but was taken into Gloucester's custody. It was only four days until the king's coronation, but he was never to be crowned. Before Gloucester proceeded to London with the king, he sent his prisoners far away to his castles in the North. Rivers was despatched to Sheriff Hutton, Grey to Middleham, and Vaughan to Pontefract. Richard Haute (Hawte), Edward V's comptroller, seems to have been arrested and imprisoned as well, although he was apparently later pardoned. Clergymen, the king's tutor and others in the king's party were also later released from Gloucester's custody.

Gloucester, Buckingham and the king did not reach London until the day of the planned coronation, 4 May. Gloucester had been careful to arrange for the reception of Edward V by the citizens of London. Taking his time to reach the city, he had sent in advance letters to the king's council and to the mayor. He told them that he had rescued the king from treason. Gloucester placed four cartloads of weapons in front of the king's procession, claiming that they had been stored outside the capital by the queen's family to use against Gloucester himself. The independent Italian observer Mancini reported that this charge was obviously false, as the weapons had been stored when war was being waged against Scotland. Gloucester rode into London in procession behind Edward V, proclaiming, 'Behold your prince and sovereign!' to the cheers of the crowds. Notably, he is not known to have declared Edward as king, but still as a 'prince'. A great council of nobles was next held, declaring Richard of Gloucester 'Protector of the king and kingdom'. Lord Hastings supported Gloucester's formal installation as Lord Protector and collaborated with him in the royal council. One of Gloucester's first acts as Protector was to illegally confiscate the estates of Dorset, Grey and Rivers and other members of the Woodville family, as if they had been forfeited by Act of Attainder. He redistributed them among his followers, but they were given back to the surviving Woodvilles by Henry VII.

In council Gloucester argued that the small force of Rivers guarding the new king had been planning to ambush him, but the council was not convinced by the rather obvious untruth. Gloucester also accused Edward IV's's half-brother Lord Richard Grey, his brother Thomas Grey, Marquis of Dorset, and Earl Rivers of 'hostile and treasonable designs'. The queen's brother Edward Woodville was said by Gloucester and Buckingham to have taken treasure from the Tower of London and sent a force to sea. This is not true, but his fleet took gold coins from a ship at Southampton before he sailed to join Henry Tudor in France. Actually Richard sold royal plate to pay for 4,000 Northern troops to come and secure his coronation, and his accusation was probably meant to cover his own actions. The council accepted Richard as Protector, but refused his demands for the immediate execution of the queen's brother Rivers, son Richard Grey, son Dorset and the venerable and faithful Vaughan. The council could find 'no certain case' that Rivers was planning to take Richard, and argued cogently that it could not have been treason because Richard then held no public office.

Councillors asked Gloucester if Rivers would have ridden to spend a night in the 'enemy' camp if he was planning to capture Gloucester. Would he have taken such a small force? Would his men have capitulated without a fight? What would be the point of Rivers trying to strengthen his position vis-à-vis Gloucester? When Edward V was crowned, the Woodville family would still have controlled the country, so Gloucester would have been no threat. Gloucester's apologists uniformly and pointedly ignore the abduction of the king, the later murder without trial of the nobles protecting him and the refusal to crown the new king, in their attempts to transform Gloucester's image.

Gloucester summoned armed help from the North, and at least one of his letters survives. It is dated 10 June 1483, and was delivered to the Mayor and City of York, by Sir Richard Ratcliffe, a knight of Richard's household. Its terms are revealing:

The Duke of Gloucester, brother and uncle of Kings, Great Chamberlain, Constable and Admiral of England – Right trusty and well beloved, we greet you well, and as ye love the weal of us, and the weal and surety of your own selves, we heartily pray you to come unto us in London in all the diligence ye can after the sight hereof, with as many as ye can make defensibly arrayed, there to aid and assist us against the Queen, her blood adherents and affinity, which hath intended and daily doth intend to murder and utterly destroy us and our cousin, the Duke of Buckingham, and the old Royal blood of this Realm, and as it is now openly known, by their subtle and damnable ways plotting the same, and also the final destruction and disinheriting of you and all other men of property and honour, as well of the north parts as other counties that belong to us.

William, Lord Hastings, had been the best friend and Chamberlain of Edward IV and had, more than anyone, ensured that Gloucester's faction held its own in court and held against the queen's party. The new council came to be biased towards Gloucester's side, with Woodville power vastly diminished. The queen-consort had fled into sanctuary at Westminster Abbey on 1 May with her remaining children when Edward V was taken by Gloucester. Gloucester, however, also wanted the heir presumptive, Prince Richard, in his power. One has to ask why. Hastings thus gave his personal promise to the Archbishop of York, Thomas Rotherham, that the queen-consort's remaining son, Richard of York, would be safer with Gloucester. However, according to Barnard and other sources, Gloucester had agreed a course of action with Buckingham, who had rapidly risen in power and wealth to become Gloucester's main ally, and Sir William Catesby. It appears that they took Hastings into their confidence that Richard was going to take the throne, but 'the loyal Hastings, shocked at the thought of Richard assuming the regal diadem, declared he would support the interest of the young princes, and not only at the expense of his own fortune, but with the last drop of his blood'.

Gloucester, possibly the next morning, called a council meeting in the Tower on 13 June 1483, ostensibly to discuss the coronation of Edward V. Gloucester conversed 'affably' with its members, and gave the final directions for the long-deferred coronation of Edward V, and then left. (This was six weeks after the original agreed date.) However, he returned in a rage after about an hour, shouting 'My lords, what punishment do those deserve, who have conspired against my life?' Hastings answered, 'Whoever was guilty of such a crime, deserves to suffer the death of a traitor.' Gloucester and Buckingham then accused Hastings and other council members of having conspired against Gloucester's life with the Woodvilles. They said that Hastings' mistress Jane Shore had acted as a go-between. Gloucester shouted at Hastings, 'I arrest thee for high treason.' In this fait accompli, soldiers seized the unsuspecting Hastings, along with Lord Thomas Stanley, the Archbishop of York and Bishop Morton of Ely. Hastings was allowed a confession to a priest and immediately beheaded on Tower Green. Gloucester had packed the council with his supporters, and from now on acted as king. There could have been no treason from Hastings as Gloucester was not yet king. This whole sequence of stage-managed events is unexplained by Ricardians, desperate to create a noble king out of Gloucester.

According to Thomas More, as soon as Edward IV died, Gloucester had started stirring up opposition between the queen's party and the nobles, telling them of the inequality of blood between the queen's commoner relatives and the nobles. Buckingham seemed to be complicit in and aware of Gloucester's duplicity, but Hastings seemed too trusting. Hastings also put too much trust in his assistant Catesby, who had also been secretly recruited by Gloucester. On the other hand, Lord Thomas Stanley, Earl of Derby, who was a close friend of Hastings, distrusted Gloucester and criticised him for having two councils. More tells us that Gloucester asked Hastings' adviser Catesby to sound Hastings out as to whether he would support Richard's plans to usurp the kingdom; 'but Catesby whither he assayed him or assayed him not, reported unto them, that he found him so fast [steadfast], and heard him speak so terrible words, that he durst no further breke [reveal]'. Hastings was completely taken in by the friendship that Richard and Buckingham then showed towards him.

Let us briefly examine the case of Elizabeth, known as 'Jane' Shore. She was a mistress of Hastings after becoming Edward IV's mistress from 1476 until his death in 1483. She had also been also a mistress of Edward IV's stepson, Dorset. The new Protector, Gloucester, accused her of plotting treason with the absent Dorset, Hastings and the Woodvilles, and summoned her to appear before the king's council upon charges of conspiracy. No proof was found against her, despite the Woodville party now being in the minority. She was then sent by Gloucester to be tried in the spiritual court for adultery. Shore was sentenced to do public penance before being sent to Ludgate Gaol, eventually marrying the solicitor-general. Thomas More met her when she was an old woman, and it seems that some of his information was given by her.

Of the others arrested along with Hastings, the most important were the clergymen John Morton, Bishop of Ely, Thomas Rotherham, Archbishop of York, and Lord Thomas Stanley. A former Lancastrian, Morton was one of the executors of Edward IV's will in 1483. When he was arrested with Hastings, Oxford University in vain petitioned for Morton's release, and after some weeks in the Tower he was entrusted to Buckingham's charge at Brecon Castle. Here, it seems that he influenced Buckingham against Gloucester. The second clergyman arrested was Thomas Rotherham (1423–1500), Archbishop of York. He had been appointed by Edward IV as Keeper of the Privy Seal in 1467, and in 1474 was made Lord Chancellor. The archbishop was one of the celebrants of Edward IV's funeral Mass in 1483, and sided with the dowager queen Elizabeth Woodville as she tried to deprive Gloucester of his role as Lord Protector of the new king, her son Edward V. When Elizabeth sought sanctuary after Richard had taken her son Edward V, the archbishop released the Great Seal to her. Although he later recovered it and handed it over to Thomas Bourchier, Archbishop of Canterbury, Richard III dismissed him as Lord Chancellor. Rotherham was charged with being involved in the conspiracy between Lord Hastings and the Woodvilles against Richard and imprisoned in the Tower, but released only a month later. The *London Chronicle* related that Rotherham was also sent into Buckingham's custody at Brecon, so there would have been two of Henry Tudor's main supporters in close contact with Buckingham.

The third so-called accomplice of Hastings was Lord Thomas Stanley. After the death of Edward IV, Stanley tried to maintain a balance of power between Gloucester and the Woodvilles. Stanley's own son and heir, George, Lord Strange, was married to the queen's sister, Joan le Strange, the daughter of Jacquetta Woodville. In the council meeting Stanley was hit with a battleaxe when Hastings was taken, but his life was saved as he sank, injured, under a table. This must have affected his feelings towards the House of York. However, 'In preparing the ground for the usurpation and in consolidating his position, Richard found it more expedient to appease than to alienate the house of Stanley.' Thus Lord

Stanley was freed, continuing as steward of the royal household, and bore the great mace at Richard III's coronation. His wife, Henry Tudor's mother Margaret Beaufort, carried the new queen's train. Stanley was also appointed to the Order of the Garter, taking the place of the executed Hastings. Thus not one of the three main persons arrested by Gloucester for alleged treason alongside Hastings received any real punishment.

Learning on 30 April that her brother Rivers and her sons Edward V and Richard Grey had been captured by Gloucester, Elizabeth Woodville had fled into sanctuary at Westminster Abbey precincts. She took her other son by Edward IV, Richard, Duke of York, and her five daughters. Elizabeth's eldest son Thomas Grey, Lord Dorset, was also in sanctuary with the queen, but managed to slip away and elude Richard's men, to join Henry Tudor in exile. Gloucester now bestowed nearly all the Grey and Woodville holdings upon his own men. He had then made a motion in council, asking the queen to give up the Duke of York to assist in the preparations for Edward V's coronation. He told his supporters that the queen's distrust would incite factions, so bringing the heirs together would unite the nation. He said that if Prince Richard of York remained in asylum, the queen could 'raise commotions'.

Gloucester proposed that the Archbishop of York should convince her that Richard of York would come to no harm, saying that if the matter did not end peacefully, it would have to be resolved by force. Hastings went to the London palace of Thomas Rotherham, Archbishop of York, assuring him that no harm would ever come to Edward V and that Gloucester was sincere in his protection of the infant king. The archbishop found the queen distressed, sitting on the floor and crying about the fate of her children. He gave her Hastings' assurances, which gave her no comfort, but then promised that if Edward V was killed, he would instantly crown the infant Richard, giving her the Great Seal as a promise of his sincerity.

Gloucester found out, and ordered the Archbishop to immediately retrieve the Great Seal from the queen. Gloucester gave it to the Bishop of Lincoln, who became Lord Keeper of the Great Seal until 1485, when Henry VII returned it to the Archbishop of York. The queen heard of Hastings being killed, and still refused to leave, but on 16 June Richard kept to his word and surrounded the abbey with troops. He now sent the aged Archbishop of Canterbury, Thomas Bourchier (1404–86), to plead with her. The queen eventually gave in to the clergyman's continued pressure, on condition that Richard of York was returned to her after the coronation. On or before 20 June 1483 she let Richard be taken away, while staying in sanctuary with her daughters. It was the last she saw of Prince Richard. Bourchier had sworn to Edward IV to be faithful to Edward V, but crowned Richard III later in 1483. Both princes were now in the royal apartments in the Tower of London.

Plans were still seemingly in motion for Edward V's delayed coronation upon 24 June. However, Robert Stillington had been Edward IV's Lord Chancellor and was the Bishop of Bath and Wells. In 1473 he was dismissed by Edward IV, and in 1478 spent some weeks in prison for associating with the disgraced Clarence. Sometime between the end of April and 13 June 1483, Bishop Stillington had told Gloucester that he had witnessed the contract of betrothal between Edward IV and Lady Eleanor Butler, daughter of the Earl of Shrewsbury. This was before Edward's clandestine marriage to Elizabeth Woodville, mother of Edward V and his younger brother Richard. A contract of betrothal was as binding as a marriage contract, and under English common law of the time Edward IV's subsequent marriage to Elizabeth Woodville could be thus thought bigamous. There is no documentary proof of Stillington's claim, and there were no other witnesses, but this gave Gloucester a valid reason to take the throne. With all his enemies in custody, sanctuary or exile, Gloucester declared the marriage of his brother Edward IV invalid.

Edward V and his brother were thus declared illegitimate on the grounds that Edward IV was pre-contracted to Eleanor Talbot when he married Elizabeth Woodville. There may have been a legal justification, but breaking pre-contracts was quite normal at the time. If any question of legitimacy had arisen then ecclesiastical dispensation or parliamentary instruments could have been sought. They were never required because the issue had never been raised, and time and custom had conferred legitimacy upon Edward IV's marriage. There was also the question of whether it was a 'morganatic marriage' to Woodville. In the context of royalty, a morganatic marriage is one between people of unequal social rank, which prevents the passage of the husband's titles and privileges to the wife and any children born of the marriage.

Whether Stillington was lying or not, Richard could now depose Edward V and Richard, Duke of York, on the grounds that they were illegitimate. Also, Clarence's son Edward was debarred by his father's attainder, so the crown could pass to Gloucester. Gloucester had transformed himself into the only legitimate heir of the

House of York. To add to his claims, Gloucester and supporters now claimed that his brother Edward IV had been illegitimate. Edward IV was not physically like his small, dark father Richard of York, being for that time an exceptionally tall 6 feet 4 inches. Richard Neville, Earl of Warwick, had raised the question of adultery in 1469, when he fell out with the king. The rumour had been repeated by Edward's brother, Clarence (who was later sentenced to death by Edward in 1478). In Edward IV's case, the suggestion was that his real father might have been an archer called Blaybourne. Gloucester was accusing his mother of adultery leading to at least two illegitimate sons.

From 14 July to 21 August 1441, the time of conception for Edward, who was born in April 1442, Edward's father, the Duke of York, was on campaign at Pontoise in France. Pontoise was several days' march from Rouen, where his wife Cecily Neville was quartered. The christening of the couple's first-born son Edward was a small ceremony in a small chapel in Rouen. However, the christening celebration of Edmund, Earl of Rutland, the second son of York and Cecily, was a much more lavish affair, which led to the rumours about Edward IV being a bastard. Once he gained the throne, Richard III did not persist with the story of his brother's illegitimacy.

Upon 22 June 1483 Dr Ralph Shaa gave a sermon at St Paul's, 'Bastard slips [children] shall not thrive', alleging that both Edward IV and Clarence were illegitimate, unlike Gloucester. Shaa publicly declared Edward IV's children bastards and Gloucester the rightful king. The citizens of London, nobles and commons were convened, and a petition was drawn up asking Gloucester to assume the throne. On 25

June a packed assembly of lords and commoners, with most Woodville supporters absent, and many others cowed by the example of Hastings' murder, endorsed the claims. The council had been powerless in the execution of Hastings and the arrests of others. Richard of Gloucester accepted on 26 June and was crowned Richard III at Westminster Abbey upon 6 July 1483. His title to the throne was confirmed by Parliament in January 1484 by the document *Titulus Regius*.

Kings usually proceeded from the Tower of London to Westminster in procession to their coronation, and this had been Richard's excuse for placing the princes in the Tower. They were never seen in public, nor heard from, again. Hastings had done more than anyone in London to prevent the Woodvilles taking over the apparatus of state after the death of Edward IV, and was regarded as perhaps Gloucester's closest advisor and confidante. However, something had drastically and suddenly altered in the relationship between the two men. It appears that Hastings was loyal to Edward V, his friend's son, and disagreed with Gloucester's true intentions towards the 'Princes in the Tower'. Upon 13 June Hastings had been murdered, upon 20 June Prince Richard was taken to join his brother in the Tower, upon 22 June Shaa gave his illegitimacy sermon, upon 25 June Rivers, Grey and Vaughan were beheaded, and upon 25 June Richard was asked to be king. This was a well-oiled takeover of the monarchy.

On 25 June, on explicit orders from Gloucester to Sir Thomas Radcliffe, the governor of Pontefract Castle, Edward V's closest advisers were killed. In 1473, Anthony Woodville, Earl Rivers, the brother of Elizabeth Woodville, had been appointed as governor to the three-year-old Prince Edward, and had been at his side for ten years. Richard Grey, Elizabeth Woodville's younger son by her first husband, was probably in his twenties at the time of his death. Michael Hicks describes him as being 'the most visible Wydeville in Wales in the mid-1470s', serving on local commissions of the peace. Thomas Vaughan, in his fifties at his death, had been a royal servant since the 1440s and loyal to the Yorkist cause for well over two decades. Having held a number of responsible positions during his career in royal service, he had been Edward V's Chamberlain since July 1471, when his charge was still an infant. A soldier who had fought in numerous battles, he carried Prince Edward in his arms on state occasions and was knighted at the same time as Edward in 1475. Having spent most of the past decade with the young prince at Ludlow, far from the politics of court, he represented little threat to Richard.

Before their executions, Rivers and Grey had been moved to join Vaughan at Pontefract, where the Earl of Northumberland and Sir Richard Ratcliff presided over their executions. Their deaths were witnessed by troops making their way toward London at Gloucester's command, in case trouble arose over Gloucester's claim to the throne. There is no record of any trial, but Rivers made his will on 23 June, while still at Sheriff Hutton. This, and more especially the ballad he wrote ('Such is my dance/Willing to die'), indicates that he knew that if he did receive a trial, it would be only for show.

Lewis Glyn Cothi had written a tribute to the heroic Syr Thomas Fychan ab Syr Rhosser Fychan (Sir Thomas Vaughan). The Welsh bard, having been informed of the death of Edward IV, seemed to have some foreboding that Richard of Gloucester would directly succeed him. In this excerpt Lewis Glyn Cothi styles Richard 'y brenin Rhisiart', that is, 'the king Richard', but Richard was still the Duke of Gloucester when the poem was written. After stating that Sir Thomas Vaughan had served Edward IV faithfully in eighteen engagements, Lewis Glyn Cothi assumed that Vaughan would now be willing to defend the white rose of Richard. It seems that the poem was written shortly before Vaughan, Rivers, Grey and the young King Edward V were captured. The reference to 'king' Richard, obviously written before Thomas Vaughan was taken by him, is extremely puzzling. This, and other contemporary writings and poems referring to Richard and Henry, need full academic study. We read the following lines in an *Awdl arall i Syr Thomas Fychan ab Syr Rhosser Fychan o Dre y Twr* ('Another Awdl to Sir Thomas Vaughan son of Sir Roger Vaughan of Tretower'). An awdl is a long poem in one of 24 strict metres, using a rhyming form called cynghanedd, and is one of the finest achievements of any Welsh poet.

Cryv oedd ar gadoedd, deunaw gwart gadarn;	He [Vaughan] was strong in battle, eighteen strong defenders;
Gyda'r brenin Edwart; A chwedi ev o awch dart,	With King Edward And after as sharp as a dart,
I gadw rhos gyda Rhisiart.	To keep the rose with Richard.
Y brenin Risiart, barnai'n wrestig,	King Richard, he judged forcibly,

Yw tarw crvv-vraisg
tyrau caer Evrog;

The bull [Richard] is
the strong and powerful
towers of York;

A vaidd dyn heddyw,
vaedd danneddog!

A boar man today, a boar
[Richard] with teeth
[tusks]!

... Syr Tomas curas y
gwyr caerog,

... Sir Thomas defeated the
men of the castle,

Asur yw ei helm, a ser
hoeliog;

His helmet is azure, with
stars attached;

A mwg o rubi ar helm
gribog;

And a ruby mane on top
of his helmet;

Ar ymyl ei ŵn aur
melynog;

On the border of his
golden gown;

Aur Rhisiart a vydd ar
osog rhyvel,

Richard's gold will be on
the goshawk [warrior] of
battle,

Aur yn vur uchel; arain
a farchog...

Gold on a high wall; a
knight in silver...

Upon 26 June, Richard III began his reign, and he was crowned upon 6 July 1483. According to Hutton, Richard had to sell the crown plate, 'consisting of 275 pounds 4 ounces, for 3s 4d an ounce, to pay a body of 4,000 sorry troops, hired from the North, to secure his coronation'. Incidentally Richard had falsely accused Edward Woodville of taking Crown treasure. Accusations were circulating that the princes had been murdered on Richard's orders, but Richard now felt secure enough in his power base to mop up any loose ends. Richard simply could not have got away with the murders of Edward V's closest advisers Rivers, Grey and Vaughan if the young king had assumed power. The very fact of killing them meant that Richard never could allow the princes to live. It is absurd to think that Edward V would have backed his uncle Gloucester against his mother and family. The Woodvilles' massive landholdings were given to Richard's supporters.

Fenn records, as recounted by William Thomas, a letter dated 23 June 1483 from Gloucester to the people of England, where he persuades them

> to resist Henry Tudor, and his attainted traitors; whom he pronounces murderers, adulterers, extortioners, rebels to God, honour, and nature; who obey his ancient enemy the French king; and under Henry their bastard leader, begotten in double adultery, intend to enter his kingdom, and, by conquest, despoil his subjects of life, liberty, and goods; to destroy all the honourable blood in the realm; and seize their possessions, therefore advises every man to lift up his hand against them. He tells them the French king lends assistance, in consideration of Normandy, Anjou, Gascoigny, Guisnes, Cassel, Hammes, Calais, and the marches given up, and the arms of France being forever dissevered from those of England; and that Henry hath already hath bestowed upon the foes of the kingdom, the bishoprics, and spiritual dignities, with the duchies, earldoms, baronies, and inheritances of knights, esquires, and gentlemen; that the old English laws are to be abolished, and those of a tyrant established among the people. That Henry Tudor and his wicked followers will commit the most horrid murders, slaughters, and robberies, that were ever heard of in a Christian country; every true Englishman therefore, is commanded to furnish himself with arms, to oppose the rebels, in defence of his wife,

children, and possessions; and the king himself will most courageously expose his most royal person, to every labour and hazard, to subdue their enemies, and comfort his faithful subject; and calls forth every man to defend his king in battle.

Could this perhaps be termed Ricardian propaganda?

In July 1483, there was some sort of plot to free the princes. Soon after 16 June 1483, perhaps on 20 June, the queen had been forced to send her son Richard of Shrewsbury, Duke of York, to join his brother Edward V in the Tower of London. The queen and her daughters remained in the sanctuary of Westminster Cathedral. The princes were seen playing together soon after they met, and then never seen in public again. In July, several men conspired to release them but were discovered. The circumstances are still unclear, but those executed at the Tower as a consequence of the failed conspiracy were John Smith, a groom of stirrup under Edward IV; Stephen Ireland, a wardrober in the Tower; Robert Rushe, Russe or Ruffe, sergeant of London; and William Davy, pardoner of Hounslow. A pardoner was an ecclesiastic who was authorised to raise money for religious works by issuing papal indulgences, i.e. who forgave sins in exchange for money.

It seems that they started fires across London, in the hope that the Tower garrison would rush out to deal with the flames, and the princes would be left unguarded. The existence of such a plot is confirmed by a contemporary account of Thomas Basin, a Frenchman who reported, in the words of historian Michael Hicks, 'a plot by fifty Londoners on the princes' behalf which failed to attract support and led to the execution of four of them'. Hicks and Horrox point out, this plot may be the unnamed '*enterprise*' to which Richard III alluded in a letter to his chancellor on 29 July 1483. Rumours immediately arose that the princes were dead. The men were all beheaded upon 26 February 1484, presumably after six months of torture to reveal other enemies of the king.

The plot involved Lord John Cheney (or Cheyne) and Margaret Beaufort at its head. Their plans were to set fire to parts of London as a distraction, storm the Tower and rescue the princes, restoring Edward V to the throne supported by an invasion by Jasper and Henry Tudor from France. Over fifty conspirators were arrested and included men who had worked under Cheney in the royal household. Cheney had been Edward IV's Master of Horse and master of his bodyguard, and also had been appointed a knight of the body to Richard, attending his coronation. In Buckingham's rebellion of 1483, one of the centres of revolt was Salisbury, and John Cheney became one of the leaders in the Salisbury rising. The risings began shortly after the failure of the rescue plan. In October 1483 the risings in Kent, the central south and the west, with the Duke of Buckingham as its nominal head, presented the first challenge to Richard III's reign. The men involved in the London fire plot were also accused of having sent letters to Henry Tudor. Cheney fled to France. A huge man at 6 feet 8 inches, his presence in Henry Tudor's bodyguard at Bosworth possibly prevented Henry Tudor's death.

Henry Stafford, 2nd Duke of Buckingham, had risen to be Richard of Gloucester's right-hand man, and was in an unparalleled position after the execution of Hastings. Bishop Morton of Ely had been placed in Buckingham's charge at Brecon Castle after being arrested with Hastings, and it seems that Morton encouraged Buckingham to rebel against Richard, putting him into contact with Henry Tudor, Margaret Beaufort and Elizabeth Woodville. Buckingham may well have felt threatened. If Gloucester could kill the bodyguards of Edward V, and his former great ally Lord Hastings, could Buckingham ever be safe? Also Buckingham (1455–83) himself had claims to the throne. He was known to be haughty, even by the standards of his times. He had seen how easily Gloucester took the crown, and the remaining royals had been bastardised or attainted. Gloucester had no surviving heir, so Buckingham was one death away from the throne. The Staffords were descended directly from Thomas of Woodstock, youngest son of Edward III.

In 1464, Edward IV had purchased the wardship of young Buckingham from the late duke's executors, and in 1465, Henry was recognised as 2nd Duke of Buckingham. Buckingham was placed as the ward of Elizabeth Woodville, Edward IV's queen. In 1466, Elizabeth married ten-year-old Henry to her thirteen-year-old sister Catherine, in her ongoing process of building up Woodville power and estates. Henry resented the forced marriage to an 'inferior' family and disliked the rest of the Woodvilles, so he had naturally allied himself with the rising Gloucester in his struggles with the queen's family.

The deaths in 1471 of Henry VI and his son Edward of Lancaster left Buckingham as sole heir to the de Bohun fortune. Buckingham had angered Edward IV by adopting the royal arms of Thomas of Woodstock, and this was a large factor in the king's refusal to allow

Buckingham's claims to the de Bohun lands and titles. The de Bohun inheritance was also part of the legacy of Henry VI, and an acknowledgement of Buckingham's rights would have also amounted to recognition of Henry Tudor's rights to the throne, putting Edward's own crown in danger.

With the end of the direct Lancastrian royal line, the inheritance and the earldom of Hereford should have passed to the Staffords, but the Yorkists had held on to their lands. When Richard III became king in 1483, Buckingham was at last granted restoration of the portion of de Bohun lands which had been disputed and held by the Crown. Buckingham, as the senior surviving Plantagenet, may well have been named Richard's heir if he had died childless. The execution of Clarence had brought not only Richard, but Buckingham, one step closer to the crown. Buckingham had been High Steward of England for the trial and execution of Clarence, and benefited greatly from his cousin's downfall, gaining numerous Clarence estates and rents. Buckingham was only Steward of England for the period of the trial and execution of Clarence, and this was the last office he held under Edward IV. He had become virtually *persona non grata* with the king and court, 'denied all the offices and responsibilities which his rank might expect, he had even been excluded from all commissions of the peace except the county of Stafford'. Edward had been suspicious of Clarence's ambition, and for the same reason had kept Buckingham close at court but largely powerless. Buckingham resented his lack of power and royal offices.

Under Richard III, Buckingham became Lord High Chamberlain (Steward) of England again for Richard's coronation. He was effectively the second-most powerful man in Britain after years of being in the cold. However, Buckingham rebelled against his new king. Whatever the reason for Buckingham's volte-face, Hume related that Henry Tudor's mother Margaret Beaufort and Elizabeth Woodville plotted with Morton and Buckingham, financing a rebellion against Richard in 1483:

But it was impossible, that so extensive a conspiracy could be conducted so secretly as entirely to escape the jealous and vigilant eye of Richard; and he soon received intelligence, that his enemies, headed by the duke of Buckingham, were forming some design against his authority. He immediately put himself in a posture of defence by levying some troops in the North; and he summoned the duke to appear at court, in such terms as seemed to promise him a renewal of their former friendship. But that nobleman, well acquainted with the barbarity and treachery of Richard, replied only by taking arms in Wales, and giving the signal to his accomplices for a general insurrection in all parts of England.

But there happened at that very time to fall such heavy rains, so incessant and continued, as exceeded any known in the memory of man; and the Severne, with the other rivers in that neighbourhood, swelled to a height which rendered them impassable, and prevented Buckingham from marching into the heart of England to join his associates. The Welshmen, partly moved by superstition at this extraordinary event, partly distressed by famine in their camp, fell off from him; and Buckingham finding himself deserted by his followers, put on a disguise, and took shelter in the house of Banister, an old servant of his family. But being detected in his retreat, he was brought to the King at Salisbury; and was instantly tried, condemned, and executed, according to the summary method practised in those ages [on 2 November]. The other conspirators, who took arms in four different places, at Exeter, at Salisbury, at Newbury, at Maidstone, hearing of the duke of Buckingham's misfortunes, despaired of success, and immediately dispersed themselves.'

Many writers state that Humphrey Banister did not receive the promised reward from Richard, as he had betrayed his lord, noting Richard's sense of loyalty and honour in doing so, and neglecting the fact that Richard actually offered a huge sum. Kimber relates, 'Banister demanded the thousand Pounds promised in the Proclamation, but Richard refused to pay him, saying, He that would betray so good a Master, would be false to any other.' However, this is not true. Banister was rewarded with 'the manor of Yalding in Kent, to hold by knight's service'. It had belonged to Buckingham, and Henry VII gave it back to Buckingham's son.

The same terrible weather that affected Buckingham's rebellion, where his troops began to starve and deserted, prevented Henry from landing and joining the revolt. Interestingly, Buckingham's widow Katherine subsequently married Jasper Tudor, uncle and mentor to Henry Tudor. A series of simultaneous revolts across the west, south and south-east of England were easily crushed because of lack of leadership. Bishop Morton escaped from Brecon Castle to Flanders, and devoted his energies during the next two years to working for the interests of Henry Tudor. Many of the unsuccessful rebels fled to Brittany to join his cause and thereby hoped to regain their forfeited lands. Henry Tudor, former Earl of Richmond, and his uncle Jasper Tudor, former Earl of Pembroke, were formally attainted in Richard III's parliament of January 1484 for the Rising at Brecon, 18 October 1483. Henry Tudor's mother Margaret Beaufort, Countess of Richmond, was also attainted in Richard III's parliament, January 1484, Third Act: 'Mother to the King's great rebel and traitor. She wrote to Henry, telling him to come and make war. She gave great sums of money in London and elsewhere for treason, conspired to destroy the King and assisted Buckingham.' She was given into the care of her husband, Lord Thomas Stanley.

Thomas Grey, Marquess of Dorset, was attainted for the risings at Exeter, 18 October 1483, and was the eldest son of Elizabeth Woodville by her first husband John Grey. He and his young son Thomas joined Henry Tudor in exile, as did John Welles, esquire of the body and Robert Willoughby of Broke in Wiltshire, knight of the body, attainted in Richard III's parliament, January 1484 for the Risings at Exeter, 18 October 1483. Lionel Woodville, Bishop of Salisbury, attainted in Richard III's parliament, January 1484, Second Act was the brother of Elizabeth Woodville. He joined Henry Tudor in exile and died there in 1484. Edward Woodville, another brother of Elizabeth Woodville, joined Henry Tudor in exile. His brother Richard Woodville, knight of the body, was attainted in Richard III's parliament, January 1484 for the risings at Newbury, Berkshire, and elsewhere, 18 October 1483.

Examining some of the other men involved in rebellion, we can see the extent of the flare-ups against the new king, all across the south of England. One must also ask why many, although pardoned, still preferred to take their remote chance with Tudor rather than stay in England or Wales. One of the strangest incidents was the case of Sir Richard Haute or Hawte, esquire of the body, and through his mother, a first cousin of the queen Elizabeth Woodville. In February 1483 he joined the Council of the Duchy of Lancaster. Haute took part in Buckingham's rebellion in Kent. He became one of the rebel leaders at Maidstone, and was among the armed band which was forced to abandon its attempt to take London. Haute was later captured, handed over to Lord Cobham and his lands and fees legally confiscated. He was attainted in Richard III's Parliament, January 1484 for the 'Risings in Kent and Surrey, at Maidstone, Gravesend, Guildford, and elsewhere between October 18 and October 25, 1483'. Richard Haute is often listed as having been executed by Richard at Pontefract upon 25 June 1483, along with Rivers, Grey and Vaughan, so may have been arrested with them. Somehow, upon 14 March 1485, Haute was pardoned of all offences committed before 11 March 1485, but in August he still joined Henry Tudor's invading army. One wonders whether he was related to Richard III's former mistress, Katherine Haute.

His brother William Haute was also a ringleader in the Kentish rising, and also attainted. William had been associated with the young Prince Richard of York's household and had been prominent in the Woodville-dominated wedding celebrations of infant Richard and Anne Mowbray in January 1478. He had been appointed constable of Swansea and steward of the Gower lordship, acquired by Prince Richard through his wife. Thomas Arundel of Lanherne in

Cornwall, knight of the body, was attainted in Richard III's parliament, January 1484 for the risings at Exeter, 18 October 1483. He had served the Crown in the South West and managed to escape and join Henry Tudor in exile. William Berkeley, knight of the body, was also attainted in January 1484 for the risings at Newbury, Berkshire, and elsewhere on 18 October 1483. Berkeley had been constable of Southampton and Winchester, and had hosted Margaret of York when she visited England in 1480. He was suspected of collusion with Southampton mayor Walter Mitchell and he fled to Henry Tudor in exile. Thomas Bourchier of Barnes, knight of the body, was a younger son of Lord Berners. He was a leading rebel in Somerset, according to royal indictments, November 1483–84. His brother John Bourchier joined Henry Tudor in exile.

Thomas Brandon joined Henry Tudor in exile. His brother William Brandon, esquire of the body, was attainted in Richard III's parliament, January 1484 for the Risings in Kent and Surrey, at Maidstone, Gravesend, Guildford, and elsewhere between 18 October and 25 October 1483. He was also a leading rebel in Norfolk and Suffolk, according to royal indictments of November 1483–84. William Brandon refused to relinquish his Essex estate to Thomas Tyrrell in mid-December 1483. A riot ensued as 300 men threatened to burn him out, and Brandon was ejected by his enemy Thomas Bruin with a large band of men. William Brandon had been a key London connection in Buckingham's revolt, along with his brother Thomas and his brother-in-law, Wingfield. Brandon was pardoned in March 1484, but still sailed in November to France, where he was supposedly joined by his wife, who gave birth to their eldest son in Paris. He joined his brother Thomas Brandon in the relief of the Hammes fortress. William Brandon, Henry Tudor's personal standard-bearer, was one of the few notable fatalities in Henry's army at Bosworth. Sir Thomas Brandon became Henry VII's master-of-horse, and William's son Charles was made 1st Duke of Suffolk by Henry.

James Blount, constable of the Hammes Castle garrison guarding Calais, had served Edward IV and had fought for him to regain his crown. He was the warden of John de Vere, Earl of Oxford, the Lancastrian who had been imprisoned in the Hammes garrison on Edward IV's orders since 1475. Upon 29 October 1484, Richard III ordered Oxford's return, having heard of a plot to rescue him. However, James Blount and John Fortescue, porter of Calais, defected to Henry Tudor, taking Oxford with them. In December, Lord Dynham, governor of Calais, attacked Hammes and captured it, holding several as prisoners, including Blount's wife. In January 1485, Oxford, the Brandons and others returned to Hammes to rescue them. In a truce, the Yorkist Calais force allowed those disaffected to leave. They joined Henry Tudor.

Humphrey Cheney, gentleman, was attainted in Richard III's parliament, January 1484 for the risings at Salisbury, and elsewhere 18 October 1483. His brother Robert Cheney, gentleman, was also attainted, as was a third brother John Cheney, esquire of the body. All three brothers joined Henry in exile. John was known as the 'Great Rebel of Wiltshire', and had been Edward IV's master of horse, involved in the Tower fire plot and the Exeter Rising. John Cheney, later Baron Cheney, was unhorsed at Bosworth by

Richard III personally, while acting as bodyguard to Henry, possibly saving Henry's life.

Edward Courtenay, esquire of the body, the disinherited heir of the Earl of Devon, was attainted in Richard III's Parliament, January 1484 for the risings at Exeter. Courtenay joined Henry Tudor in exile, along with his brother Peter Courtenay, Bishop of Exeter, who was also attainted. Although Peter Courtenay had supported Henry VI's readeption, he had later served Edward IV as his secretary and councillor, and had been awarded the bishopric in 1478. Giles Daubenay, knight of the body, had been Sheriff of Somerset, Dorset, and Devon and also constable of Bridgwater, but was attainted for the risings at Salisbury and elsewhere. Daubenay escaped to join Henry, later becoming Baron Daubenay, his major military leader. Richard Edgecombe or Edgecumbe, a leading rebel in Devon, according to royal indictments in November 1483-1484 also joined Henry.

Other men who flocked to Henry in France were Richard Fox, Evan Morgan, Sir John Fortesque and John Gaynesford, esquire of the body, who was attainted in January 1484 for the risings in Kent and Surrey, at Maidstone, Gravesend, Guildford, and elsewhere between 18 October and 25 October 1483. (An esquire of the body is a man of rank, directly below a knight.) He was the son of Nicholas Gaynesford of Carshalton in Surrey, esquire of the body, who was attainted, and escaped to France. Edward Poynings, esquire of the body, was attainted, joining Henry Tudor in exile. He became Henry VII's future deputy in Ireland. Poynings was the step-son of the executed George Browne.

Others were not so lucky. The greatest casualty of

the October 1483 rebellion was Henry Stafford, Duke of Buckingham, executed 2 November at Salisbury. Upon 13 November, Thomas St. Leger, knight of the body (the brother-in-law of Edward IV and Richard III through their sister Anne Plantagenet), was executed at Exeter. He had served Edward IV as controller of the mint and master of the king's harthounds. He and John Fogge had spearheaded the household resistance to Warwick and his rebels in 1469–70 and had gone into exile with Edward IV in 1470.

Sir Thomas St Leger (c.1439–83) had married the king's sister, Anne, Duchess of Exeter, in 1472 and became friendly with the important family of Bourchier, of whom Thomas was Archbishop of Canterbury from 1454–86. A member of Edward IV's household, he was friendly both with Edward's most intimate friend, William Lord Hastings and the Woodvilles. In the political confusion and in-fighting that followed the unexpected death of Edward, St Leger remained loyal to the late king's family. His opposition to Gloucester's coup to seize the throne led to his involvement in the risings of October to November 1483, commonly known as 'Buckingham's Rebellion', first in Surrey and then in the South West, where he was captured and executed at Exeter. Driver tells us, 'It was his objection to Richard of Gloucester's aim to deny the young Edward V his throne that determined his rebellion in October 1483, which cost him his life.' St Leger was involved in his brother-in-law Richard's coronation, but soon became involved in rebellion.

The opposition to the king was a 'roll-call of the leading aristocracy and governors in every shire from Kent to Oxfordshire and Cornwall'. In Kent prominent among the rebels were Sir George Browne of Maidstone and Nicholas Gaynesford of Carshalton, Surrey, both of whom had associations with St Leger. In Surrey Thomas St Leger appeared to have had an important role. However, there was a lack of co-ordination between the rebels, and when Buckingham was betrayed and executed at Salisbury on 2 November the revolt began to crumble. Richard moved to Exeter to deal with opponents in the South West now led by St Leger. Taken at his place at Torrington, the wealthy St Leger tried to bargain for his life, but the king was not disposed to leniency, and he was executed at Exeter on 13 November. Action quickly followed to take control of all of Sir Thomas St Leger's properties. On the very day of his execution orders were issued to deliver monies which belonged to him into the hands of the Crown and, at the same time, his castle and manor of Torrington were granted to one of the king's Northern followers. All his other lands were forfeited. For a Yorkist such as St Leger, the king's brother-in-law and friend of Edward IV, to have risen means that he either knew Edward V was in danger or more likely that he was dead.

Sir George Browne of Betchworth in Surrey, knight of the body to Edward IV, was attainted in Richard III's parliament, January 1484 for the risings in Kent and Surrey, at Maidstone, Gravesend, Guildford, and elsewhere between 18 October and 25 October 1483. Browne's father Thomas had been killed by Warwick in 1460, but George entered Yorkist service, probably under the influence of his father-in-law Thomas Vaughan. Browne was Sheriff of Kent in 1480–81 and a regular commissioner of the county. He was MP for Guilford in 1472 and for Surrey in 1478, and carried the flag of St George at Edward IV's funeral. He was beheaded at the Tower upon 4 December 1483, along with Sir Roger Clifford, esquire of the body. All of these men, either executed or fleeing to join Henry, had been faithful servants of Edward IV, and wished his son to be crowned king or Richard to be punished for their disappearance. If Richard had just shown the king and prince to be alive, he could have quelled the revolts sooner.

William Collyngbourne, a sergeant of pantry to Edward IV, was a member of the household of Cecily Neville, the Duchess of York. Cecily was the mother of Edward IV and Richard III. In July 1484, he was said to have conspired with others to send Tom Yate to Brittany with an invitation for Henry Tudor to invade England. In July 1484, Collyngbourne tacked a poem to the door of St Paul's Cathedral, noting the three main advisers of Richard III (the 'hogge'), whose heraldic emblem was a white boar: 'The Catte, the Ratte and Lovell our dogge, Rulyth all England under a hogge.' The 'catte' was Sir William Catesby (1450–85), one of Richard's main councillors, serving the new king as both Chancellor of the Exchequer and Speaker of the House of Commons. The 'ratte' was Sir Richard Ratcliffe, a close confidant of Gloucester in the north of England, who was chosen to organise an army in the North to help Gloucester when he was proclaimed Protector. As king, Richard III made Ratcliffe a Knight of the Garter, hereditary High Sheriff of Westmoreland, and gave him many estates such as those of the Earl of Devon. Now hugely wealthy, Ratcliffe died at Bosworth Field.

The 'dogge' was Francis Lovell, 9th Baron Lovell, later first Viscount Lovell and a great friend of Gloucester. He was one of the wealthiest barons in

England not holding an earldom or dukedom. His wife was the first cousin of Richard's wife, and he had served in Scotland under Richard. Richard appointed Lovell Lord Chamberlain to replace the executed Hastings. 'Dogge' refers to Lovell's heraldic symbol of a silver wolf. In June 1485, Lovell was appointed to guard the south coast to prevent the landing of Henry Tudor, and it seems fairly certain that he fought for Richard at Bosworth. Collyngbourne was captured, and suffered the gruesome hanging, drawing and quartering while still alive, at the Tower in October 1484.

Parliament was dissolved on 20 February 1484, and there were ninety-five attainders, representing those who had taken part in the recent rebellion or had fled to join Henry Tudor. The three bishops involved in the rebellion – Rotherham of York, Courtenay of Exeter and Morton of Ely – had all their property confiscated. Margaret, Lady Stanley, was effectively shut up in her husband's Lathom Castle, was declared incapable of holding any dignity or title, and all her property was forfeited to the crown, i.e. Richard, the forfeiture only to take place after the death of her husband Lord Stanley.

Richard already possessed a large share of the huge former de Vere estates but, determined to acquire the remainder, as Miller reminds us, 'he had harried the aged Elizabeth, Dowager Countess of Oxford to her death'. Interestingly, all grants to the dowager Queen Elizabeth were now resumed as part of Richard's attempt to get her and her daughters to leave sanctuary. However, the continuous positioning of his Northern supporters in the South, and giving them local offices of influence was creating enormous resentment.

Although the risings in favour of Henry Tudor and

Edward V had failed, Richard III realised that Henry was still a threat to his new reign. Henry's followers across the Channel were increasing in numbers, and his attempts to have Henry returned to England had failed. Richard also realised that Henry Tudor was being favoured by Margaret Beaufort and Elizabeth Woodville as a husband for Edward IV's daughter Elizabeth of York. Richard's need for a male heir was increasingly desperate. His only son, Edward of Middleham, Prince of Wales, after Richard usurped the crown, died aged ten in April 1484. After his death, Anne had effectively adopted Edward, Earl of Warwick, the nine-year-old son of George of Clarence and her sister Isabel, who were both now dead. The boy was a nephew of both Richard and Anne, and Richard had made the boy his heir presumptive, probably in deference to Anne's wishes. However, Edward of Warwick was not only debarred by his father Clarence's attainder, but also described by some as 'simple-minded'.

Lord Thomas Stanley and his brother William had stayed on Richard III's side during the 1483 rebellions, being rewarded from the forfeited estates of several rebels. Lord Stanley was appointed to Buckingham's position as Lord High Constable of England. However, it is almost certain that Stanley was involved in the Buckingham uprising. His wife, Margaret Beaufort, was a key conspirator, and had been arranging the marriage alliance of her son Henry Tudor and Edward IV's daughter Elizabeth of York. If Henry Tudor had been able to land with his small army in 1483, perhaps the Stanleys would have joined him. Stanley swore to Richard to keep his wife Margaret Beaufort in custody and to end her plotting. Henry's mother was thereby saved from attainder, the immediate confiscation of her great estates and possible execution. Her estates would legally go to Richard in the event of her husband's death, however. Gloucester was still unsure of Stanley's position in the summer of 1485, when Stanley sought permission to leave the court and return to his base at Lathom Castle in Lancashire. Gloucester insisted that Lord Stanley's son Lord Strange should take his place at court as a token of his father's allegiance.

Edward IV's widow Elizabeth Woodville and her daughters had been in sanctuary from Richard since 1 May, after they heard the news of her son Edward V's seizure on 29 April 1483. On or before 20 May 1483 Gloucester took Prince Richard from her and despite her pleas she never saw either of her sons again. In autumn of that year she had given consent for her daughter Elizabeth of York to marry Henry Tudor, who had then undergone a betrothal ceremony in exile in Rennes. Some time after Easter 1484, after around a year in confinement, Elizabeth and her daughters gave in to Richard's promises of safe conduct and good marriages. They left sanctuary and her two elder daughters entered Richard's court. Ricardian novelists and others would have us believe that this is the time that her tall, attractive eldest daughter, the eighteen-year-old Elizabeth of York, fell in love with the little king who had imprisoned her brothers, killed her kinsmen and exiled others.

During the Christmas festivities of 1484, Richard had complained to Thomas Rotherham, Archbishop of York, of his queen's barrenness. Others would have been present, and almost definitely Queen Anne would have heard of it. Still only thirty-two, Richard desperately wanted a male heir. Perhaps he and the court had known that the sickly Anne could not produce another child, as they had been married for almost twelve years, producing only one sickly son, who was now dead. He had fathered illegitimate children, so Richard knew that he could produce heirs. He was fertile, but his wife did not seem to be so. At the Christmas banquet, it was noticeable to the Croyland Chronicler and others that the king was paying special attention to Elizabeth. She was dancing and disporting herself with the gayest abandon while dressed in robes of the same cloth, colour and cut as those of the queen herself. (Another source says that she was wearing similar clothes to the king.) This was a breach of protocol, and Anne furiously demanded that the girl should be reprimanded by the Lord Chamberlain, or at least by her mother Elizabeth. Richard refused.

Shortly into the New Year of 1485, Anne took to her bed. A tale spread that the king was determined to marry Elizabeth, either after Anne's death or as the Croyland Chronicler tells us 'by means of a divorce for which he believed he had sufficient grounds'. When Anne became sick a few days after Christmas, the rumours of divorce were now superseded by whispers of poison. The queen was gravely ill, and according to the *Croyland Chronicle*, Richard was spurning his consort's bed, but this may have well been so as not to catch any illness. Queen Anne died on 16 March 1485 at the age of twenty-eight. Anne may have died of tuberculosis (often known as 'consumption'). The day she died, there was an eclipse, which some took to be an omen of Richard's fall from heavenly grace. She was buried in an unmarked grave to the right of the high altar in Westminster Abbey, next to the door to the Confessor's Chapel. There are no known plans of any funerary monument, which Ricardians ascribe to Richard's preparations for Henry Tudor's invasion.

The *Croyland Chronicle* reports that in the days following Anne's death, Sir William Catesby and Sir Richard Ratcliffe told Richard bluntly that if he did marry his niece, he would lose the support of his Northern friends. They did not care for what would have been incest and would certainly turn against him. The clergymen who had apprehensively accompanied Catesby and Ratcliffe told Richard that the Pope could never sanction a union of such close relatives as an uncle and a niece. Suspicion that Anne really had been poisoned was addressed, and as Anne was a Neville, her name was still revered in the North. Richard was in a quandary – instead of freeing his hand, the death of his wife was causing immense problems, related to him by his most trusted advisers.

Two weeks after Anne's death, upon 30 March 1485, Richard called the mayor, Mercers' Company, aldermen and citizens of London and the available lords to the great hall of the Hospital of St John to address them. Here he made an astonishing and humiliating public denial of poisoning Anne and intending to marry Elizabeth of York. Did he intend to marry Elizabeth? Intriguingly Elizabeth's half-brother Thomas, Marquis of Dorset, was told by his mother to return home from exile with Henry to share in the family's new-found fortunes. If Elizabeth Woodville had ensured her family's security by her daughter marrying Richard, Dorset would surely be safe and honoured. As the court was celebrating Twelfth Night upon the eve of 5 January 1485, Richard's agents had brought news that Henry was going to invade in the coming summer. Hume tells us that Richard believed that he could squash all potential support for Henry Tudor by marrying Elizabeth of York, and was trying by all means to convince Elizabeth Woodville of his good intentions:

... he paid court to the Queen-dowager with such art and address, made such earnest protestations of his sincere good-will and friendship, that this princess, tired of confinement, and despairing of any success from her former projects, ventured to leave her sanctuary, and to put herself and her daughters into the hands of the tyrant. But he soon carried farther his views for the establishment of his throne. He had married Anne, the second daughter of the earl of Warwick, and widow of Edward prince of Wales, whom Richard himself had murdered; but this princess having born him but one son, who died about this time, he considered her as an invincible obstacle to the settlement of his fortune, and he was believed to have carried her off by poison; a crime for which the public could not be supposed to have any very solid proof, but which the usual tenor of his conduct made it reasonable to suspect. He now thought it in his power to remove the chief perils which threatened his government. The earl of Richmond, he knew, could never be dangerous but from his projected marriage with the princess Elizabeth, the true heir of the crown; and he therefore intended, by means of a papal dispensation, to espouse himself this princess, and thus to unite in his own family their contending titles.

The whole affair dented the Richard's prestige. Any hopes of marrying his niece collapsed. There was also a marriage deal being considered at this time involving

Richard and a Portuguese princess, and Elizabeth and a Portuguese prince. After Anne died, Richard seems to have named another nephew to replace Edward, the son of Clarence, as his heir presumptive. This was John de la Pole, Earl of Lincoln.

The question of poison should be addressed. We know that Richard had a ruthless nature. He had ordered Somerset and others to be put to death after Tewkesbury upon 6 May 1471. Richard has also been directly implicated in the murder of Edward, Prince of Wales, after that battle. He was also accused of the murder in the Tower of London of Henry VI during the night of 21/22 May 1471. His presence did not engender trust among nobles or commoners. His brother Clarence believed that his own wife, Anne's sister, had been poisoned. It could be that Richard had been involved. In 1478, Richard may well have been instrumental in having Clarence brought to trial and killed by poison, drowning or other means. Edward IV was possibly poisoned, dying of a 'violent fever'. Richard definitely was responsible for the murders of Hastings, Rivers, Grey, Vaughan, Fauconberg and others. All contemporary sources seem to hold Richard responsible for many deaths, and especially greed over land ownership, well before Shakespeare further blackened his name.

There was a high likelihood of high-ranking individuals having some kind of food taster. But such a person could be circumvented by a slow-acting poison. In addition, in regular food poisoning, the effects are not felt for up to two days, although four to six hours is also common. The usual method was to conceal the poison in either food or wine. A bribe to the proper servant could mean the demise of the victim, or a murderous banquet-goer might conceal a small quantity of poison in his ring. The most common poisonous herbs in the Middle Ages were arsenic, belladonna, hemlock, monkshood (also known as wolfsbane or aconite), cyanide, hellebore, henbane, foxglove and mushrooms.

Many historic figures have allegedly died of poisoning, but it is virtually impossible to offer any meaningful opinion. Firstly, the standard of diagnosis was negligible, and symptoms are often not recorded in any sufficient detail. With treatment then confined to a mixture of herbalism and magic, there could be no diagnostic value in observing a positive reaction to treatment. Gastrointestinal disease was rampant due to the poor hygiene of the times and diarrhoea and vomiting were often ascribed to poisoning when they were equally likely to be from gut infections. A death from dysentery could be ascribed to a fast poison and a lingering death from tuberculosis could be blamed upon the cumulative effects of a slow poison. A terminal pneumonia was a very common end result secondary to a host of basic infections and diseases.

Historians sometimes over-interpret from vague descriptions, but hard fact is now impossible to get in almost all cases, as there were no analytical methods until the nineteenth century. Even the cause of Napoleon's death is impossible to determine with any accuracy, as the attribution of arsenic in his wallpaper is complicated by the fact that he was given arsenic as a medicine when young. What we can say is that nearly every important death in his time was connected with Richard contemporaneously.

4

Henry Tudor & the Path to the Battle of Bosworth

To a great extent the achievements of Henry Tudor have been overlooked, being sandwiched between two of the most famous kings in English history. It is necessary to study his life alongside that of Richard of Gloucester to assess some of the truths and untruths written about each man. Ricardians call Henry a usurper, conveniently neglecting that Richard III certainly was one, along with many of his Norman-Plantagenet precursors. Indeed, when we regard English history and royal succession throughout the ages, the very concept of a 'royal bloodline' begins to seem absurd. Early writers favouring Henry VII blackened Richard's name, just as current writers favouring Richard III denigrate Henry. Nearly every year of Henry's life was spent in danger, custody or exile, and this shaped his character as much as Richard's background shaped his. Henry had little power and few prospects until he became king, whereas Richard was born into power, the son of a would-be king and the brother of a king. Richard was a warrior shaped by his environment, basing his judgements upon his continuing experience of the world around him at the centre of war and rule.

We also must not neglect the treatment of Henry VII by the writers of his son's day. It was not in the interests of the courtiers, writers and historians of Henry VIII's day to write that he was only the second king in an infant, unproven dynasty. The Plantagenets had effectively wiped each other out with familial, fratricidal and patricidal strife, with the great nobles influencing the court, council and events. Henry VII virtually emasculated these great houses from major influence, not by violence but by setting up new mechanisms with checks and balances to control the state. Henry VII founded an effective and efficient monarchy capable of proper tax gathering and centralised power in the person of the king and his advisers. Henry VIII's writers virtually ignored his father, concentrating on the 'glory' of the new, and far more ruthless, king. Tudor achievements were to be Henry VIII's achievements. Later, Tudor greatness would be personified by Elizabeth I, greatly assisted by the flowering of England's greatest writers.

Thus the reputation of Henry VII has suffered from both Ricardian sympathisers, in their belief that Richard was somehow a 'good' king who did not deserve to lose the throne he had himself usurped, and from the reign of his larger-than-life successor Henry VIII. Henry VII was undoubtedly one of England's greatest kings, which is not to say that any deserve that epithet. Alfred the Great never ruled all of England, and it is difficult to make out a case for any monarch except Elizabeth I to aspire to greatness among all the Norman, Plantagenet, Tudor, Stuart and Hanoverian/Windsor monarchs. People write blithely of 'Tudor propaganda' but there were none of the 'spin doctors' we suffer today. To state the obvious, Henry VII did not have a Goebbels, Saatchi or an Alistair Campbell at his side – they were simpler times. Each reign in English history can be deconstructed into good, bad or indifferent, for example that of Richard the Lionheart; it often all depends upon the sympathies of the writer rather than facts. What we all can agree upon is that Henry VII was one of the unlikeliest men to take the kingship. He had no real power base, no money, a convoluted claim to the throne (much like Richard III's) and no experience as a warrior or leader.

Henry's circumstances, more than anything, made him an intelligent claimant to the crown. He grew up surrounded by shadows and threats, under the loyal guidance of his uncle Jasper, relying upon diplomacy to keep alive – this made him a totally different king, one who relied upon pragmatism, rather than the vengeance and vendettas displayed by the main characters in the wars. In effect the Plantagenets had been their own worst enemies, killing nearly all claimants to the crown from the rival houses of York and Lancaster. Even before the Wars of the Roses, sons had rebelled against kings, brothers had fought brothers, wives had fought husbands, various Plantagenets had usurped the rightful monarch and so on. Plantagenet history is drenched in bloodshed and intrigue, whereby power was more important than legitimacy. This is Richard III's background. There had been troubled reigns for nearly all of the seventeen Norman-Angevin-Plantagenet monarchs from 1066.

Several of Richard's predecessors had murdered their way to the crown or been usurpers, so his so-called royal bloodline was tangential at best, which we shall mention in the next chapter.

The Plantagenets thrived upon internecine strife, in a more defined black-and-white world, whereas Henry Tudor grew up in multiple 'shades of grey', always trying to seek accommodation and safety. He was in effect forced to invade England or be killed. His death would either come by assassination, as when the great Welsh captain Owain Lawgoch had been stabbed in the back upon the orders of John of Gaunt in Mortagne-sur-Mer in 1378; by incarceration and death in France or Brittany in an alliance with English wishes; or by being returned to England to be killed. As we shall see, Henry's invasion was his only option to stay alive, as both Edward IV and Richard III had tried to take him back to England and certain incarceration or execution.

While Richard's paternal family had been at the centre of the 'War of the Cousins', the War of the Roses, Henry's paternal family had been engaged in a different kind of war, that of Welsh independence against English kings and their aggressive Marcher Lords. From the first Germanic invasions of Britain in the fifth century, the British had gradually been pushed back into their last nation of British-speaking Wales. From the Norman invasion of England onwards, borders had ebbed and flowed until 1282 and 1283 when the last princes of Wales were killed. Henry Tudor's paternal family were at the very epicentre of hundreds of years of fighting off English attacks. This is an aspect very much overlooked in the story of Richard and Henry, and Henry's reliance upon Welsh support ensured that his army reached Bosworth Field. If we examine Tudor's Welsh ancestry, it seems that historians have ignored the part played by his forebears in the great Owain Glyndŵr War of Independence from 1400 to 1415. Glyndŵr, recognised as the true Prince of Wales by the Welsh nobility, fought off no less than six invasions by the military might of the English king's armies and his foreign mercenaries, in a war which nearly bankrupted Henry IV.

Henry's direct paternal ancestor was Ednyfed Fychan ap Cynwrig (d. 1246), a warrior and possible crusader, who was Lord of Criccieth and for over thirty years acted as seneschal (chief councillor) to Prince Llywelyn the Great and his son Dafydd ap Llywelyn. Ednyfed is said to have first come to notice in battle, fighting against the army of the Marcher Lord Ranulph de Blondeville, 4th Earl of Chester. Chester attacked Llywelyn ab Iorwerth, Prince of Wales, at the request of King John. Ednyfed cut off the heads of three Franco-English lords in battle and carried them, still bloody, to Llywelyn. (The great English lords, like the royal family, were still Norman-French at this time, and were called French by the Welsh. The English are called Saeson, or Saxons. In turn the invading Saxons called the British Walsci, or foreigners, which became Welsh.) The Prince of Wales commanded Ednyfed to change his family coat of arms to display three heads in memory of his valour. Ednyfed lost a son fighting the English. Prince Llywelyn's successor Dafydd also fought England after it reneged upon promises, being probably poisoned at his court at Abergwyngregyn. Thus Ednyfed had lost a son and a prince to the English. Two of Ednyfed's other sons were seneschals to another Prince of Wales, Llywelyn ap Gruffudd, who was lured into a trap and murdered in 1282 by the Mortimers after years of war with England. Wales was effectively conquered in 1482–83, although another of Ednyfed's descendants acted as seneschal for Madog ap Llywelyn when he declared himself Prince of Wales in the Madog War of Independence in 1294–95.

Ednyfed's son Goronwy ab Ednyfed (d. 1268) was also a seneschal to Llywelyn the Great from 1246 to 1256, fighting to keep Welsh independence. He was the founder of the line of the Tudors of Penymynydd, Anglesey. His son Tudur Hen was also known as Tudur ap Goronwy (d. 1311) and took part in the Madog ap Llywelyn uprising, acting as his steward, and also led a raid against Marcher Lords in Gwent in 1263. His son Goronwy ap Tudur Hen, Lord of Penymynydd (d. 1331), served the English Crown as a soldier, probably fighting at Bannockburn in 1314. Tudur ap Goronwy (d. 1367) was a wealthy nobleman who married Marged ferch Tomos, who was the sister of Elen ferch Tomos, the mother of Glyndŵr. Their three sons virtually initiated the rising of their kinsman, the Glyndŵr War, in 1400. Maredudd ap Tudor (d. 1406) was Henry Tudor's great-grandfather. His brothers were Rhys ap Tudur (hanged, drawn and quartered at Chester in 1409) and Gwilym ap Tudur (killed in 1413).

Rhys ap Tudur, Sheriff of Anglesey, had been Richard II's squire and resented the usurpation of Henry IV, and with his brothers Maredudd and Gwilym was the instigator of the Glyndŵr War, taking Conwy Castle in 1401. For more details see *Owain Glyndŵr: The Story of the Last Prince of Wales* (2009), by this author. Maredudd was pardoned but lost most of his Penymynydd estates to the English Crown. Maredudd tried to gain favour by moving to London and changing his son's name from Owain ap Maredudd to Owain Tudor, one of the first instances where a surname instead of a patronym was used by a Welshman. Had Owain taken his father's name (rather than that of his grandfather) the Tudor dynasty would have been called the Maredydd or Meredith Dynasty. This is Henry Tudor's paternal background, over 2o0 years of fighting for independence.

In London, Owain Tudor became the ward of his father's second cousin, Lord Rhys. At the age of seven he was sent to Henry IV's court as page to the king's steward. Owain fought for Henry V at Agincourt in 1415, and was promoted to squire. After the battle he was granted 'English rights' and permitted to use Welsh arms in England. Henry IV, because of the Glyndŵr War, had deprived Welshmen of many civil rights, and not until 1432 was Owain granted the full rights of an Englishman, when he was aged around thirty-two. The dowager queen Catherine of Valois, Henry V's widow, upon being denied permission by her son's regents to wed John Beaufort, Duke of Somerset, allegedly said upon leaving court, 'I shall marry a man so basely, yet gently born, that my lord regents may not object.' The daughter of Charles VI of France, Catherine married Owain when he was probably keeper of her household at Windsor, but there is no documentation extant. Catherine and Owen had at least six children including Edmund and Jasper Tudor, and she died in 1437 after childbirth.

After her death, Owen was arrested for violating the law of the remarriage of the queen dowager. He appeared before the Council, acquitting himself of all charges, and was released. On his way back to Wales, he was arrested and his possessions seized. He escaped from Newgate gaol in early 1438 but was recaptured and taken to Windsor Castle. Meanwhile, Owen and Catherine's two elder sons, Edmund and Jasper, went to live with Katherine de la Pole, sister of the Duke of Suffolk. Owen was eventually released on £2,000 bail, but was pardoned in November 1439. Sometime after 1442, Henry VI, the half-brother of Edmund and Jasper, took a role in their upbringing. Owen was treated well afterwards and was a member of the king's household until the mid-1450s.

Owain ap Maredudd came to be known as Owain Tudur and then Sir Owen Meredith Tudor when Henry VI knighted his stepfather and made him Warden of Forestries, and appointed him a Deputy Lord Lieutenant. Prior to his creation as a Knight Bachelor, Owen, though excused from duty, was appointed an esquire to the king's person. Years later, in order that he could command Henry VI's forces at Mortimer's Cross, Owen was made a Knight Banneret. Owen Tudor was beheaded after Mortimer's Cross, but was said to have expected a reprieve because of his relationship with the former royal family. Owen's son Edmund Tudor, 1st Earl of Richmond, was captured by Sir William Herbert of Raglan in 1456 and died of plague at Carmarthen Castle upon 3 November 1456.

Henry would have known intimately all the above details of his family's history of constant warfare, and was born three months after his father Edmund's death. To examine Henry Tudor's life, we must briefly return to the Lancastrian Henry VI briefly regaining power in 1470. However, Edward IV returned from exile and the Yorkists won at Barnet and Tewkesbury in 1471, and the only royal heir, Edward, Prince of Wales, was killed after the battle. The imprisoned Henry VI was quickly murdered. Aged just fourteen, Henry Tudor was suddenly the only surviving male of the House of Lancaster who was not in custody. As Edward IV said, Henry was 'the only imp now left of Henry VI's brood'. Henry's life was now in great danger and his uncle Jasper managed to smuggle him out of Wales in June 1471 into exile in Brittany. For the next twelve years, although Margaret Beaufort never saw her son Henry, she never stopped trying to secure his return. She married again, this time to Thomas, Lord Stanley, head of a powerful Yorkist family, and began trying to turn them to the Lancastrian cause.

The usurper Henry IV's parliament had issued a declaration barring the accession to the throne of any heirs of the legitimised offspring of his father, John of Gaunt, by his third wife Katherine Swynford. Henry IV was the son of Gaunt's first wife, Blanche of Lancaster, and wished to prevent his step-mother's children from having any right to the crown. However, the original Act legitimising the children of Gaunt and Swynford had been passed by Parliament and a Bull issued by the Pope had legitimised them fully, which made the legality of Henry IV's declaration questionable. Ricardians follow the line that Henry Tudor's claim was illegitimate as he came from the Swynford line, neglecting the fact the Henry IV's declaration had no backing in the eyes of the Church. The parliament of 1453 also declared Edmund Tudor and his brother Jasper to be legitimate.

Henry's main claim to the throne came via his mother Margaret Beaufort, a descendant of Gaunt and Swynford, who played a central part in Richard's downfall. She is depicted by Ricardian historians and novelists as a scheming, devious woman. Margaret may have been, but what was her alternative? Historians have noted the extremely close bond between Margaret and her son, who was only thirteen years younger than her. Her plottings were only the natural actions of a Lancastrian mother who could not have any more children, trying to prevent her only child from being killed by Yorkist Plantagenets.

Margaret Beaufort, Countess of Richmond and later of Derby, was the only surviving legitimate child of John Beaufort, 1st Duke of Somerset, who had incurred the enmity of Richard of York in the reign of Henry VI. As the great-grandson of John of Gaunt, Duke of Lancaster, Somerset was a Lancastrian throughout the Wars of the Roses. Somerset campaigned in France, and gained the bitter enmity of Richard of York. He may have committed suicide when faced with a charge of treason instigated by York. His death marked the end of Beaufort influence and paved the way for the de la Pole family to dominate the government. Margaret was a fabulously rich heiress, under a year old, upon Somerset's death in 1444. She and the rest of the Beaufort family had a lasting resentment for the House of York over the death of her father.

When Margaret was only a year old, Henry VI broke a promise to her mother and gave her wardship to the Duke of Suffolk. Margaret was then married to John de la Pole, the son of the 1st Duke of Suffolk when aged around seven, probably in January 1450. It appears that Suffolk was trying to ensure his son's future and to gain Margaret's estates, as in that month Suffolk had been arrested and imprisoned in the Tower. Suffolk was banished for five years, but on his journey to Calais his ship was intercepted, and he was executed. It was suspected that Somerset's enemy, Richard of York, was responsible for his beheading on one of York's boats. Suffolk's body was thrown overboard and later found on the seashore near Dover.

In August 1450, papal dispensation was gained for Margaret to divorce, still aged seven, upon the grounds that she was too closely related to her husband. Margaret never herself recognised the marriage. Henry VI now placed her in the wardship of the king's half-brothers Edmund and Jasper Tudor, and chose for her husband Edmund Tudor, Earl of Richmond. When informed of the change in her wardship arrangements, Margaret asked the advice of a trusted retainer, who suggested she pray to St Nicholas for guidance. Margaret stayed awake praying that night, until 'about four o'clock in the morning one appeared to her arrayed like a bishop, and naming unto her Edmund Tudor, bade her take him as her husband'. Margaret Beaufort agreed to the match, but the wedding was postponed until 1455, when she had reached the age of twelve and Richmond was twenty-four.

Richmond was shortly captured by the Yorkist Lord William Herbert of Raglan, and by the end of November 1456, he was dead of plague in prison in Carmarthen Castle, leaving his thirteen-year-old widow pregnant with the future King Henry VII. Her brother-in-law Jasper Tudor, Earl of Pembroke, took the pregnant widow into his care at Pembroke Castle, where Henry was born upon 28 January 1457. Margaret only just survived the birth and was probably unable to have more children. Her son Henry was also extremely lucky to survive. He was an ailing child, in an age when over half of those born died before the age of five. In 1461, the Yorkist Edward IV successfully took the throne, after having Henry VI imprisoned as unfit to rule.

Pembroke Castle was given to Lord Herbert of Raglan, and he also purchased Henry's wardship. Herbert was given the attainted Jasper Tudor's earldom of Pembroke, as Jasper had been forced to escape to France and Scotland to seek Lancastrian support. Herbert's earldom patent stated that he had that honour for expelling 'Jasper the rebel'. Margaret Beaufort was now separated from her five-year-old son, but Herbert ensured Henry's safety and education, as he wished for Henry to marry his daughter Maud. Henry remained in custody under Herbert at Raglan. In 1458, the fourteen-year-old Margaret was given dispensation to marry Henry Stafford, the son of the Duke of Buckingham, and her estates supplied the marriage with its income.

Stafford fought in 1461 at the Battle of Towton on the Lancastrian side but survived, being fortunate to be later pardoned by Edward IV. His and Margaret's staff included fifty servants, many of them 'gentle born', including their Receiver-General Reginald Bray (d. 1503), who went on to fight for Henry Tudor at Bosworth in 1485. Henry Stafford was with Edward IV in 1470 at the Battle of Losecoat Field where the rebel forces of Sir Robert, Lord Welles (Margaret Beaufort's stepbrother), were defeated. Papers found on the battle provided clear evidence of Warwick and Clarence's involvement in the Lancastrian uprising, and Stafford rode with the king throughout April during the pursuit of Warwick and Clarence. The rebels managed to escape to Calais. Shortly afterwards Stafford gave Margaret's mother, Lady Welles, the news of her son's execution after his capture at Losecoat Field. In September 1470,

Warwick and Clarence returned to England. Edward IV, caught out by the speed of their invasion, was forced to flee into exile in Burgundy with his brother Gloucester, later to be Richard III. Stafford, although initially arrested, was released shortly afterwards following a petition from his Lancastrian wife. On 27 October, Henry Stafford, Margaret Beaufort and Jasper Tudor attended the restoration of Henry VI at Westminster. It is believed that Henry Tudor had an audience with the king, and he spent a little time with his mother and stepfather at their mansion of Woking Old Hall before returning to the care of Jasper.

On 24 March, the 4th Duke of Somerset visited Stafford and Margaret, his first cousin, at Woking Old Hall. He wished to persuade Stafford to join the Lancastrian army being mustered to defend against Edward's return. However, because of his reprieve after Towton, Stafford decided to support Edward IV. Stafford was so badly wounded at fighting for the Yorkists at Barnet that he never recovered, and died in his bed on 14 October 1471. Somerset died at the following battle at Tewkesbury. The widowed Margaret married Lord Thomas Stanley, the High Constable of England, in 1472. Stanley was a vastly wealthy and influential Yorkist landowner. This may well have been a marriage of convenience as her will of that year specified that she wished to be buried alongside Edmund Tudor. From Henry VI's murder in May 1471 Margaret dedicated herself to the Lancastrian cause on behalf of her son, Henry Tudor. Two of Margaret's retainers, John Kymer and John Harper were involved in the Exeter rising in support of the 1483 rebellion and both later went on to fight under her servant Sir Reginald Bray at Bosworth in 1485.

Margaret Beaufort did all that she could to help her exiled son, and her marriage to a prominent Yorkist, following the marriage to the Yorkist Stafford, could have been to give her some influence in saving Henry's life if he was brought to England. However, it is only because of the determination and loyalty of Jasper Tudor that Henry Tudor was still alive at this time. Jasper had fought in Henry VI's army at St Albans in May 1455, where Henry VI was captured. Jasper then had attempted to bring together the warring houses. He was briefly successful as the rebel lords renewed their allegiance to Henry, but fighting broke out again in 1459 when Richard of York returned from exile in Ireland. Jasper was ordered to seize Denbigh Castle to block York's lines of communication between England and Ireland. However, the Yorkists defeated Henry VI's army at Northampton in 1460, leaving Jasper isolated at Denbigh. He refused to surrender and the Yorkist army stormed Denbigh, but Jasper managed to escape. Jasper left for France to seek aid for the Lancastrians.

Richard of York was then killed by Lancastrian forces at Wakefield. The Lancastrians marched south and defeated another Yorkist army at St Albans while Jasper Tudor returned from France and was gathering a fresh army in Wales. In early 1461 the Welsh force, which included Jasper's father, Owen Tudor, marched to the borders of Herefordshire to face an army led by the Duke of York's son Edward. The Battle of Mortimer's Cross was noted for the appearance of three suns in the sky. Jasper's army was defeated, and the Yorkists adopted the image of the sun as a symbol. Owen Tudor, the husband of Catherine of Valois, was captured and executed in the marketplace at Hereford.

His last words were said to have been, 'This head shall lie on the block that once lay in Queen Catherine's lap.'

Soon after Mortimer's Cross the main Lancastrian army was exterminated in a bloody battle at Towton in Yorkshire. Edward now marched to London to be crowned King Edward IV. Jasper had escaped from Mortimer's Cross in disguise, and shortly afterwards was in Tenby, writing letters in an attempt to rally resistance in North Wales. Later in the year he was a fugitive in Snowdonia. He escaped, and after a further defeat near Caernarfon, was hunted for two years in Ireland. He then was chased to Scotland but in 1468, Jasper landed in North Wales to try and relieve Harlech Castle. This defence of the garrison was the inspiration for the song 'Men of Harlech'. On three occasions before his last exile in Brittany, Jasper returned to Wales and attempted to revive opposition to Edward IV. On the first two occasions he escaped by boat from near Harlech, where he appears to have had friends among the local gentry. Finally, in the invasion of 1470, Jasper again landed in Wales.

The 'Kingmaker', the Earl of Warwick, had rebelled against Edward IV, allowing Jasper Tudor to return to Wales during the brief restoration of Henry VI from 1470 to 1471. Edward IV's soldiers had deserted him and he was forced to flee abroad. Henry VI was brought out of imprisonment and restored as king, and Jasper was restored to the Earldom of Pembroke, but Henry VI was mentally unstable. In 1471 Edward returned with a new army, and the War of the Roses was finally decided by two tremendous battles at Barnet and Tewkesbury, which resulted in the virtual destruction of the Lancastrian cause. Jasper had gathered a Welsh army but had failed to reach Tewkesbury in time for the second great defeat of the Lancastrians. Edward of Westminster, Prince of Wales, had died at Tewkesbury, and the king was then murdered. Jasper had regained his Earldom of Pembroke under Henry VI's brief readeption, but now lost it a second time. It was later surrendered by the second William Herbert to Edward IV, and the king handed it to his son Prince Edward.

Jasper's nephew Henry Tudor was now the only Lancastrian heir left who was not in custody or dead. Jasper Tudor understood the danger, and hastened to take the fourteen-year-old Henry from the Welsh Marches. The pair rode urgently towards Jasper's estates in West Wales where he still had support, and where there could be temporary protection before the Yorkists came for Henry. Besieged at Henry's birthplace of Pembroke Castle in the far south-west corner of Wales, the pair managed to break through the encircling troops, and rode 11 miles east, seeking refuge in Jasper's walled town and port of Tenby. Thanks to the town's mayor Thomas White, Henry and Jasper hid in a basement in the centre of town, and escaped towards the harbour in underground tunnels. Under cover of darkness, they shipped aboard a waiting barque at Tenby Harbour.

The Tudors had wished to land in France where Jasper had already established diplomatic relations, and where they could expect a welcome at court from his kinsman the king, but were blown off course. They were forced to land at Le Conquet in the extreme west of the Duchy of Brittany, then an independent nation and in almost constant war with France. They were taken to François II, Duke of Brittany, in his capital of Nantes. After a short stay in Vannes, the Tudors were granted asylum as privileged prisoners, but at the mercy of political manoeuvrings between England, France and Brittany. Henry and Jasper were then sent to the imposing Château de Suscinio in southern Morbihan around October 1472, just over a year after they had landed. Henry and Jasper's stay here was comfortable, as they were valuable detainees, but escape would have been extremely difficult.

Edward IV demanded that the Bretons return Henry and Jasper, to eradicate his main Lancastrian threat, but Duke François kept the Tudors in custody as a bargaining force in any future negotiations with England or France. Edward IV's ambassadors then demanded the Tudors were treated more as prisoners than guests, while the French insisted that Jasper and Henry were put under far stricter control, to stop them being captured by any English force. François II was forced to accept these terms and the prisoners' movements and privileges were curtailed. Access to the sea meant the château was exposed to the possibility of English attack and the Tudors were moved inland. However, the Château de Suscinio continued to be the main base for their Lancastrian support, with perhaps up to 500 followers being in the vicinity at various points during Henry's fourteen-year exile in Brittany and France.

Edward IV and Louis XI continued to demand the handing over of the Tudor hostages. Louis XI was also a first cousin of Jasper Tudor. His father Charles VII had been the brother of Jasper's mother Catherine of Valois, the dowager Queen of England. Louis believed that he had the right to the guardianship of his kinsmen Jasper and Henry. Duke François II therefore decided to separate Henry and Jasper, lessening the chance that both would be captured together. Jasper was taken to the mighty fortress of Josselin in central Brittany in 1473 or 1474 and Henry was taken to the Château de Largoët in 1474, 10 miles from the port of Vannes.

From 1471, both uncle and nephew had been kept under the explicit protection of the Duc de Bretagne. François II had rejected constant English demands, keeping his word to grant the Tudors asylum. Edward IV's envoys had mixed promises with bribes to try to take the Tudors, but in 1476 altered their position. The ambassadors promised to safeguard Henry back to England, saying that he would not be harmed. Henry would be granted his full Beaufort inheritance and be married to a prominent Yorkist woman to further ensure his safety. It was even said that Edward IV wished to marry Henry to his own daughter Elizabeth of York, to integrate Henry into the Yorkist line. The young Henry refused to go. His father had died in a Yorkist gaol before he had been born, and all of his nineteen years had been spent in care, custody or exile. Henry had become a pragmatist, even separated from his beloved uncle. The French diplomat Philippe Commines met Henry in Brittany and France, and wrote of him, 'Without power, without money, without right ... and without any reputation but what his person and deportment excited; for he had suffered much, been in distress all the days of his life, and particularly a prisoner in Bretagne to Duke Francis from the eighteenth year of his age who treated him as kindly as the necessity of his imprisonment would permit.' Commines recorded that as a young man, the Earl of Richmond claimed that 'from the time he was five years old he had been always a fugitive or a prisoner'.

After five years of pressure from both France and

England, and having succumbed temporarily to illness, in the winter of 1476 François gave in. He agreed to release Henry into English hands, accepting Edward IV's good intentions. Edward IV had also promised to reward many courtiers at the Breton court when Henry returned, so there was little opposition to the refugees being sent home. Henry's friends rushed to the Breton court and urged the duke to allow Henry to stay. Admiral of Brittany since 1432, Jean du Quelennec, Vicomte du Fou, was one of the duke's most trusted councillors. He was vehemently against the proposal, but was away from court when the duke reached his decision. The admiral rode to court, pleading for Henry's cause, saying, 'Most noble Duke, this paleness of countenance is unto me a messenger of death.' François asked what was wrong and the admiral replied that his duke had forgotten his promise and delivered instead 'that most innocent imp, to be torn in pieces by bloody butchers, to be miserably tormented, and finally to be slain'. Duke François protested, but the Vicomte du Fou insisted, 'Henry is almost lost already, whom if you shall permit to step one foot out of your jurisdiction, all the world shall not after that be able to save his life.'

In November 1476 Henry was reluctantly escorted to Vannes and given to the English envoys. He was then escorted north overland to St Malo where ships were berthed ready to take him back to England. At St Malo, Henry either feigned sickness or was actually ill, thereby missing tides and delaying the departure of the ship to England. Because of his admiral's intervention, François had now changed his mind, and the delay saved Henry's life. The duke sent Pierre Landais, his chief treasurer and main advisor, to St Malo, arriving just as the English were due to sail. Landais entered into a lengthy discussion with the envoys, saying that Duke François now wanted Henry back in his own protective custody. During the argument, Henry somehow escaped and was chased through the narrow streets to St Vincent's Cathedral, where he claimed sanctuary. The citizens of St Malo then crowded around and refused to allow the English to break sanctuary tradition by entering the cathedral armed, and the envoys were forced to sail home without Henry. Edward IV's men had held Henry for only three days, and Henry returned to court with Landais. Thus is history changed forever – we may not have seen the Elizabethan Age of Renaissance, the English Empire or England as a Protestant nation if Henry Tudor had slipped on his dash to sanctuary.

François apologised profusely to Henry, reassuring the 'comte de Richemont' that he was now safe, but also tried to appease Edward IV by making Henry's imprisonment more secure. By 1480 Henry was in captivity at the Château l'Hermine in Vannes, where he was later joined from Josselin by his uncle Jasper. Envoys from both France and England continued to pressure Duke François into giving them up. Again, in June 1482 Edward sent envoys to Brittany. He reconfirmed his desire to welcome Henry Tudor back as a treasured member of his inner court, again promising marriage into a strong Yorkist family. He again promised that Henry would receive his Beaufort inheritance, and that upon his mother's death he would receive even more. Henry would not return. However, Edward IV died suddenly in April 1483. With Edward dead, Henry and Jasper were now given greater freedom over their movements. Events moved quickly. The Earl of Richmond became the new focus for all those who thought that Gloucester was an unworthy king who had murdered his nephews.

Margaret Beaufort saw the first real opportunity to safeguard her son's life. She immediately liaised with Elizabeth Woodville, the former queen-consort, after Edward IV's death in 1483. Elizabeth's brother-in-law Gloucester accused her of plotting to 'murder and utterly destroy' him. Upon 25 June 1483 he had Elizabeth's son and brother executed in Pontefract Castle. In the *Titulus Regius* of 1484, Richard declared Edward's and Elizabeth's children illegitimate. The act also contained charges of witchcraft against Elizabeth, but gave no details and had no further repercussions. Richard became king. He also revived the allegations of witchcraft against the queen's mother Jacquetta when he claimed that she and Elizabeth had procured Elizabeth's marriage to Edward IV through witchcraft. Richard never offered any proof to support his assertions. Along with the imprisonment and probable murder of her two sons, Richard had declared Woodville's marriage invalid and stripped her of her dower rights.

In 1483, Landais persuaded the Duke of Brittany to arm Henry with ships, men and arms to invade Britain, to coincide with Buckingham's rebellion. When Henry attempted to land on 10 October (or 19 October), storms meant that his fleet was scattered, and he arrived too late to join Buckingham. Buckingham's rebellion demonstrated the weaknesses inherent in Richard III's regime. Edward IV had successfully deposed Henry VI in 1461 because he had strong support in London and the South. He had the support of the Church, including the papal legate, and he had a justified grievance against Henry VI who had broken the Act of Accord and waged war on, and killed, Edward's father. Richard III's support was in the less populated, less wealthy and less influential North. The Church was divided in its view of him and the bishops of Ely, Exeter and Salisbury (a brother of Elizabeth Woodville), along with the Archbishop of York, all directly opposed him.

Henry met with his supporters at St Pierre Cathedral, Rennes, to pledge an oath to marry Elizabeth and unite the rival houses, upon Christmas Day 1483. Present on this day was the majority of his force, both Yorkist and Lancastrian, in addition to the Duchess of Brittany herself. As the premier minister in the land Pierre Landais was also present and through him Henry had obtained Duke François's solemn promise to support and assist in the cause. Henry had entered into a pledge which he could not turn his back on; if his invasion of England was successful and he became king, he would marry Elizabeth of York. It was in effect a marriage by proxy.

The twenty-six-year-old Henry and the fifty-year-old Duke François had become increasingly friendly during Henry's twelve years in Breton custody. Henry needed François for security, and for any prospect of defeating Richard III. François needed Henry to become King of England in order to gain a powerful ally in his constant battles with France. However, François II had grown increasingly ill and by 1484, his treasurer Pierre Landais was effectively in control of the dukedom while François was recuperating. Powerful nobles opposed Landais, and Charles VII wished to annexe Brittany to France. Landais decided that the renewal of the historic ties with England was his best hope for continuing Breton independence and his own preservation. Landais thus made an agreement with William Catesby, Richard III's principal advisor, to surrender Henry and Jasper in exchange for English protection of the Duchy of Brittany. In 1483 Bishop Morton had escaped from Brecon Castle, where he had been in Buckingham's custody, and was in Flanders. News of the arrangement reached Morton, who immediately despatched the priest Christopher Urswick (1448–1522) to warn Henry.

Urswick had been the chaplain to Henry's mother, Margaret Beaufort. Urswick stayed in exile with Henry and was with him at Bosworth Field, probably previously corresponding with Margaret Beaufort and her husband Thomas Stanley. Henry now urgently needed to escape across the border into France, for asylum in the court of the new French king Charles VIII. Leaving Vannes at some point in September under the pretence of visiting a friend, around 5 miles later Henry suddenly left the road and rode into the woods where he changed into the clothes of a peasant. He then rode fiercely for the French border. Landais, hearing of his flight, sent armed troops to head Henry off, but the Bretons arrived at the border just one hour too late. Jasper had crossed the border unnoticed two days earlier in a similar manner. Louis XI had died in August 1483, and the new king Charles VIII was just thirteen, so his regents were his eldest sister Anne de Valois of France and her husband Peter II, Duke of Bourbon.

At Angers Henry met Jasper and was received by Charles VIII. The Tudors were useful pawns to Charles, Anne and Peter to ensure that Richard III did not interfere with French plans to annex Brittany.

(Just four years later Duke François II of Brittany died, after seeing British-speaking Brittany fall to France when Charles VIII attacked and forcibly married his daughter and heir Anne de Bretagne. Breton was basically the same language as those of the Britons of Wales and Cornwall). Luckily for Henry, John de Vere, Earl of Oxford, now escaped from Hammes Castle near Calais, after ten years' imprisonment. Oxford had escaped with the help of the castle's custodian, Sir James Blount. Oxford, Blount and Sir John Fortescue rode to Paris with others including Richard Fox, later Bishop of Winchester, to offer their services to Henry.

This was an incredible boost to Henry's bleak prospects, as Oxford was one of the greatest military men of his day. It appears that one Brereton, a retainer of Lord Thomas Stanley, Henry's father-in-law, also brought money for Henry to use in an invasion. Anne de Valois, in the name of Charles VIII, helped to raise French troops and more money to help Henry. Richard sent out a force from Calais to regain Hammes Castle, whose garrison supported the Lancastrian cause, but Oxford and Thomas Brandon reinforced it. The whole garrison was allowed to leave on honourable terms with their arms and joined Oxford, Jasper and Henry in Paris.

Duke François, recovered from his illness, had been furious with Landais for losing Henry, his main bargaining device for securing English aid against France. Landais was hung from the walls of the Breton capital, Nantes, upon 19 July 1485. However, François bore no ill will to Henry. Ashamed of the incident, the duke sent his regrets to Henry. Rather than punishing Henry's supporters left behind in Brittany, the duke provided them with safe conduct to France and helped to finance the move, allowing 400 Lancastrian supporters to leave for France to rejoin their Tudor leaders.

Provided with extra funds from Charles VIII's treasury, plans were developed to launch a fresh invasion from the coast of France. Henry began to appeal to other nobles across Wales and England to support his claim. Henry no longer was the exiled Earl of Richmond but styled himself as the real King of England. He began to be addressed and address others in this manner, signing his letters with the solitary initial 'H', as opposed to his previous 'Henry de Richemont'. Yorkist propaganda called Henry a bastard, and Lancastrians in turn named Richard a tyrant and usurper. Henry gathered a force of Lancastrians, dissident Yorkists and French mercenaries at Honfleur.

Upon 16 March 1485, Richard's queen, Anne Neville, died and rumours spread across the country that she was murdered to pave the way for Richard to marry his niece, Elizabeth. The loss of Elizabeth's hand in marriage would shake the foundations of the alliance between Henry's Lancastrian supporters and those who were Yorkist loyalists to Edward IV. Henry expected Richard to marry Elizabeth of York, and desperately sent messages to the new Lord Herbert of Raglan, proposing to marry his sister Katherine. He also sent messages to the Earl of Northumberland, who had married another sister, Maud Herbert, seeking a Yorkist bride. Henry needed Yorkist support, and these urgent attempts demonstrate that there was a strong belief that the king was about to marry his niece. Morgan of Kidwelly, attorney-general to Richard III, arrived to let Henry know that Sir John Savage and Rhys ap Thomas would support him, and that Reginald Bray had raised money to pay for his troops. Anne of Valois and Charles VIII were encouraging Henry's planned invasion but began hedging about financial support. However, with the support of Philippe de Commines, an influential diplomat, Henry pressed Charles and his regent to request money from the French parliament. The French king did so on 4 May 1485 and returned with Henry to Paris about a month later.

Charles VIII was a minor, so the French force was despatched by the regent, Anne of Beaujeu, also known as Anne of France and Anne de Valois. Besides around 400–500 English exiles (who were likely to be men at arms and their households), some Scots and perhaps 1,000 men, apparently recruited by 'emptying all the gaols in Normandy', there was also a contingent of perhaps 500 discharged soldiers from a base at Pont de l'Arche led by Philibert de Chandée, a Savoyard captain in French service. Chandée's expert soldiering during the actual battle and the use of tactics copied from the Swiss may have swung the Battle of Bosworth in Tudor's favour. Chandée was knighted and made the 1st Earl of Bath, being one of the very few men elevated to the peerage by Henry VII, and died after 1486 in Brittany. Henry's English supporters were placed under the command of Richard Guildford.

On 1 August 1485, Henry and his followers left Harfleur and sailed down the Seine into the Channel. Some accounts state it was Honfleur, a few miles away near Le Havre. On 7 August, they sailed into Milford Sound near sunset. Henry landed at Mill Bay, Pembrokeshire, on Welsh soil for the first time since he was forced into exile fourteen years earlier. He fell to his knees, kissed the soil and was heard to cry, 'Judge me, Lord, and fight my cause.' The story of Henry's fast march through Wales, picking up support along the way, needs to be told in greater detail in another book, but will be recounted briefly.

This was a strange invasion. It seems that Richard underestimated the danger from a ragtag force of around 2,000 men, or that he felt that his loyal nobles in Wales would stifle it, just as happened in the series of rebellions across southern England in 1483. There was no urgency in Richard's reaction to the invasion, but Henry's motley force raced up and across Wales at around 20 miles per day, foraging for provisions. With hindsight, Richard should have moved to force as early an engagement as possible, as Henry was daily picking up new support. Through the agency of the bards, the Welsh were conditioned for the return of Henry Tudor, as the realisation of a prophecy that Wales would regain its power against England.

The force marched to Haverfordwest, the county town of Pembrokeshire. Richard's main officers in South Wales, Sir William Herbert and his brother Walter, failed to move against Henry, and some of Herbert's officers, Richard Griffith and Evan Morgan, deserted to Henry with their men. Arnold Butler of Johnston, Pembroke, a relative of the powerful Butlers of Dunraven, joined at Haverfordwest, where the castle, like that at Dale, was not defended. Henry's marched north, keeping near the coast and potential rescue, from Haverfordwest to Cardigan. From Cardigan Henry wrote letters to Gilbert Talbot, the Stanley brothers and others saying that he would cross the Severn at Shrewsbury, asking them to meet him with troops.

Henry's most important supporter in the early stages of his invasion was Rhys ap Thomas, the most powerful lord in South Wales, who had declined to support Buckingham's revolt. When Richard III appointed officers to replace those who had joined the revolt, he made Rhys ap Thomas his principal lieutenant in south-west Wales. Rhys was told to send his son Gruffydd ap Rhys to the king's court at Nottingham as a hostage. However, he excused himself from doing so by claiming that nothing could bind him to his duty more strongly than his conscience. The support of Rhys ap Thomas was crucial to an invasion, and it appears that at he had been in previous contact with Henry Tudor. It seems that Henry had successfully offered the lieutenancy of all Wales in exchange for Rhys's loyalty. Henry marched north, along the Ceredigion coast to Aberystwyth and there to Machynlleth (around 100 miles from the landing).

Here Henry wrote a letter to Sir Roger Kynaston, the guardian of the Grey estates. To pass safely to Shrewsbury, Henry needed – at the very least – Kynaston's inaction. Outside Machynlleth Henry stayed with Dafydd Llwyd at Mathafarn, before heading north-east to Newtown, Welshpool and then Shrewsbury. Rhys ap Thomas of Dinefwr took a more easterly route, acting as a buffer army against possible Herbert attacks, and recruiting 500 more Welshmen before reuniting with Henry near Welshpool. Henry VII had sent a letter to the Welsh gentry, seeking their support before Bosworth: 'To free this, our Principality of Wales of such miserable servitude as they have long piteously stood in.'

En route to Shrewsbury, supporters marched to join Henry, bringing along much-needed supplies. From the south-east, Walter Herbert, a childhood friend of Henry's, joined with some forces from Gwent, despite the fact that he and his brother were prominent Yorkists. It was vital, however, that the army passed Shrewsbury and into England unopposed. Sir Roger Kynaston was based at Plas Kynaston, just south of Wrexham in Denbigh, and Henry had to pass through the Grey estates that Kynaston guarded to reach Shrewsbury. Kynaston had been Constable of Denbigh and Harlech castles, High Sheriff of Shropshire and was High Sheriff for life of Merionethshire. A prominent Yorkist, he effectively won the Battle of Blore Heath in 1459 by personally killing James Tuchet, 5th Baron Audley.

While the Herberts had grown up as children with Henry and had divided loyalties, which accounted for their refusal to engage with him, Kynaston had fought throughout the Wars of the Roses, and was expected to definitely delay or even halt Henry's progress. Incidentally, Kynaston was defending the estates of Edmund Grey, Lord of Ruthin and 1st Earl of Kent, whose treachery had given victory to the Yorkists at Northampton. Grey raised no forces for Richard III at Bosworth, despite being JP for Merioneth and a former Lord Treasurer of England. Kent's warrior son George Grey also did not attend Richard at Bosworth, and as 2nd Earl of Kent later became one of Jasper Tudor's commanders in France and Cornwall. One must ask why so few Yorkists rallied to Richard's cause – did they believe that he had killed Edward V and was a usurper?

Flintshire men joined under Richard ap Hywel of Mostyn. William ap Griffith from Penrhyn joined, bringing men and food supplies in the form of herds of cattle. Around 15 or 16 August, Henry's army had crossed the border, heading for the important town of Shrewsbury. Supporters sent money to pay the mercenary troops. Since 22 June, Richard had known of Henry's impending invasion and had ordered his lords to maintain a high level of readiness. News of Henry's landing reached Richard on 11 August, but it took three or four days for his messengers to notify his lords of their king's mobilisation. On 16 August, the Yorkist army began to gather. The Duke of Norfolk headed for Leicester, the Yorkist assembly point. Simultaneously the Duke of Northumberland had gathered his men and ridden to Leicester.

At Shrewsbury, the prominent Yorkist Kynaston brought men to fight for Henry at Bosworth. Another Welsh contingent was led by Rhys Fawr ap Meredydd, who had travelled from his mansion at Foelas, outside Ysbyty Ifan, Conwy. He may have met up with Henry and Rhys ap Thomas at Long Mountain near Welshpool. Shrewsbury opened its gates on 15 August after one day's parleying. Henry's forces headed eastwards and on 17 August Sir Gilbert Talbot, uncle and guardian of the young Earl of Shrewsbury, joined him with 500 of the retainers of his old Lancastrian house. Sir Thomas Bourchier joined, as did Sir Walter Hungerford, who had deserted Thomas Brackenbury's Yorkist force. More deserters from Richard's forces joined. Although its size had increased substantially since the landing, Henry's army was not yet large enough to fight, and Jasper Tudor slowed down the pace of the army through Staffordshire, trying to gather more recruits.

Henry's strategy of landing in Wales and heading east into central England had depended on the reactions of his kinsmen Sir William Stanley, as Chamberlain of Chester and North Wales, and those of Lord

Thomas Stanley, who owned much of Cheshire and Lancashire. Learning of the invasion, Richard III had ordered the Stanleys to raise the men of their region to fight Henry. Henry had been communicating on friendly terms with the Stanleys for some months, and the Stanleys had actually mobilised their forces upon hearing of Henry's landing, before the message from Richard. The Stanley armies ranged themselves ahead of Henry's march through the English countryside, meeting twice in secret with Henry as he slowed his progress through Staffordshire. On 20 August Henry rode with his bodyguard well in advance of his army to meet William Stanley, proof that he did not fear the Stanleys capturing him. At the second meeting, at Atherstone in Warwickshire, they conferred 'in what sort to arraign battle with King Richard, whom they heard to be not far off'.

When Richard discovered that Sir William Stanley had effectively cleared the path for Henry, he ordered his older brother Lord Thomas Stanley to join him immediately. Lord Stanley replied that he was too unwell to answer Richard's summons. Stanley's son Lord Strange was caught trying to escape from Richard's camp, and admitted that both he and Sir William had been plotting with Henry Tudor. Richard seems to have thought that Henry's rising would peter out in Wales, mainly because of his trust in William Herbert, who was inactive. William Herbert's Yorkist father William ap William ap Thomas ap Gwilym ap Jankyn (c. 1423–69) anglicised his name, to be known as William Herbert after a remote Norman ancestor. A great warrior known as Black William, he had been executed by Warwick after Edgecote Moor, so it was expected that Herbert would have strongly supported the Yorkist cause.

In 1467, Herbert had married Elizabeth Woodville's sister Mary Woodville (c. 1456–81). The bride was about ten or eleven years old, and William Herbert was fifteen. This link between William Herbert and the Woodvilles may well have affected William Herbert's decision not to attack Henry on his invasion. Herbert was governing South Wales for York, but he had been forced by Edward IV to give up the second earldom of Pembroke in 1479 in exchange for that of Huntingdon, and a less valuable endowment in Somerset and Dorset. In 1484, Herbert took as his second wife Katherine Plantagenet, the illegitimate daughter of Richard III – whether this was a forced marriage is unknown, and there were no children. Thus William Herbert not only had links with the Woodvilles, but his incomes and estates had been slashed by the Yorkist king he faithfully served. He had also grown up with Henry Tudor, so his loyalties would have been mixed at best.

Henry's wardship in the Herbert household seems to have played a massive role in his path to the kingdom. Indeed, upon acquiring the throne, Henry and Anne Devereux, the widow of William Herbert, Earl of Pembroke, killed at Edgecote in 1469, kept on extremely friendly terms. She had been as a mother during Henry's years at the great Raglan Castle, when Henry was aged between four and twelve. Pembroke's daughter Maud Herbert, whom Pembroke had wished to marry Henry, had married the Earl of Northumberland at some time between 1473 and 1476. Northumberland did not engage his reserve army at Bosworth, possibly because of the influence of Maud. In Henry's eight years in custody at Raglan until 1469, he aged from four to twelve, while Maud aged from thirteen to twenty-one, the eldest son and heir William from ten to eighteen and the second-eldest son Walter from nine to seventeen. In effect Henry grew up with Herbert's children, learning martial arts and courtly behaviour along with them. When William succeeded his father in 1469, he had been growing up with Henry for almost a decade. William Herbert was ordered to intercept Henry's invasion army in Wales, but did not move, and his younger brother Walter Herbert actually took a force of men from Gwent to join Henry's invading force. The Herberts were Yorkists but felt no loyalty to Richard III, especially as he had not returned the Earldom of Pembroke to them, taken by Edward IV. It is known that Richard was thrown into 'a fierce rage' when he found that Henry had 'traversed Wales unopposed'. He had expected loyalty from the Herberts, Rhys ap Thomas, Kynaston, Grey and the Stanleys.

5

Bosworth Field
22 August 1485

The king was at Nottingham when he heard of Tudor's landing four days earlier. He publicly rejoiced, as he thought there was no real threat, summoned an array, and went out hunting to celebrate the news. He would be able to extinguish the only remaining threat – he knew from his agents that Henry did not have much of an army. Richard sent out a call to the City of York on 15 August, but the citizens ignored it to celebrate the Feast of the Assumption. Discussing the summons the next day, it was decided to send to Richard for 'more information'. On 19 August, just eighty men were despatched, but probably arrived too late. There is no evidence that any men from the city actually arrived to fight for Richard. His scouts watched the Lancastrian army of around 5,000 men straggle through Lichfield, heading west into Leicestershire. Henry had come to Lichfield and camped outside the walls. The next day he was, as Hutton relates, 'joyfully received in the town, which the Lord Stanley, two days before, had evacuated as if flying before him.' Both Stanleys were clearing the path toward London for Henry.

The main royalist army of 6,000 under Richard III marched from the south to link with Norfolk and Percy. Approaching from the east into Leicestershire was the newly created Duke of Norfolk with 4,000 Yorkists. It is said that there were verses posted on the Duke of Norfolk's tent before the battle – 'Jockey of Norfolk, be not bold, / For Dickon thy master is bought and sold' – indicating treachery by the Percys or Stanleys. This may have even been sent by Northumberland.

Hutton relates that a letter survives from the Duke of Norfolk, which must have been written a few days before the battle, to Sir John Paston, Sheriff of Norfolk and Suffolk, saying that

> the enemy was landed, that the king would march on Tuesday August 16th, and that he himself, should rest at Bury [St Edmunds] in his way to the army, and desires the sheriff to meet him at Bury with the men he had promised the king, and bring besides, as large a company of tall men as he can procure, dressed in jackets of the Duke's livery, and he would reimburse his expense, when they met.

Paston did not move, and indeed Henry in 1486 used him to chase Lord Lovell. Hutton also records that Richard 'was no favourite; they [his men] were pressed into his service; Henry's were volunteers. If Richard won the battle, his men could not be gainers, nor much losers if he lost it; they were indifferent, and indifference is seldom crowned with success; some were determined not to fight'.

Henry Percy, Earl of Northumberland, was moving at last from the north, with 3,000 troops. Percy had links with the Woodvilles, land disputes with the

House of York, and Henry Tudor had sent messages to him. He was also married to Maud Herbert, with whom Henry Tudor had spent his childhood. Percy's father was the first cousin of Edward IV, Clarence and Richard III but had been killed fighting for the Lancastrians at Towton in 1461. Henry Percy had been imprisoned in the Fleet Prison and then the Tower by the Yorkists, not being released until 1469, aged twenty. He swore fealty to Edward IV, but his earldom was not restored to him until 1473. Northumberland then held important government posts in the north of England. Percy's experiences may have made him less than sympathetic to Richard's cause, and he had been surprisingly slow to raise a force for the battle.

Around 13,000 Yorkists under Richard, Norfolk and Northumberland were committed to take on Henry's force of 5,000 or so, intercepting it south of Market Bosworth. Another two Yorkist armies from the north-west, under the Stanley brothers, came to the site of battle. Sir William Stanley and Lord Thomas Stanley brought around 3,000 North Walians and Cheshire men and 4,000 Lancashire men respectively to the battlefield, ostensibly giving Richard a huge army of 20,000 well-armed men, over four times the size of the Lancastrian force. Thomas Stanley had married Henry's mother Margaret, Countess of Richmond, in 1482, but Richard had taken Lord Stanley's son as hostage to ensure Stanley's support against their kinsman Henry. However, Richard knew that William Stanley had colluded with Henry Tudor. If Richard won, William would not be certain of his fate.

There were only about 100 knights and noblemen who had responded to Richard's summons. A significant comment is made by Ross: 'For all its special ties with

Right: 1. 'Richard II. He was Born at Windsor December 6 1421 – Ascended the Throne August 21, 1422, & Murdered in the Tower of London, June 20, 1471.' (From Barnard's *New, Comprehensive, and Complete History of England*, 1783)

Below: 2. 'Edward IV. He was Elected King, March 5, 1464 – He caused his Brother the Duke of Clarence who joined the Earl of Warwick in his Rebellion & used some rash expressions against the King to be drowned in a Butt of Malmsey in 1478 – and Died of an Ague at Westminster April 9, 1483, Aged 40.' (From Barnard's *New, Comprehensive, and Complete History of England*, 1783)

Below right: 3. Richard, Duke of York (1411–1460), father of Richard III and Edward IV.

4. Henry VI (1421–1471), the son of Henry V, was king from 1422 to 1461 and 1470 to 1471.

Right: 5. Richard III (1452–1485), possibly his best known likeness.

Below: 6. A grassy mound and a block of masonry protected by railings is all that remains of Fortheringhay Castle, birthplace of Richard III.

RICHARD III.

Left: 7. 'Richard III. He was made Protector of England, May 27, 1483 – Elected King, June 20, and Crowned July 6, 1483 – and was Slain by Henry Earl of Richmond, afterward Henry VII, at Bosworth in Leicestershire, August 22 1485, Aged 32.' (From Barnard's *New, Comprehensive, and Complete History of England*, 1783)

Below: 8. Anne Neville, daughter of Richard Neville, the 'Kingmaker', and wife of Richard III (centre), Prince Edward of Lancaster, Anne's first husband (left) and Richard III (right).

9. Margaret of York, Richard III's sister.

Left: 10. Richard Neville, Earl of Warwick, 'the Kingmaker' (1428–1471).

Below: 11. Richard III and Anne Neville (1456–1485). *Richard, Duke of Gloucester, and the Lady Anne,* Edwin Austin Abbey, 1896.

12. 'Edward V. He succeeded to the Crown, April 9, 1483 & was murdered in the Tower about three months after by order of his Uncle Richard 3, who had previously usurped the Throne.' (From Barnard's *New, Comprehensive, and Complete History of England*, 1783)

13. 'Edward V & the Duke of York his Brother smothered in the Tower of London by Tyrrell & his accomplices, which assassination was ordered by the Duke of Gloucester, their Uncle afterwards Richard III.' (From Barnard's *New, Comprehensive, and Complete History of England*, 1783)

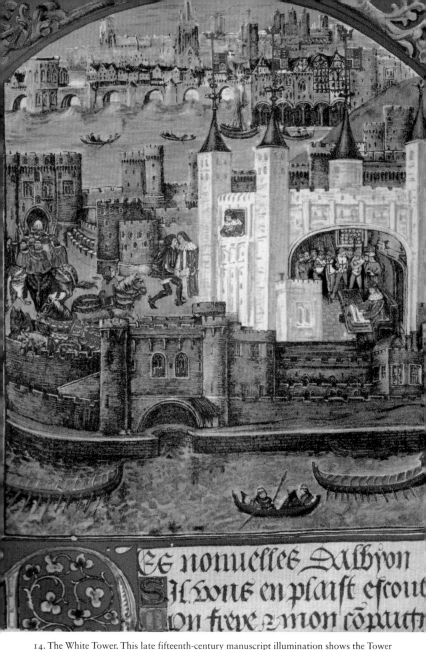

14. The White Tower. This late fifteenth-century manuscript illumination shows the Tower of London much as it would have looked in 1483.

Right: 15. The north-west tower staircase.

Below: 16. Edward V (1470–1483).

Below right: 17. Elizabeth Woodville, mother of the Princes in the Tower and Richard III's sister-in-law.

18. *The Princes in the Tower* (1832) by J. E. Millais.

Above: 19. Richard III carved in a misericord as a hunchback.

Below: 20. On 12 October 1483 Richard wrote to the Chancellor, John Russell, ordering him to bring the Great Seal to him at Grantham. The postscript referring to 'the malice of him that had best cause to be true, the Duke of Buckingham, the most untrue creature living' is in his own hand.

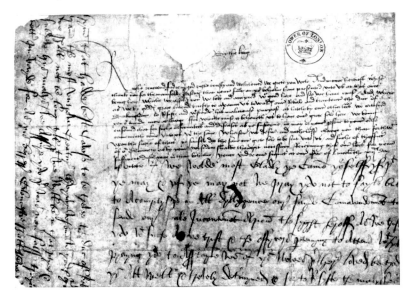

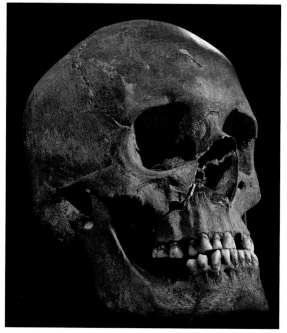

Above: 21. Middleham Castle, Richard III's principal residence in the North.

Left: 22. Skull of Richard III.

HENRY VII.

Elizabetha R

Above: 23. 'Henry VII. Being elected King, he was crowned Oct. 30 1485 – and Died at Richmond April 22, 1509.' (From Barnard's *New, Comprehensive, and Complete History of England*, 1783)

Right: 24. Elizabeth of York, Richard III's niece.

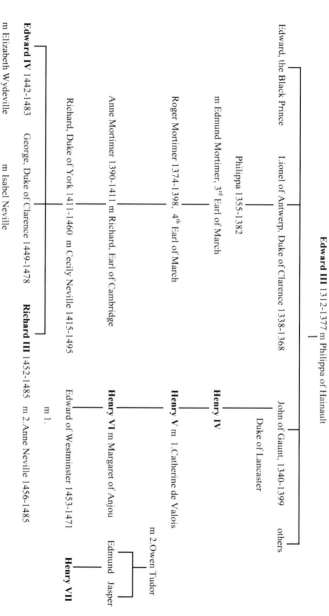

25. The Yorkist and Lancastrian lines.

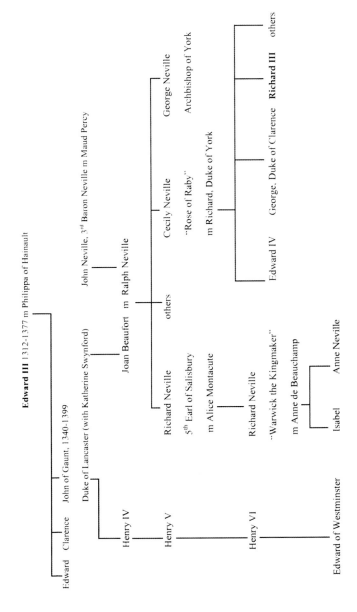

26. The descent of Richard III and Anne Neville.

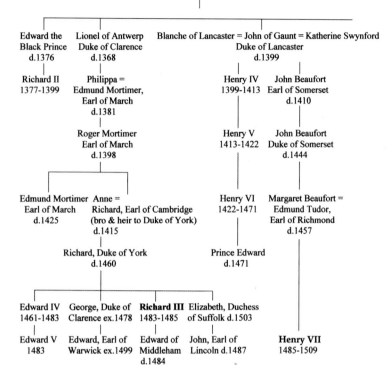

27. The lines of York, Lancaster and Tudor.

him, it [York] produced no more than eighty men at this time of supreme crisis in its patron's fortunes, and York, like Norwich, was one of the largest cities in the realm ... When news came of Richard's death at Bosworth a "great heaviness" fell upon the town, but in truth it had scarcely strained its resources to help him.' This may have been caused by Percy's dilatoriness in raising support in the North, and it is not even certain that any men from York arrived in time for battle. There is little information available upon the battle that forever altered England's history. However, the actions, and more interestingly non-actions, of the participants reveal Richard's support across his kingdom. His assistance from the more heavily populated south of England was negligible.

Commissions of array were important to raise extra troops in times of invasion or war. John Hardwick of Lindley Hall, Leicestershire, was the local commissioner of array to Richard, responsible for gathering local men for his army. However, with some mounted retainers, it is said that Hardwick had ridden to Henry at the Three Tuns, Atherstone, and offered to act as a guide towards Richard's army. He advised that the 'White Moors' on Redemore Plains was the best place for Henry to position his army, which gave him the defensive advantage of a great marsh to protect his right flank, when about to engage with Richard. He also advised that Henry's troops should fight with the sun at their backs.

A fascinating but little-known fact about the ensuing battle was that William Gardiner, one of Rhys ap Thomas's Lancastrian force, was supposed to have been the mercenary and 'Welsh halberdier' who killed Richard III. An acquaintance of Gardiner's for many years was fellow mercenary Roland Warburton. Warburton was noted for his arrival at Bosworth Field on 21 August 1485, the eve of the battle, with money to pay the 3,000 men under William Stanley's command. His arrival did much to lift the morale of the troops, making them more eager for action. Was this money sent by Margaret Beaufort?

Contemporary records indicate that the battle was fought on Redmoor, or Redemore Plain, between Market Bosworth to the north, Sutton Cheney to the east, Stoke Golding to the south and Upton to the west. There was once a great marsh, since drained. Henry issued a proclamation that Richard of Gloucester was killed at 'Sandeford in the county of Leicester', and the locations of the camps of Richard, Henry, Northumberland and the two armies of the Stanleys are still disputed. Sir John Savage, Lord of Clifton in Cheshire and married into the Stanleys, probably joined with Sir Simon Dygby and Sir Bryan Sandford (Sandforth) upon 19 August, all deserting with their men from Richard's army.

Fortified by local knowledge, defections from Richard's camp and lack of opposition, Henry's army was however split between his French and British soldiers, with frequent arguments breaking out. He had to separate the troops to stop fighting between the Welsh and French. However, Henry had prepared well, and had the hopes, rather than definite knowledge, that Richard's troops were fairly demoralised in following a king about whom rumours swirled. He also quite probably believed that the Stanleys would support him, and may well have known that Northumberland would refrain from battle. Hutton relates that the end of Henry's speech to his troops before the battle reads, 'Should we be conquered what mercy can we expect from a man who shewed none to his friends, his brother, his nephews, and his wife? We cannot retreat without destruction. What though our numbers be few; the greater will be our praise if we vanquish, and if we fall, the more glorious our death.' The same words were echoed by Sir Henry Morgan and Winston Churchill in years to come.

Facing immense odds, Henry had no choice but to flee the battlefield or face Richard's forces alone. He gave command of his army to the Earl of Oxford, and surrounded himself with his bodyguards including Rhys ap Thomas and Rhys ap Maredudd. Henry's three main standards were the Cross of St George of England, the Red Dragon of Cadwaladr to satisfy his Welsh forces, and the Dun Cow of Guy, Earl of Warwick, in reference to Henry's noble descent from the Beauforts and Beauchamps. Seeing the long line of Richard's army strung along the ridge of the hill, Oxford decided to keep his smaller force together instead of splitting it into the traditional three battles (troop formations) of vanguard, centre, and rearguard.

Sir William Stanley and Thomas, Lord Stanley, with combined armies perhaps 7,000 strong, took up positions possibly side by side. Richard advanced over Ambion Hill with the intention of deploying his army in the traditional manner, with three 'battles' drawn up in a line opposite the enemy. However, the Earl of Northumberland brought his 'battle' to a halt on the hill while still far away from the rebels. This may have been either to better defend against an attack by the Stanleys or to await the outcome of the battle.

Henry's army did not have the cannon or archery power of Richard's force, so the determined Oxford led an advance towards Richard's men. Oxford had been locked up for years and his lands confiscated – a battlefield veteran, he had nothing to lose. The Lancastrians were harassed by Richard's cannon as they manoeuvred around the marsh, heading for firmer ground. Norfolk's battle and several contingents of Richard's force started to advance on this better ground as Oxford cleared the marsh. After suffering more casualties from arrows, and faced with a much greater body of soldiers, Oxford's line began to thin and lengthen. Aware of the danger of his line breaking, Oxford ordered his troops to stay within 10 feet of their banners, otherwise small individual groups would be surrounded and overwhelmed. Various individual groups of fighting men now clumped together. This shortened and concentrated the Lancastrian line, consolidating it into a single large mass. Hutton states, 'Oxford seems to have taken an imprudent step in closing his ranks, because the king would out-flank him. But he was apprised, no doubt, of the determinations in the little close at Atherstone, and narrowed his front with a view to make way for Stanley.'

The battle, once joined, according to Vergil was short, lasting only two hours. In response to Oxford's all-out attack on his vanguard, Richard drew up his centre behind Norfolk and proceeded to reinforce him. While the Earl of Oxford was slowly pushed back, the Stanley brothers remained non-committal to either side. It appears that the royalists were demoralised by the Stanley brothers and Northumberland staying out of the battle. Also they had been impressed to fight, whereas the Lancastrians had nothing to lose. The Lancastrians fought with the knowledge that defeat would probably mean death. Oxford's force held its

ground in grim hand-to-hand combat, with some of
Norfolk's southern English recruits fleeing the field. It
now appears that Oxford and Norfolk met in combat
with Oxford being wounded in the left arm but striking
off Norfolk's visor. Norfolk did not press home the
attack and was killed by a chance arrow into the brain
as his visor was missing. Surrey saw his father fall and
with Sir Richard Clarendon and Sir William Conyers
fought his way towards the body, but the knights
were killed and Surrey badly wounded as Talbot and
Savage, the leaders of Henry's cavalry wings, joined the
central melee. Talbot took Surrey as his captive. News
of their leaders' death and capture would have spread
through the royalist army, which was making no major
inroads upon Oxford's men.

Around this critical time, Lord Thomas Stanley led
his 4,000 men towards Northumberland's position
on a nearby hill. It may be that Thomas Stanley and
Northumberland communicated by envoys with each
other at this time, for both held back their forces.
Northumberland now took no action when urgently
signalled to assist Richard's army. It is possible that
he could not advance through Stanley's men, and the
land only otherwise allowed a long, difficult flanking
movement. This would expose him to attack, so he
held his troops back rather than endanger their lives.
More likely, he had come to an agreement with Henry
and Stanley to hold back his army. Richard now
spotted Henry and Jasper Tudor with their bodyguard
under the Red Dragon banner, on the slopes behind
Oxford's men. Henry had ridden off towards the
Stanleys, probably to beg them to join Oxford's
troops, and seemed isolated. With Northumberland
uncommitted, Richard feared that the Stanleys would

join Henry, and saw the opportunity to kill Henry and end the battle.

Richard now charged downhill with his knights past the unengaged William Stanley's army, towards Henry and Jasper. Richard personally unhorsed the giant Sir John Cheney, who was Henry VII's personal bodyguard. Henry's standard-bearer, William Brandon, was killed, the flag going down with him. Brandon's brother Thomas fought in Henry's bodyguard, and Brandon's son was later made Duke of Suffolk. In the midst of the fighting Henry was almost killed, but his Welsh bodyguards surrounded him and succeeded in keeping Richard's nobles away. William Stanley saw Henry's flag fall, but also that Richard and his small body of knights were separated from the main Yorkist army, and took his chance to enter the combat. His troops were mainly Denbighshire Welsh, and he probably would have been attainted by Richard. His whole force charged in behind Richard, to assist Henry.

Lord Thomas Stanley still held his 4,000 men back, as did the Earl of Northumberland with his 3,000-strong army. They watched the battle develop around Richard's small and rapidly diminishing force. Richard's standard-bearer lost his legs but held the Yorkist banner aloft until he was hacked to death. Richard's horse became mired in soft ground and he was forced to continue the fight on foot. Overwhelmed by the masses of Welsh spearmen around him, the last Yorkist king died on the battlefield. Hutton states, 'Richard at length fell, fighting an army! His body was covered with wounds. His helmet, which, like a colander, was full of holes, had lost the crown, and was beaten into every form but the right. Had a stranger afterwards examined the field, the most abused helmet he could find, he might safely conclude had been Richard's.' Richard's forces quickly disintegrated as news of his death spread. Northumberland's men marched away to the north upon seeing the king's fate, while the earl surrendered himself.

Jean Molinet was historiographer to the Burgundian court and sympathetic to the Yorkist cause. His account of Bosworth was written around 1490:

The Earl of Northumberland, who was on the king's side with 10,000 men, ought to have charged the French, but did nothing except to flee, both he and his company, and to abandon his King Richard, for he had an undertaking with the Earl of Richmond, as had some others who deserted him in his need. The king bore himself valiantly according to his destiny, and wore the crown on his head; but when he saw this discomfiture and found himself alone on the field he thought to run after the others. His horse leapt into a marsh from which it could not retrieve itself. One of the Welshmen then came after him, and struck him dead with a halberd, and another took his body and put it before him on his horse and carried it, hair hanging as one would bear a sheep.

Like the Croyland Chronicler, Molinet states that the Earl of Northumberland was unengaged in the battle, and in this instance accuses him of treachery.

It seems that the battle was decided at Henry's meeting at Atherstone with the two Stanleys. Hutton relates,

Lord Stanley hated Richard for the cruel attack he had made, two years before, upon his life [when Hastings was taken], for the murder of his friend Hastings, and the young Princes; but durst not espouse Henry's cause for the danger of his son ... What passed at this triumvirate council of war, never appeared to the light, but it is plain from succeeding events, it was resolved ... That the Stanleys should seem to avoid him, as if friends to Richard. That Richmond would march directly to the field. That Lord Stanley should keep at a distance on the right, and Sir William on the left. That when the two armies of Richard and Henry were drawn up face to face; Lord Stanley should form, and cover the opening between Richard's left and Richmond's right, and Sir William do the same on the opposite side, but join neither; so that when the four armies were marshalled they would form a hollow square. That while the king and the earl were engaged, the two brothers should stand neuter. That if the Earl could overcome the King, which was probable, for they knew Northumberland, who commanded a large body for Richard, would decline fighting, they should not interfere; but if Richard proved too powerful, they should run all hazards and assist Henry.

Henry Percy, Earl of Northumberland, was mainly responsible for Richard's defeat. Northumberland was briefly imprisoned soon after the battle, but released under surety on 6 December, restored to his offices and sent north, where Henry VII had discovered he could not do without his authority. The stronger army had lost, although facing Henry's single force had been the armies of Richard, Norfolk, Northumberland, Lord Thomas Stanley and Sir William Stanley. Northumberland and Thomas Stanley did not participate, and William Stanley took Henry's side. Only Norfolk was loyal to the king.

Henry's success had been largely due to Welsh support, and the emissary for Venice reported to the Doge that 'the Welsh may now be said to have recovered their independence, for the most wise and fortunate Henry VII is a Welshman'. Francis Bacon later commented that 'to the Welsh people, his victory was theirs; they had thereby regained their freedom'. Richard had been killed because he lacked support from nearly all major nobles after the fall of Buckingham. His murder of Hastings, Rivers and Grey had already alienated many former allies. Richard had also alienated the former Lancastrian Henry Percy, Earl of Northumberland, by appointing John de la Pole, Richard's nephew and heir designate, as leader of the Council of the North, a position that Percy had expected. The Stanleys had little trust of Richard, Thomas having been injured when Lord Hastings had been taken and murdered. The only magnate to fight for Richard was John Howard, Duke of Norfolk, who had just been elevated to the dukedom by Richard. The Wars of the Roses had weakened the power of all the major nobles to raise substantial numbers of troops, and those who could were not inclined to support Richard. This alone tells us something about the esteem in which he was held by his peers during his reign. They neither liked nor trusted him, despite the recent rewriting of history making him a 'good king'. As soon as Richard's active supporters realised he was dead, they fled. There were few casualties in Henry's army, the only casualty being Sir William Brandon, but equally astounding is the mass of survivors on Richard's side.

6

Henry VII's Actions 1485–1509

The preface of this book tells us that 'history is not exact'. In attempting to create a different version of history, a sympathetic view of Richard III, it has been necessary to blacken the character of his successor, Henry VII. However, one could easily write a book showing Henry to be perhaps the greatest and wisest of English kings. According to Bindoff, 'the man whom the battle made a king was to be the seventh and perhaps the greatest of those who bore the name Henry'. Today, we see Henry VII subjected to a history replete with pejorative adjectives, which have no place in a work of non-fiction. The 'History Book of the Year' in 2011–12 was Thomas Penn's *Winter King*, lauded by all the national press and famous historical novelists such as Hilary Mantel and Philippa Gregory. The latter calls it 'a definitive account that will alter the view not just of Henry VII, but of the country he dominated and corrupted'. These are strong (and also strange) claims. The book has been lauded by authors belonging to its publishing house, Penguin, and marketed with all the strength that an English subsidiary of the largest publishing firm in the world (Bertelsman of Germany) can muster. Tariq Ali calls it a 'chilling and enticing portrait' of Henry, and with a marked lack of knowledge of four centuries of English history, Diarmaid McCulloch calls Henry a 'weird man' and says that the 'book should be the first port of call for anyone trying to understand England's most flagrant usurper since William the Conqueror'.

How is Richard III himself not a flagrant usurper? Other 'flagrant usurpers' include William II, Guillaume the Bastard's third son, in 1087; Henry I, who probably had William II killed in 1100; Stephen, who usurped both his elder brother Theobald, and Matilda in 1135; John, who fought against his father and tried to usurp Richard and usurped and had killed Geoffrey's son Arthur in 1199; Henry IV, who murdered Richard II in 1399; and Edward IV, who murdered Henry VI in 1271. The facts of Henry's actions do not justify such comments. Penn actually states, in his introduction, his belief that Henry VII is missing from Shakespeare's plays, 'one suspects, because the reign was simply too uncomfortable to deal with'. This is history written via value judgements made to justify a hypothesis, whereas one should use proofs. To sell history books, one has to have an 'angle' in these times, whether it has any validity of not. Henry's reign of twenty-four years was incredibly peaceful and generous compared to those of Shakespeare's other English rulers. What great events could he write about? By Penn's logic, Elizabeth I's reign must also have been 'too uncomfortable to deal with'. In Henry's last decade as king, he was ill and intent upon securing the succession for his surviving son Henry. In doing so his financial advisers squeezed nobles and people alike to swell the treasury. There was undoubted financial hardship, but none of the vindictiveness laid at Henry VII's door by Penn.

Penn records dismissively that even the Tudor apologist Bacon called Henry a 'dark prince'. This is a selective and misleading quotation – its proper context is a far more revealing:

Towards his Queen he was nothing uxorious, nor scarce indulgent; but companiable and respective, and without jealousy. Towards his children he was full of paternal affection, careful of their education, aspiring to their high advancement, regular to see that they should not want of any due honour and respect, but not greatly willing to cast any popular lustre upon them.

To his council he did refer much, and sat oft in person; knowing it to be the way to assist his power, and inform his judgment. In which respect also he was fairly patient of liberty, both of advice, and of vote, till himself were declared. He kept a strait hand on his nobility, and chose rather to advance clergymen and lawyers, which were more obsequious to him, but had less interest in the people; which made for his absoluteness, but not for his safety. Insomuch as, I am persuaded, it was one of the causes of his troublesome reign; for that his nobles, though they were loyal and obedient, yet did not co-operate with him, but let every man go his own way. He was not afraid of an able man, as Lewis [Louis] the eleventh was: but contrariwise, he was served by the ablest men that were to be found; without which his affairs could not have prospered as they did. For war, Bedford, Oxford, Surrey, Daubeney, Brook, Poynings: for other affairs, Morton, Fox, Bray, the prior of Lanthony, Warham, Urswick, Hussey, Frowick, and others. Neither did he care how cunning they were that he did employ; for he thought himself to have the master-reach.

And as he chose well, so he held them up well; for it is a strange thing, that though he were a *dark prince* [authors' italics] and infinitely suspicious, and his times full of secret conspiracies and troubles; yet in twenty-four years' reign, he never put down, or discomposed counsellor, or near servant, save only Stanley the lord chamberlain. As for the disposition of his subjects in general towards him, it stood thus with him; that of the three affections which naturally tie the hearts of the subjects to their sovereigns, love, fear, and reverence; he had the last in height, the second in good measure, and so little of the first, as he was beholden to the other two.

He was a Prince, sad, serious, and full of thoughts, and secret observations, and full of notes and memorials of his own hand, especially touching persons. As, whom to employ, whom to reward, whom to inquire of, whom to beware of, what were the dependencies, what were the factions, and the like; keeping, as it were, a journal of his thoughts. There is to this day a merry tale; that his monkey, set on as it was thought by one of his chamber, tore his principal note book all to pieces, when by chance it lay forth: whereat the court, which liked not those pensive accounts, was almost tickled with sport.

He was indeed full of apprehensions and suspicions: but as he did easily take them, so he did easily check them and master them; whereby they were not dangerous, but troubled himself more than others. It is true, his thoughts were so many, as they could not well always stand together; but that which did good one way, did hurt another. Neither did he at some times weigh them aright in their proportions. Certainly, that rumour which did him so much mischief, that the duke of York should be saved, and alive, was, at the first, of his own nourishing; because he would have more reason not to reign in the right of his wife. He was affable, and both well and fair-spoken; and would use strange sweetness and blandishments of words, where he desired to effect or persuade any thing that he took to heart. He was rather studious than learned; reading most books that were of any worth, in the French tongue, yet he understood the Latin, as appeareth in that cardinal Adrian and others, who could very well have written French, did use to write to him in Latin...

This is not the portrait of a 'dark prince' but of a deeply astute ruler of a new dynasty in extremely difficult times. If we examine Henry's reign dispassionately, we may effectively despatch many such canards. Penn tells us that after Henry's victory at Bosworth 'nor was there any detail of his genealogy, of precisely what his claim to the crown consisted in [sic]'. There was – Henry proclaimed his lineage not only through the Beaufort and Beauchamp royal lines, but via Cadawaladr and Arthur of Wales with his use of the red dragon in battle and heraldry. By descent, Henry VII was a quarter Welsh, a quarter French and half-English. Henry VII was descended in direct male succession from Ednyfed Fychan, seneschal (steward) of Llywelyn the Great. The Tudor surname first appeared in the ancestry of Henry VII in the 1420s, when Owain ap Maredudd ap

Tudur ap Goronwy ap Tudur ap Goronwy ap Ednyfed Fychan abandoned the Welsh patronymic system and adopted a fixed surname.

Had he, as was generally the custom, adopted his father's name, the English throne would have been occupied for a century by the Maredudd dynasty. The Tudors of Penmynydd in Anglesey had in effect started the Glyndŵr War. The historian David Powel claimed in 1584 that Henry VIII inherited England from his father Henry VII, heir to John of Gaunt and Edward III, and Wales from his mother, heiress to the Mortimers and Llywelyn the Great. The use of 'Machiavellian' as meaning cunning or unscrupulous threads its way through Penn's book, but in truth 'Machiavellian' correctly means the intelligent process of securing power and security for a ruler.

'Machiavellian', if one actually reads *The Prince*, is associated with the establishment of constitutional legitimacy in a post-feudal state. Machiavelli defined how a principality, i.e. a territory ruled by a prince, could be run according to constitutional law and order after the prince had passed on. This order would be accepted by the next ruler of the principality, and the principality had to be strong enough to withstand invasions by rival states. Unintentionally, Penn has used the correct description of Henry VII's reign – he passed on a secure kingdom to his son. Unfortunately, Prince Arthur was dead and Henry VIII did not follow his father's precepts.

Throughout Penn's much-lauded work, adjectives such as 'chilling', 'remorseless', 'paranoid' and 'ruthless' describe Henry's motives and conduct. Let us examine reality. The dead Richard was indeed slung over a horse from Bosworth to Leicester, as the easiest way to transport the corpse over churned-up paths and highways. He was naked as his armour would have been stripped, as would have been the armour of any dead or dying soldiers. Richard was said to have been flung 'like a dog in a ditch', but was buried in the monastic community of Greyfriars in Leicester, which was founded around 1255. Richard's body was displayed for at least two days, as was the custom, to demonstrate to as many people as possible that the king was indeed dead. In 1495, Henry VII paid £50 for a marble and alabaster monument to mark the grave. Using the University of Exeter's 'current value of old money' website, this in today's money would be worth £34,000 (retail price index), £287,000 (labour value) or £958,000 (income value).

Let us also examine how, in the immediate aftermath of battle, the new king treated his defeated opponents in his strange new country. By the standards of previous English kings, he was noted as being 'remarkably merciful'. Almost immediately after his coronation, Henry showed his lack of greed and his intentions for peace and reconciliation. He issued an edict that any gentleman who swore fealty to him would, despite any previous attainder, be secure in his property and person. His actions both after the battle and during his reign denote a very different and much more accommodating character than that of Richard Plantagenet. Richard's close advisor, Sir William Catesby, was captured in the flight, and was executed at Leicester along with two yeomen of the king's chamber, a father and son from the West Country named Bracher. These were the only lives taken in cold blood by Henry. Catesby, plotting with Landais, had almost managed to extricate Henry from Brittany to face certain death at Richard's hands. It is thought that Catesby may have made a deal with the Stanleys before the battle, as in his will he asked them 'to pray for my soul as ye have not for my body, as I trusted in you'. Dugdale's *Warwickshire* gives us Catesby's will and proves him alive on 25 August, three days after the battle. 'It also proves him, under his own hand, a dishonest man, in amassing a fortune by unfair means. He expresses a friendship for Lovell, and seems angry with Stanley and Strange. He was descended from a very ancient family at Lapworth, near Birmingham, was bred to the law, in which profession he had acted for Buckingham, Hastings, and the Stanleys.'

The Brachers were almost certainly only killed because local interests resented their role in suppressing rebels in the west of England in 1483, and taking some Somerset estates. William Bracher is described as 'yeoman of the crown', and had been at the court of Edward IV where his rewards had been unexceptional. However, in Richard's court, Bracher received favours more appropriate for an esquire or even a knight, with income-earning opportunities from new Somerset and Dorset estates. One historian notes that William Bracher 'remains a shadowy figure and the reasons behind his unusual gains and the brutality of his treatment after Bosworth are unknown'. He may have been a spy, but Skidmore suggests the deaths of him and his son were due to some 'private vendetta'.

Sir John Buck of Hartshill was Richard's comptroller, and it is uncertain whether he was executed or died in battle. The only source for his execution alongside Catesby seems to be his descendant George Buck, the Ricardian author and sympathiser. Richard's friend and advisor Lovell, and Humphrey and Thomas Stafford, escaped from Bosworth to sanctuary in Colchester and were left alone. All those who escaped to sanctuary later rebelled, which we shall note later. This is in marked contrast to the Yorkists' treatment of those nobles dragged from sanctuary in the abbey and executed after the Battle of Tewkesbury in 1471.

Northumberland was not among those attainted in the November parliament. Henry had taken him into comfortable custody after the battle until December 1485, when Northumberland was freed under conditions of good behaviour. He now swore allegiance and loyally served the new king, retaining all his titles and lands and returning to his old posts. The Percy earls of Northumberland traditionally held the Northern Marches, in effect as buffer states against the Scots on the eastern side of England, while the Neville earls of Westmorland held the west. However, in spring 1489, Henry VII allied himself to Duchess Anne of Brittany against Charles VIII of France, and Northumberland was assassinated near Thirsk. Adams states that a note placed by Northumberland's body blamed him for Richard's death. He had been asked to speak to protesters against high taxes to pay for military action. Yorkist-leaning historians tell us that Henry took over the huge Northumberland estates, and let the matter rest there, with the assumption that Henry, like Richard, was greedy to take lands off the great houses. However, Henry merely (and sensibly) held them temporarily for the twelve-year-old 5th Earl of Northumberland, who faithfully served both Henry VII and Henry VIII. Henry was scrupulously fair in matters of estates, fees and ownerships, as a result rarely coming into conflict with the major nobles or gentry. A fuller account of Northumberland's death follows later.

The *Ballad of Bosworth Feilde* tells us that Ralph Neville, 3rd Earl of Westmorland (1456–99), fought for Richard III, but this may not be so. The ballad was written by a Stanley retainer who was probably present at the battle. Westmorland was arrested along with Northumberland and Surrey after the battle, so possibly was with Northumberland's army to witness the conflict. Westmorland was quickly released and entered into bonds to Henry of £400 and 400 marks, to be paid if he rebelled against the king. In December 1485 Westmorland gave the king the custody and marriage of his eldest son and heir, Ralph Neville (d. 1498). Westmorland held a command in the army sent into Scotland in 1497 after James IV supported the pretender Perkin Warbeck. Upon his death he was succeeded by his grandson, and the earls of both Westmorland and Northumberland served the Tudor dynasty.

Thomas Howard, Earl of Surrey, had carried the sword of state at Richard's coronation. Surrey had been badly wounded and taken at Bosworth, where his father the Duke of Norfolk had died. Surrey was attainted by Henry's first parliament and his estates were forfeited. He was also committed to the Tower, where he remained in comfort for over three years, receiving an excellent allowance of £2 a week for his board. (This is £1,230 per week using the Retail Price Index, but £11,000 using average earnings.) In June 1487, Lincoln invaded England, and the lieutenant of the Tower offered to open the doors to Surrey, but he refused the chance of escape. Henry VII realised that Surrey could be a loyal and useful official, and in January 1489 released Surrey, restoring him to his earldom in May. Henry for the time being kept the greater part of Surrey's forfeited lands, and trusted him to put down the Yorkshire Rebellion. The care of the Northern borders was given to Surrey, who became lieutenant-general of the North. Henry did not punish Richard's supporters for their loyalty, but did legally and rightfully restore some lands which had been confiscated by Edward IV and Richard and given to them.

Over time Surrey became the leading military commander of the Tudors. He slowly gained Henry's confidence and was named one of the executors of Henry's will, being present on all great occasions at the court. Henry VII, shortly before his death, made a full restoration of Surrey's forfeited lands and fees. Surrey became the chief adviser to the new king Henry VIII, and the most influential member of the Privy Council. Apart from John de la Pole, the Earl of Lincoln, Northumberland, Westmorland and Surrey were the three leading surviving opponents from the Battle of Bosworth, and all were fully restored by Henry to their honours and estates, which then stayed in their families. The Earl of Lincoln escaped the field, but was not attainted and swore an oath of allegiance to Henry, which he later reneged upon.

It is interesting to note the fates of the other notable Yorkists at Bosworth. Richard III had died heroically in battle, upon his bloody charge to try and kill Henry. Accompanied by his banner-bearer, Sir Percival Thirlwall, he had gathered his close companions about him. These included Sir Robert Percy, controller of the household, and knights of the body such as Sir Ralph Ashton, Sir Thomas Broughton, Sir Marmaduke Constable, Sir John Grey, Sir James Harrington, Sir Thomas Markenfield, Sir John Neville, Sir Thomas

Pilkington and Sir Richard Ratcliffe. Some accounts also give Catesby (who was captured), Sir John Byron and Sir Gervis Clifton (who was killed) as being in the last fatal charge. With a force of perhaps 200–400 mounted men, Richard led his cavalry downhill to crash into Henry's bodyguard. Among those who died around him were Sir Robert Brackenbury of Denton, Durham, lieutenant of the Tower of London (killed by Hungerford). Sir Percival Thirlwall of Thirlwall Castle, Northumberland, had his legs chopped off as he held Richard's flag. The king's councillor and confidant Sir Richard Ratcliffe was also killed in the melee that developed around Henry and Richard.

Sir James Harrington of Hornby, North Yorkshire, had helped capture Henry VI in Lancashire, and he and his brother Robert were in Richard's select band of retainers. They were deadly enemies of the Stanleys, after Hornby Castle and their Lancashire estates had been given to that family. Some believe that their support for Richard was a critical factor in the Stanleys siding with Henry. James Harrington was possibly killed in the charge, along with his brother. According to Horrox, 'both Harringtons were attainted for their part in the battle, and the family tradition was that James died there'. Their attainder seems to have been forced through by Thomas Stanley, and the Harrington family also related that James was left in great poverty because of Stanley's enmity.

The effigy of Sir Thomas Markenfield, High Sheriff of Yorkshire from 1484, can be seen in Ripon Cathedral. He was with Richard in the charge, but was pardoned and also became Henry VII's first sheriff in Yorkshire, helping to repress a tax revolt in the North in 1489 for the new king. By 1497 the Markenfields were serving

Thomas Stanley, Earl of Derby, stepfather to Henry VII. Sir Thomas died at his manor of Markenfield Hall near Ripon in 1497. Sir John Neville was an illegitimate son of the 2nd Earl of Westmorland, whose half-brother the 3rd Earl of Westmorland was captured at Bosworth, but as with Sir John Grey in Richard's bodyguard, it is unknown if he survived the battle.

Sir Thomas Pilkington, of Pilkington, Lancashire, survived the charge. One of Richard's inner circle, he was said to have died fighting for Lambert Simnel at the Battle of Stoke in 1487. However the *Victoria County History of Lancashire* states that he was not killed there, and it is recorded that his lands were confiscated and given to Thomas Stanley in 1489. Pilkington was pardoned by Henry VII in 1506, dying in 1508. Sir Robert Percy of Scotton near Knaresborough, controller of the household, was said to have been killed, but survived after fleeing the battlefield. In 1488 he received a general pardon and restitution of goods.

Sir Robert Ashton (Assheton) of Fritton-in-Redesdale, Yorkshire, was pardoned in 1486, and died aged sixty-nine, three years later. Hated by his tenants, he was known as 'The Black Knight', and his effigy was burned at Ashton near Middleton annually until the 1950s. Sir Thomas Broughton, lord of the manors of Witherslack and Broughton-in-Furness, was in Richard's bodyguard, but was pardoned after Bosworth. However, Broughton played an important part in the Simnel Rebellion in 1487, dying fighting for the Yorkists at Stoke. According to Horrox, it is unclear whether Sir Marmaduke Constable ('the little') of Flamborough fought at Bosworth. He may well have been with Northumberland's inactive army, rather than in Richard's personal cavalry charge. He was not attainted, and was granted a pardon on 18 November 1485. He became a knight of the body to Henry VII by May 1486, and accompanied him to the wars in France in 1492, dying in 1518.

These are the known men who rode alongside Richard III when he was killed, and we can not see any vindictiveness by Henry personally to any survivors, nor any battlefield executions of captured nobles as normally practised by Richard and his brothers. Apart from the king, the most notable Yorkist casualty was Sir John Howard, 1st Duke of Norfolk, who commanded the main army. Others who died away from Richard, in the main battle, included Lord Ferrers of Weobley, Herefordshire. Ferrers had fought at Towton as far back as 1461, and also at Barnet and Tewkesbury. Devereux was slain during the initial fight with the opposing van under Oxford, fighting next to the young John, Lord Zouche. An in-law, Sir John Ferrers, was also killed at Bosworth.

Sir John Babington of Dethick (High Sheriff of Derbyshire in 1479) died at Bosworth, slain by John Blount, but his family did not suffer. His son Thomas and his grandson Anthony both served as High Sheriff of Derbyshire. Other dead included John Kendal, Richard's secretary, and Chris Skidmore relates that

of the commissioners of array who assembled for Richard, ten were likely to have been killed at the battle: in Buckinghamshire, Thomas Hampden of Kimble and Thomas Straunge; William Allington in Cambridgeshire; John Coke in Essex; John Kebyll in Leicestershire; Richard Boughton and Henry Beaufort in Warwickshire; Sir Thomas Gower and Sir Robert Percy in Yorkshire all are listed among the inquisitions post mortem as having died around the date of the battle.

He points out that others died later, possibly as the result of injuries.

Of the main battlefield Yorkist survivors, Thomas Howard, Earl of Surrey, and son of the dead Norfolk, was imprisoned and later released to become the 2nd Duke of Norfolk. Lord Zouche, John de la Zouche of Harringworth, Northamptonshire, was allowed his freedom but his honours were passed to his son, and Zouche died in 1526. Lord Henry Grey of Codnor, Derbyshire, was made commissioner of mines by Henry VII, and died in 1496, after making arrangements for his uncle, John Zouche, to purchase Codnor Castle and other properties.

Sir John Huddleston of Millom, Cumbria, like Ratcliffe and Pilkington, was one of Richard's inner circle, and Sheriff of Cumberland. His son Sir Richard was thought to be killed in the battle, as he died around this time but is not in any list of those killed there. Perhaps he died of wounds. Sir Richard had been married to Margaret Neville, a daughter of Warwick the Kingmaker. Huddleston and his son Henry went into hiding after the battle, and were eventually summoned to give themselves up. They were pardoned by the new king. Sir John had also fought at Tewkesbury and died in 1494.

Roger Wake of Blisworth, Northamptonshire, has a tomb dating from 1503–04. His father-in-law was Richard Catesby of nearby Ashby St Ledgers, Chancellor of the Exchequer and Speaker of Parliament. Catesby was subsequently beheaded at Leicester. Wake was temporarily imprisoned, and had his lands forfeited.

By Act of Parliament Wake's lands were later restored to him. Sir William Conyers was thought in the *Ballad of Bosworth Feilde* to have died fighting for Richard, but in 1490 his title and estates were succeeded to by his grandson, and he is not listed in any contemporary accounts of the dead. Sir Robert Ughtred, of Kexby, Yorkshire, was a former Sheriff of Yorkshire and a king's knight of the household, and died in 1487 or 1488, aged almost sixty. It seems that his estates passed through his family. Sir William Gascoigne ('the younger') of Gawthorpe, JP for the West Riding of Yorkshire, died in 1487, and his estates were not confiscated.

Lord John Scrope, of Castle Bolton, Yorkshire fought for Richard but was pardoned by Henry VII. However, Scrope then supported the Yorkist pretender Lambert Simnel and in 1487, with Thomas Scrope, Baron of Masham, Yorkshire, unsuccessfully attacked Bootham Bar in York. John Scrope had to pay a heavy fine and remain within the London area. In 1497 he fought for Henry against the Scots and assisted in raising the siege of Norham Castle. He died in 1498, and Thomas Scrope in 1493, with both Scrope estates passing intact to their heirs.

The leniency shown by the new king to his opponents was astonishing by the standards of the day. The ablest were integrated into his government. Henry almost immediately paid off and dismissed the mercenaries in his force, retaining only a small core of fifty Welsh soldiers to form the 'Yeomen of his Garde', known today as the Tower of London's 'Beefeaters'. The first parliament reversed Henry's attainder and recorded Richard's kingship as illegal, although Richard's reign remains official, like that of Edward V, in English monarchic history.

The proclamation of Edward IV's children as illegitimate was also reversed almost immediately, restoring Elizabeth of York's status to a legitimate royal princess suitable for marriage to a king. *Titulus Regius* was the parliamentary statute of 1483, which made Richard, Duke of Gloucester, into Richard III. The 'king's deed' describes how Parliament had found that the marriage of Edward IV and Elizabeth Woodville was bigamous, declaring that the Princes in the Tower and their sister Elizabeth of York were illegitimate and ineligible to inherit the throne. Henry ordered that all copies of the statute, and all documents related to it, should be destroyed, unread. He did not want his future bride, Elizabeth of York, to be legally bastardised. Only one copy of the law survived, transcribed by a monk of Croyland Abbey into the *Croyland Chronicle*, discovered by Sir George Buck in the reign of James I. The repeal of *Titulus Regius* made the claim of the vanished princes stronger than that of Henry, Earl of Richmond, so it is fairly obvious that Henry believed that they were dead, but equally he appears to have had no idea of what had happened to them.

There was a general royal pardon on 11 October, but on 7 November 1485 the king and council met, and *Rotuli Parliamentarium* (the Parliamentary Record) records an Act of Attainder. This Act dated Henry's reign from 21 August, making the assembly of men under Richard the day before Bosworth a rebellion against the king. Thus the rebels could have their titles taken as well as their estates. Ricardians such as Penn call the Act 'sinister' and 'rewriting history', but basically it gave Henry an excellent bargaining counter to ensure those few Yorkists who fought for Richard would now be loyal. Their titles and estates could be forfeit for treason at any time if they rebelled again. This helped to bring peace in the kingdom. Indeed, the *Croyland Chronicle* states that the Act was 'far more moderate than anything of the sort which had been seen in the days of King Richard or King Edward'.

The Act of Attainder names 'Richard, late duke of Gloucester, calling and naming himself, by ursurpation, King Richard the Third'. It listed the late Thomas Howard, Duke of Norfolk and Earl of Surrey; Francis Viscount Lovell; the late Lord Ferrers; John, Lord Zouche; Robert Harrington; Richard Charlton; Richard Radcliffe (Ratcliffe); William Berkeley of Weobley; Robert Brackenbury; Thomas Pilkington; Robert Middleton; James Harrington; Walter Hopton; William Catesby; Roger Wake; William Sapcote; Humphrey Stafford; William Clerk of Wenlock; Geoffrey St German; Richard Watkins, Herald of Arms; Richard Revel of Derbyshire; Thomas Poulter junior of Kent; John Walsh alias Hastings; John Kendal, secretary; John Buck; Andrew Ratt; and William Bramton of Burford. The acts states that upon 21 August, in

the first year of the reign of our sovereign lord, assembled to them at Leicester ... a great host, traitorously intending, imagining and conspiring the destruction of the king's royal person, our sovereign liege lord. And they, with the same host, with banners spread, mightily armed and defenced with all manner [of] arms, as guns, bows, arrows, spears, glaives [a polearm – a single-armed blade on the end of a pole], axes, and all other manner [of] articles apt or needful to give and cause mighty battle against our sovereign lord.

Keeping the host together, they led them on 22 August to a field in Leicestershire, and 'there by great and continued deliberation, traitorously levied war against our said sovereign lord and his true subjects there being in his service and assistance under a banner of our said sovereign lord, to the subversion of this realm, and common weal of the same'.

There were no real reprisals. Estates were not confiscated by the Crown, as we can see above. Henry sensed that the nation wanted peace. Possibly the most pragmatic of English kings, he rewarded his own supporters only in the short term. As he came to understand his kingdom and the power factions, he began to appoint and promote the brightest and best and those who best served his interests. Yorkist followers could see that Henry was never vindictive, and was attempting to heal the nation. The great Northern Yorkist nobles were left virtually untouched as Henry tried to reconcile the competing parties. Northumberland, Westmorland, Scrope of Castle Bolton, Scrope of Masham, Dacre, Fitzhugh and Lumley all kept their lands and honours. Henry needed the North to be kept secure against the Scots. It is notable that Richard Charlton of Edmonton, who died at Bosworth, was the only Southerner to be attainted in this very limited Act. There is no space to go into the details of each attainder, but in the case of Charlton, most of his estates passed to his sister Agnes and her husband Sir Thomas Bourchier the Younger.

Yorkists in the South had been no real allies of Richard as king. Richard's closest advisers were all attainted, but Kendal, Brackenbury, Catesby and Ratcliffe were not part of the great families of England and their punishment would not cause any harmful resentment. Eight of the only twenty-eight men attainted were dead, and another two, Lovell and Zouche had escaped from the battle. Nearly all were later pardoned and their estates returned. Of the thirty-eight great peers in Richard's 1484 parliament, only five were attainted. These men were the dead Norfolk and Ferrers, the imprisoned Surrey, Lovell, who escaped, and Zouche, who was captured after the battle. Zouche slowly regained his lands and titles by 1495, and died in 1526. More than anything, the Act shows how limited was Richard's support at Bosworth among the noble houses of England, and how generous Henry was to the Yorkists.

Sir Thomas Lovell was the fifth son of a Lancastrian Norfolk family, and had been attainted in Richard III's first parliament. He had returned to England with Henry, fought at Bosworth and had his attainder reversed. In 1485, he was appointed Chancellor of the Exchequer for life, represented Northampton in Parliament, became Speaker of the House of Commons, Secretary of the Treasury and treasurer of the king's and queen's chambers. He was made a knight of the king's body. Lovell headed the Commons on 10 December 1485, when they requested the king to marry Elizabeth of York.

The agreed wedding to Elizabeth of York was delayed until after Henry's coronation on 30 October 1485, and he had established himself strongly enough to halt any further attempts on the kingship from Elizabeth's relations. Perhaps a majority of people still saw Elizabeth, the daughter of Edward IV, as having the stronger claim to the crown. Henry and Elizabeth married upon 18 January 1486. Their first son, Arthur, was born on 20 September 1486, and titled in Welsh the same as

Llywelyn the Great: 'Tywysog Cymru ac Arglwydd Eryri' (Prince of Wales and Lord of Snowdonia). Arthur was probably conceived two months before the couple wed, and recent Ricardian novelists are attributing this to a 'forcible rape' by the king, without any shred of evidence. Henry did not have Elizabeth crowned as his queen-consort until 25 November 1487, over two years after Bosworth Field, again ensuring that he was seen as the true king and not merely as king-consort.

Henry VII's first parliament conferred upon his mother Margaret Beaufort, Countess of Richmond and Derby, the lands and grants taken from her by Richard III. She was also given the rights and privileges of a 'sole person, not wife nor covert of any husband', allowing her personal control over her extensive properties. This was very unusual for the times. Beaufort was just thirteen years older than her son, and would become his closest counsellor. Straight after Bosworth, Henry spent two weeks in close consultations with his mother learning about the ways of government, the powers at court and the like. Called 'my Lady the King's mother', she now signed herself 'Margaret R' and became extremely influential at court. Some recent sources state that there was thus friction between Henry's Lancastrian mother and his Yorkist wife, but it is difficult to find any real evidence.

Certainly Henry bowed disproportionately to his mother's wishes, and chroniclers place her position as being higher than that of Elizabeth Woodville at court. Modern writers seem to judge medieval relationships by today's standards, with equality hopefully being the norm, but until the 1884 Married Women's Property Act women were still chattels, or possessions, of their husbands in English law. Applying today's standards of female influence upon their spouses is unreasonable for half a millennium ago. Henry also gave his mother the wardship of Edward Stafford, son of her kinsman, the late Duke of Buckingham. Margaret brought Stafford up as if he was her own son. Lord Thomas Stanley was rewarded with the Earldom of Derby; William Stanley was made Henry's Chamberlain and acquired lands and power, and Oxford regained his forfeited estates. Oxford was also appointed Constable of the Tower of London, and admiral of England, Ireland, and Aquitaine. The utterly faithful Jasper Tudor, now in his mid-fifties, was well rewarded and made Duke of Bedford.

Henry VII annulled Henry IV's penal laws upon Welshmen, to the annoyance of English burgesses in Wales. His quarter-Welshness had been of critical importance in easing Henry's path to the throne, for the only possible route to battle was through Wales, picking up followers. In his first proclamation, on 25 August 1485, Henry announced his titles to be 'Prince of Wales and lord of Ireland' as well as King of England and of France. This was the first time any king who had not himself been invested with the principality, as heir apparent, had appropriated the title of Prince of Wales. Henry was placed to heal the millennium-old racial tension between the Welsh and the English, and he developed a deliberate policy to accomplish this. The House of Tudor ruled England, Wales and Ireland from 1485 to 1603. Henry VII showed some favour to Wales, and his granddaughter Elizabeth I had a strong Welsh presence at court.

In the early sixteenth century, letters of denizenship conferred English status upon Welshmen, charters of privileges were granted, and various civic disabilities imposed by the penal laws of Henry IV and Henry V were removed. Welshmen were allowed to settle in the bastides, or plantation boroughs. The Venetian ambassador wrote in his *Relation* to the Council of Ten: 'The Welsh may now be said to have recovered their former independence for the most wise and fortunate Henry VII is a Welshman.' His Welshness was more prominently displayed in the symbolism of his regality than in acts of favouritism. Henry was only a quarter Welsh – his grandfather was Owen Tudor; a quarter French by Owen's wife Catherine of Valois; and half-English through his mother's parents John Beaufort, Duke of Somerset, and Margaret Beauchamp of Bletsoe.

We have seen the extremely lenient treatment of Richard's supporters after Bosworth, especially the lack of land-grabbing so prevalent amongst the Plantagenets. Of particular interest is Henry's treatment of Dorset. Thomas Grey was 7th Baron Ferrers of Groby, 1st Earl of Huntingdon and 1st Marquess of Dorset (*c.* 1455–1501). Dorset was the eldest son of Elizabeth Woodville and her first husband before she married Edward IV. Upon the taking of Elizabeth's sons, Dorset escaped to sanctuary in Westminster with his mother and sisters. He managed somehow to evade a ring of Richard's troops around the abbey, upon learning that his half-brothers, the Princes in the Tower, had disappeared. Dorset's younger full brother, Lord Rivers, had been murdered by Richard III, and Dorset then took up arms in Yorkshire, with a reward being offered for his capture in October 1483. He next joined Buckingham's rebellion and claimed Henry of Richmond's right to the throne in Exeter. When the rebellion failed, Dorset fled to Brittany, and eventually joined Henry at Rennes.

However, just before Henry's successful invasion of England in August 1485, Dorset learned that his mother and sisters had left the sanctuary of Westminster Abbey. Elizabeth Woodville had been colluding in the Tudor invasion. It may be that Richard was threatening to confiscate the rest of the Woodville estates, or it was a feint to show Richard that there was no plot against him, or that her daughters had been promised rich marriages and safety. There seems to be no reason for 'trusting' the man who had killed her brother and son and had locked up her other sons, Edward V and Richard, Duke of York, and made them bastards. For some reason in August 1485 Dorset was persuaded to leave Henry and head for England.

Perhaps he had succumbed to lies or promises or simply believed that Henry's little group had no prospect of success. In 1485 his mother had written to him, urging him to return to England. One suspects it was because she had agreed to her daughter Elizabeth marrying the king, but such was the national opposition that the scheme fell apart. Dorset was at Paris, and secretly left for Flanders, intending to sail to England. Henry quickly despatched Humphrey Cheney, who intercepted Dorset at Compiègne, and brought him back to Henry. Dorset did not take part in the invasion, as Henry, now mistrusting his intentions, left him behind at Paris with John Bourchier as surety for the repayment of a loan by the French government.

Dorset was Henry's new queen's half-brother, but was not permitted to recover his former influence when Henry redeemed his loan. In 1485 Dorset's attainder was reversed, and in November 1486 he received confirmation of his titles. When Lambert Simnel led a rising, Dorset fell under suspicion, and was for a short time in 1487 committed to the Tower. Not until after the Battle of Stoke was he restored to full favour. Dorset accompanied Henry on his expedition to France in 1492, but he was obliged to commit himself in writing to ensure he did not commit treason. He was allowed to assist in suppression of the Cornish Rising in 1497, and died peacefully in London in 1501.

Bishop Morton of Ely, who had plotted Henry's path to the throne, became his principal adviser. Morton had even travelled to Rome to inform the Pope of Henry's intent to take the throne from the usurper Richard III. Morton succeeded Thomas Bourchier (*c.* 1404–86) as Archbishop of Canterbury, and succeeded Alcock as Lord Chancellor in 1487. Alcock had been one of the clerics arrested with Hastings, Rivers, Vaughan and Edward V in 1483, and also one of those who canvassed openly for Henry to marry Elizabeth of York. Morton became responsible for much of the diplomatic and financial initiatives of the reign, strengthening the Crown and weakening the nobility. In 1493 Morton was created a cardinal, and in 1495 was elected Chancellor of the University of Oxford. He encouraged learning, admitting Sir Thomas More into his household and wrote a Latin history of Richard III, which some believe More translated into English.

Morton is almost certainly the primary source for More's *The History of King Richard III*, which would obviously considerably bias it against that king. His taxation strategy, known as 'Morton's Fork', was that 'if the subject is seen to live frugally, tell him because he is clearly a money saver of great ability he can afford to give generously to the king. If, however, the subject lives a life of great extravagance, tell him he, too, can afford to give largely, the proof of his opulence being evident of his expenditure'. Archbishop Morton incurred great unpopularity for Henry VII, and was blamed for a number of taxes inflicted on the people. He was personally named by the Cornish rebels when they revolted in 1497. Morton died, most likely of plague, in 1500, aged around eighty.

In 1486 and 1487 came what is known as the Lovell Rebellion. Francis, Lord Lovell, had replaced the executed Hastings as Lord Chamberlain in 1483, and along with Catesby and Ratcliffe had been the closest friend of Richard III. Lovell, together with the Stafford brothers Humphrey and Thomas, had escaped from Bosworth, finding sanctuary at Colchester Abbey in Essex. In April 1486, the king left London to tour the north of England, and Lovell and the Staffords left sanctuary to seek support to overthrow Henry in favour of Clarence's son the Earl of Warwick, who was in comfortable quarters in the Tower. They were followed by Henry's agents. Lord Lovell headed to Yorkshire and Middleham Castle, where a few Yorkist retainers came out to support him. Henry heard of the rebellion while in Lincoln, and moved north to York to suppress it with a large armed force. His uncle Jasper Tudor, now Duke of Bedford, was sent ahead with a few men into Yorkshire, promising to pardon everyone except Lovell. The rebels quickly disbanded.

Henry sent Sir Richard Edgecombe and Sir William Tyler to arrest Lovell. Lovell rode west to Furness Fells in Cumberland and passed some time in hiding with Sir Thomas Broughton. Broughton and Sir John Huddleston had briefly kept Yorkist resistance going in the north-west of England. Lovell then managed to flee to Richard III's sister, Margaret of York and

Burgundy, in Flanders. The Stafford brothers escaped from sanctuary to ride to Worcestershire in the West Midlands, but few people joined them. Hearing that Lovell had fled, and that Henry's army was moving west towards them, the Staffords were followed by Henry's scouts to Culham Abbey, where they again claimed sanctuary. They were forcibly removed from sanctuary on the night of 13 May by John Savage.

The Stafford brothers were put on trial, rather than summarily executed as under Plantagenet rulers. They were found guilty of treason, with the judges declaring that the rules of sanctuary did not apply in such cases. Pope Innocent VIII supported Henry VII and declared that sanctuary could not be claimed by rebels against the king. The judges also stated that it was unreasonable for attainted traitors to be allowed sanctuary a second time. The Staffords were sent to the Tower, with the elder brother Humphrey being beheaded at Tyburn in July 1486. Note that he was not hanged, drawn and quartered, the normal penalty for treason. The younger brother Thomas pledged allegiance, was pardoned and remained loyal to Henry. Other rebels were also treated with leniency. Sir John Conyers, who was suspected of being involved in the Lovell revolt and was a major office holder in Yorkshire, lost his stewardship of Middleham and had a £2,000 bond imposed. The Abbot of Abingdon, who had secured sanctuary for the Stafford brothers, was given a 3,000-mark allegiance bond.

John de la Pole, Earl of Lincoln, fought for Richard at Bosworth and escaped the battlefield. Henry had no wish to alienate Lincoln's powerful family, and Lincoln had taken an oath with others in 1485 not to maintain felons. On 5 July 1486 he was appointed a justice of oyer and terminer. However, suddenly he left England in the early part of 1487 to sail to Brabant. Here he was joined by Lovell in Flanders at Margaret of Burgundy's court, and thence came the first real threat to Henry's reign. Margaret of Burgundy was Richard III's sister, also known as Margaret of York. The rebels had a priest instruct Lambert Simnel, a ten-year-old boy, to impersonate Edward Plantagenet, Earl of Warwick. Warwick had been imprisoned in Sheriff Hutton as a potential rival to the crown by Richard III, and Henry had taken him to royal apartments in the Tower.

The Earl of Lincoln also had a claim to the throne, seemingly having being named by Richard III as his heir in 1485, although there was no public proclamation. Under *Titulus Regius*, Clarence's son Warwick, who had a superior claim, had been attainted so could not succeed. Lincoln had been travelling across France and Ireland, looking for support for a Yorkist rebellion in Warwick's name. A rumour was started that Warwick had escaped from the Tower. Lincoln probably wanted to use Simnel as 'the true heir' to gain support, but could have then reverted to reusing the *Titulus Regius* to proclaim himself king.

With a mercenary army led by Martin Schwarz, Lincoln and Lovell followed the pretender Lambert Simnel to Ireland, where they were supported by Gerald FitzGerald, Earl of Kildare, who wished to see a return of Yorkist rule in England. The Yorkist kings had allowed Irish self-government with FitzGerald as almost the 'uncrowned king of Ireland'. On 24 May 1487 Lincoln, Lovell, Margaret and others installed Simnel as Edward VI in a ceremony in Dublin. With an army of mercenaries, paid for by Lincoln's aunt Margaret, Lincoln had sailed to Ireland, and his army rapidly increased in size with Irish recruits led by FitzGerald's brother. They then landed at Piel Island in north Lancashire on 4 June 1487, and were joined by a number of the local gentry. These were led by Sir Thomas Broughton, and included Sir Thomas Pilkington, James Harrington and Robert Hilton. Broughton, Pilkington and Harrington had all been pardoned after Bosworth. Edward of Warwick was taken from the Tower and displayed in public at St Paul's Cathedral in 1487, in response to the presentation of the impostor Lambert Simnel as the 'Earl of Warwick' to the Irish lords.

Lincoln's Yorkist army of 8,000 included German, Swiss and French mercenaries and 4,500 Irishmen, and marched over 200 miles in five days to Bramham Moor, near Tadcaster in Yorkshire. On 10 June, Lovell led 2,000 men on a night attack against 400 Lancastrians, led by Lord Clifford. The result was an overwhelming Yorkist victory. The Earl of Northumberland now employed delaying tactics for the Lancastrians, refusing to give battle, while Henry and Jasper Tudor gathered an army with Lord Strange. On 16 June, Henry's vanguard, commanded by the Earl of Oxford, found the Yorkist army. Lincoln, Lovell and FitzGerald had no real experience of command and probably that task was given to Schwarz. The battle was bitterly contested for over three hours, but eventually, the lack of body armour on the Irish troops meant that they were cut down in increasing numbers. Unable to retreat, the mercenaries fought to the last. Lincoln, Schwarz, FitzGerald and Broughton were killed at the Battle of Stoke Field, and Simnel was captured. He was pardoned by Henry in a gesture of clemency, as Henry realised that Simnel was merely a puppet for the leading Yorkists.

Henry gave him a job as a spit-turner in the royal kitchens, and Simnel later became a falconer, dying a free man in his fifties. The Irish nobles who had supported Simnel were also pardoned, as Henry needed their support to govern Ireland effectively. No one seems to have been executed after the battle, and Henry's clemency to Simnel was remarked upon across Europe. Here was a new type of monarch who did not believe in precedent, and preferred accommodation to revenge.

Lovell was reported to have been killed at Stoke, but was seen trying to swim the Trent on horseback, and seems to have escaped to his house at Minster Lovell, Oxfordshire. Perhaps Lovell escaped to Scotland or returned to Burgundy. On 4 November 1488, James IV of Scotland issued safe conducts to forty-two exiled Yorkists, including Lovell. It is unknown if he ever collected it. Lovell had been attainted after Bosworth, but not until after Stoke Field were his lands confiscated; they were later granted to Sir William Stanley. Minster Lovell was given to George, the heir of Lord Thomas Stanley. Most of Lovell's Northamptonshire estates were given to Henry's mother, the Countess of Richmond.

In 1489, came what is known grandly and variously as 'The Yorkshire Rebellion' or 'The Northern Rising' or even 'The Northern Rising Rebellion'. Parliament granted Henry a subsidy of £100,000 to help Anne, Duchess of Brittany, in her defence against France. Henry knew that keeping Brittany independent was the only key to England re-establishing its lost French territories. However, people in Yorkshire felt that this war did not concern them as they were so geographically removed from it. Traditionally, people in the South funded wars against France while people in the North funded wars against Scotland. The great Northern counties of Northumberland, Westmoreland and Cumberland had been exempted from taxation on account of poverty. They thus were angered that Henry Percy, 4th Earl of Northumberland, was going to lead the commission to raise taxes. The North had also been affected by very bad harvests in 1488. Upon 20 April 1489, a meeting protesting against the taxation was held at Ayton in Yorkshire, led by John á Chambre. The protesters marched towards Thirsk to show their feelings. The Earl of Northumberland heard about the march and arranged to meet the protesters at one of his homes in South Kilvington, near Thirsk. On 28 April the protesters accused Northumberland of being one of the king's chief advisers of the new taxation. A scuffle broke out and they killed Northumberland along with some of his servants. A note was said to be placed next to Northumberland's body accusing him of being responsible for the death of Richard III. These were the only casualties in the 'rising'.

The protesters then asked for pardon but were denied it by Henry. He sent a large army of 8,000 to the North, led by Thomas Howard, Earl of Surrey. The rebels quickly dispersed, and their leader, John á Chambre, was hanged at York for treason. An illegitimate member of the Percy family, Sir John Egremont, took over as leader, but almost immediately fled to Flanders and the court of Henry's enemy Margaret of York, Duchess of Burgundy. Henry visited York to demonstrate his displeasure. However, he withdrew from attempting to enforce the new taxation, and was thus unable to raise the funds for the Breton mission.

This particular tax had caused widespread resentment as it was an early form of income tax, whereas many other taxes could be paid in kind as opposed to cash. Just £27,000 of the necessary £100,000 was raised. Henry became aware of the lawless nature of the North of England, and only six leading rebels were tried and executed, with 1,500 receiving a royal pardon. Surrey remained in Yorkshire as the King's lieutenant and President of the Council of the North until 1499, completing his rehabilitation after having fought against Henry at Bosworth. The Earl of Northumberland's estates were reassigned to the Crown, as the 5th Earl was only twelve. He stayed at court until his majority and in 1498 all his lands were returned to him by Henry. This 5th Earl faithfully served both Henry VII and Henry VIII. Again we see the king's leniency against his enemies, a trait virtually invisible among Plantagenet rulers.

The next Yorkist pretender, the young man known as Perkin Warbeck, was a far more dangerous threat to Henry, during the eight years from 1491 to 1499. Warbeck first appeared, aged around seventeen, in Cork in autumn 1491. Ireland was still a Yorkist stronghold and the people of Cork believed that Warbeck (who spoke poor English) was the Earl of Warwick. However, Warbeck then claimed to be Richard of York, the younger of the Princes in the Tower. He said that he had not been murdered like his 'brother' Edward V, but had been spared by the killer and allowed to escape. Henry seemed to have no idea of what had happened to Prince Richard, and treated this new threat seriously. Chrimes believes that Warbeck's appearance in this Yorkist stronghold was planned by Margaret of Burgundy and Charles VIII of France, the latter because of Henry's support for Brittany.

Warbeck probably spent 1487–91 being groomed by Yorkist sympathisers in Portugal, where he was known as the 'White Rose'. Before that that he had been in the Duchy of Flanders, now northern Belgium and then part of the Hapsburg Empire. There was little that Henry could do about Margaret's machinations for Simnel and Warbeck, as she was protected by Maximilian of Hapsburg. In 1492 Charles VIII invited Warbeck from Portugal to France, keeping him at court until he moved to stay with his protector Margaret in Brabant, a duchy in the Hapsburg Netherlands. A small fleet was assembled with Imperial and Burgundian funds, preparing to invade England at some point in 1495. For eight years, in Portugal, Flanders, Ireland, France and Brabant, Warbeck had been being prepared to take the dead Prince Richard of York's role as the true King of England.

However, Henry's agents, including Sir Robert Clifford, infiltrated the pretender's court at Malines (Mechelen, near Antwerp), and at the end of December 1494, Clifford revealed information in return for the huge amount of £500. Among his revelations was that Henry's Lord Chamberlain, Sir William Stanley, had vaguely said that he would back Warbeck if he knew him to be the genuine prince. Henry, although reluctant, was advised to make an example of Stanley and other chief conspirators by beheading them. £10,000 was found in a search of Stanley's home, enough to fund an invasion force. Lord Fitzwalter, Henry's steward, was also beheaded. It appears that Stanley did not expect to be executed, as he had done nothing except say that he would give his support to the true king. By giving a full confession, and because he had effectively decided the Battle at Bosworth, and because his brother was married to the king's mother, Stanley thought that Henry would be merciful. However, Henry feared that by doing this he would be putting himself in danger by encouraging others to undertake a similar act of supporting pretenders. The act does not appear to have affected Henry's relationship with Lord Thomas Stanley – perhaps Margaret Beaufort had influenced the decision. The Cliffords were sworn enemies of the Stanleys, and Robert Clifford's role in Warbeck's court and Stanley's death is intriguing but outside the scope of this book.

By spring 1495 there appeared to be no threat from within England, but Warbeck invaded in July, with fourteen small boats. A skirmish ended quickly on the beach at Deal, and Warbeck sailed away to Scotland. In September 1496, with the support of James IV of Scotland, 'Prince Richard of York' invaded Northumberland. Warbeck again fled the scene of the skirmish. In July 1497, Henry's army marched towards Scotland, and James IV sent Warbeck away by sea, intending him to invade England from the South West. Around 8,000 Cornishmen in this discontented corner of England joined Warbeck, ironically annoyed with the taxes raised to pay for the Scottish invasion to deal with Warbeck.

The Cornishmen besieged Exeter but failed to take the city, and after marching to Taunton Warbeck yet again panicked and fled a third time. He next surrendered to Henry VII at Taunton, in October 1497, and put his signature to a confession that stated that he was, in fact a Fleming, 'Piers Osbeck', but that name may have been false. However, testimonies at

Setubal, Portugal, in 1496 seemed to corroborate his name. Edward Brampton (*c.* 1440–1508), who had brought him to Portugal, called him 'Piris Uberque' while Tanjar, a herald at the Portuguese court, called him 'Piris Osbeque'. Henry pardoned his closest English supporters, but they started again plotting on 'York's' behalf two years later. Henry had taken Warbeck into his court 'at liberty' and had treated him like a captured nobleman, to the amazement of contemporaries. Warbeck was allowed to see his wife, though not to sleep with her, to avoid the risk of prolonging his claim through his heirs.

Henry allowed Warbeck to remain at court where he could be watched. However, Warbeck tried to run away, which seemed to emphasise his disloyalty. Warbeck was put in the stocks, humiliated and sent to the Tower. After being so generous to the pretender, Henry's patience had run out. In 1499, Warbeck was charged of plotting to escape with the imprisoned Earl of Warwick, the last true Yorkist heir. Warwick pleaded guilty in a trial by his peers, presided over by the Earl of Oxford. Both were found guilty, and Warbeck was hanged (instead of being hanged, drawn and quartered) and Warwick beheaded on 23 November 1499. In his treatment of prisoners, Henry throughout his reign was an exceptionally merciful king. To what extent Warwick was culpable is impossible to know.

If we return briefly to the 'Cornish Rebellions' of 1497, we can see Henry's treatment of rebels. Before the raising of war taxes by Henry VII, Cornwall had been exempted all taxes of 10ths or 15ths of income. The blacksmith Michael Joseph, known in Cornish as An Gof (The Smith), and the lawyer Thomas Flamank led another Cornish army into Devon, attracting more recruits in the West Country, including Baron Audley at Wells in Somerset. Henry's main forces were heading to Scotland to suppress Scottish support for Warbeck. The rebels marched past Bristol and Salisbury to Blackheath, where their force was defeated in the Battle of Deptford Bridge by Daubeny upon 17 June 1497. The leaders were captured, and Lord Audley was tried for treason, found guilty and beheaded at the Tower on 28 June 1497. An Gof and Flamank were sentenced to hanging, drawing and quartering while alive, the normal sentence for non-nobles guilty of treason, but Henry commuted the sentence to being hanged until dead before they were disembowelled and quartered on 27 June 1497. From Edward I onwards, the Plantagenets had insisted upon the disembowelling being carried out upon a living traitor, but Henry was somewhat less of a barbarian, possibly knowing that it could have been his fate if captured in the 1470s or 1480s.

In 1501 there was yet another intrigue against Henry, the 'Suffolk Plot'. Edmund de la Pole, Duke of Suffolk, was the son of Elizabeth of York, the younger sister of Edward IV. His eldest brother John de la Pole, Earl of Lincoln (c. 1464–87), had been heir apparent to his maternal uncle, Richard III. However, upon the accession of Henry VII, Lincoln had taken the oath of allegiance to the new king. In 1487, Lincoln had supported Lambert Simnel, being killed at the Battle of Stoke Field. Following the death of his older brother, Edmund became the leading Yorkist claimant to the throne, succeeding to the title Duke of Suffolk in 1491, although in 1493 being demoted to the rank of Earl of Suffolk. In 1501, Edmund unexpectedly fled into voluntary exile with the help of Sir James Tyrrell, who helped him on the Continent.

Sir James Tyrrell was an important Yorkist who missed Bosworth, being in France on the king's business at the time. He returned to England in 1486 and was twice pardoned by Henry VII. The first pardon was issued on 16 June 1486, as one of the general pardons issued by Henry VII for those who opposed him at Bosworth. The second on 16 July 1486 may have been a clerical error. Richard III apologists try to make a case that Henry chose the Yorkist Tyrrell to kill the Princes in the Tower in this month, three years after their last sighting. Henry made Tyrrell in 1486 Governor of Guisnes, in the English possession of Calais. When Henry in 1501 learned that Tyrrell had assisted Suffok, he was recalled, accused of treason, and tortured. Thomas More wrote that Tyrrell confessed to the murders of Edward V and his brother Richard. He also implicated two other men; despite further questioning, however, he was unable to say where the bodies were, claiming that they had been moved. It may be that Brackenbury's chaplain had moved them. Tyrrell was beheaded at Tower Hill on 6 May 1502, together with one of his accomplices in aiding Suffolk, Sir John Wyndham.

Suffolk had gone to the court of Maximilian, the Holy Roman Emperor, to ask for assistance against Henry. However, in 1502 Maximilian agreed to a treaty not to back de la Pole, should he make an attempt on the throne of England. In 1506, Maximilian's son, Philip of Burgundy, was blown off course and came into Henry's custody. Needing to set sail again in order to claim his wife's inheritance (Castile), Philip of Burgundy was persuaded by Henry to hand over the Earl of Suffolk. Henry agreed to the proviso that Suffolk would not be harmed and restricted himself to imprisoning the earl. The next king, Henry VIII, did not feel bound to this agreement and had Suffolk executed in 1513. Edmund's younger brother Richard declared himself Earl of Suffolk, and was the leading Yorkist pretender until his death in battle at Pavia in 1525.

Henry asked chroniclers to portray his reign as a 'modern age' with its dawn in 1485. He had effectively ended the Wars of the Roses and laid the basis for a stable constitutional monarchy. The Elizabethan antiquary George Owen called Henry 'the Moyses who delivered us from bondage'. By the Treaty of Étaples, he cleverly took money from the French in return for not fighting them. Despite threats from Scotland and the Continent, Henry refused to engage in war, instead building up the royal coffers to ensure stability and a Tudor succession. Henry built trade and alliances, and under his Royal Commission John Cabot reached Nova Scotia in 1497.

Henry VII had brought up his eldest son and heir, Arthur, as a Welsh speaker, living in the Marcher administrative capital of Wales, Ludlow. Arthur was married with great ceremony to Catherine of Aragon in 1501, cementing the Spanish alliance. Arthur's untimely death in 1502 gave the nation his brother Henry VIII and changed the course of British history – without it Britain would probably still be a Catholic country. Henry VIII's daughter Queen Elizabeth I oversaw the greatest flowering of culture, in the British Isles, under this Tudor dynasty. For the first time Britain became a player on the world stage in the arts, and its ships began the origins of the British Empire. Bosworth Field marked the end of medieval England and the beginning of more modern government, with a conscious attempt to integrate Wales into England.

Henry had laid the basis for a stable constitutional monarchy. Exhausted by the supervision of every detail of government, he began complaining of poor health by his mid-forties. The loss of Arthur, Prince of Wales, in 1502 and of his beloved wife in 1503 hastened his decline. Worn out, ill and aged only fifty-two, Henry Tudor died at Richmond in 1509, leaving a peaceful country, a full treasury and an easy succession for Henry VIII. G. M. Trevelyan pointed out the influence of Bosworth Field and the Tudors: 'Here, indeed, was one of fortune's freaks: on a bare Leicestershire upland a few thousand men in close conflict foot to foot ... sufficed to set upon the throne of England the greatest of all her royal lines, that should guide her through a century of change down new and larger streams of destiny.' The 'founder of the new England of the sixteenth century', Francis Bacon called him 'a wonder for wise men'.

There followed the most formative period of English history, with the relationships between Crown, nobility and Church altering radically. The emergence of a middle class, increasingly dominant in government and Parliament, began a fundamental transformation of the political system. Henry Tudor changed Britain for the better. Margaret Beaufort outlived her son and lived to see her granddaughter and namesake become Queen of Scotland when the twelve-year-old Margaret married the King of Scotland, James IV, in 1502. The 'White Queen', Elizabeth Woodville had colluded with the 'Red Queen', Margaret Beaufort, to bring together the factions of York and Lancaster. The greatest heiress of her time, Margaret had been imprisoned by Richard and her lands confiscated, but she had continued to work on her son's behalf, ultimately persuading her fourth husband, the powerful Lord Stanley, to abandon the king in favour of Henry. She passed her claim to the crown of England to her son, Henry VII, who gave his mother unparalleled prominence during his reign. She ended her life as regent of England, ruling on behalf of her seventeen-year-old grandson, Henry VIII.

While Henry in his long reign was never involved in any estate-grabbing scandals, Richard was immured in them. Henry redistributed estates illegally confiscated by Yorkists, but had no truck with upsetting the balance of the great houses and creating potential resentment and conflict. After Bosworth, he could have virtually ripped apart ownerships of estates, manors and fees, but left things very much alone. On the other hand, Gloucester's role in matters of land has recently been ignored. For example the disinheritance of Anne Beauchamp has been much downplayed by Ricardian writers, notably Kendall, who tells us in his non-fiction book that Richard settled for a paltry share of the Warwick inheritance before marrying his 'sweetheart' Anne Neville and escaping court 'to breathe the free air of the moors'. Richard then gallantly rescues his mother-in-law Anne Beauchamp from her enforced sanctuary at Beaulieu Abbey and has her taken north to join her daughter. When historical books are written like fiction to make characters sympathetic, we are treading upon thin ground. Reality is actually more interesting.

Gloucester may well have liked Anne Neville, whom he had presumably known when he was staying in her father's household, but he was not a lovesick boy entangled by the machinations of Clarence. Richard argued vigorously for his share of the Neville inheritance, almost going into battle against his brother. The Croyland Chronicler wrote, 'All who stood around, even those learned in the law, marvelled at the profusion of the arguments which the princes produced for their own cases.' Richard also ensured that he preserved his rights in Anne Neville's lands. Should their marriage be dissolved, he would retain a life interest in her estates, provided that he remained single.

Anne Beauchamp had been in sanctuary in Beaulieu Abbey since 1471, when her husband Warwick the Kingmaker was killed at Barnet. She was aware that she was the legal owner of the Beauchamp and Despenser lands that she had inherited from her parents, as well of her jointure and dower rights in her husband's great estates. From sanctuary, she wrote a petition, reminding Parliament that it was unfair that she was kept under guard at Beaulieu, and asking it 'to ponder and weigh in your consciences her right and true title of her inheritance, as the earldom of Warwick and Spencer's lands, to which she is rightfully born by lineal succession, and also her jointure and dower of the earldom of Salisbury aforesaid'. The petition was ignored, and her lands were partitioned between her sons-in-law, though neither Clarence nor Gloucester was happy with his shares. The argument was still going on in June 1473, when James Tyrrell finally took Anne Beauchamp out of sanctuary to Richard's estates. This gave rise to rumours that Edward IV might give all her lands to Gloucester. Horrifyingly, in an Act of Parliament in 1474, she was declared naturally dead, thereby allowing her daughters, and, more importantly, her sons-in-law, to hold her estates as if by inheritance. Richard, although he did not gain all of her estates as rumoured, took a greater share than he had before. Anne Beauchamp, Countess of Wawick, was illegally left with nothing, and was totally dependent upon her daughter and Richard.

We now know little of her activities, and she possibly spent her days in seclusion at Middleham Castle. There is no record to her attending her daughter Anne's coronation in 1483 or where she was when Richard III was killed. According to Hicks, on 1 July 1484, she was allocated £80 a year, an allowance that Hicks believes meant that she was released from Richard III's custody and allowed to set up her own household. This was a tiny sum given the wealth that she had once commanded, especially since it would have been in Richard's power as king to treat her more generously. When Henry Tudor took the throne, Anne Beauchamp's fortunes altered. Since her husband had died fighting for the Lancastrians, he was no longer considered a traitor. In 1486, she was granted lands by Henry and a pension of 500 marks a year. In November 1487, an Act of Parliament annulled the act of 1474 and restored to her the family estates. One month later, the countess conveyed most of her lands back to the Crown, except for Erdington Manor. This led to the effective disinheritance of her grandson, the young Edward, Earl of Warwick. In December 1489, she was granted many of her ancestral lands for life and appointed principal keeper of the forest of Wychwood. Anne Beauchamp died 20 September 1492, having outlived both her daughters and her sons-in-law and having lived through all or part of the reigns of Henry VI, Edward IV, Richard III, and Henry VII. She was buried at Bisham Abbey alongside her husband Warwick and his brother Lord Montagu.

There is much misinformation about Henry's treatment of Anne Beauchamp, as there is about his treatment of Elizabeth Woodville, Edward IV's widow.

Richard's sympathisers claim that Henry VII effectively banished Elizabeth Woodville from his court in 1487 and sent her to a nunnery, on the charge that she had allowed her daughters out of sanctuary to attend Richard III's court. Many believe that Henry, believing her to be behind the 1487 rebellion, imprisoned her and seized her lands. This is untrue and the remaining years of her life were spent peacefully. The dowager Queen Elizabeth indeed spent some of her last five years living at Bermondsey Abbey, but evidence from Arlene Okerlund's research indicates she was planning a religious, contemplative life as early as July 1486. At the abbey, Elizabeth was treated with all the respect due to a queen dowager, lived a regal life with small gifts from the king, and visits from her daughters. She attended the birth of her second grandchild, Margaret, at Westminster Palace in November 1489. In 1488 her brother Edward had been killed at sea, and in 1491 her only surviving brother, Richard died at the Rivers estate at Grafton. Of her other brothers, John had been beheaded by Warwick in 1469, Anthony had been murdered by order of Richard in 1483 and Lionel Woodville, Bishop of Salisbury, had died in exile in 1484. These losses, along with those of her sons, had affected the dowager queen deeply.

Shortly afterwards she entered the convent at Bermondsey. She dictated her will, in which she desired to be buried at Windsor beside her husband. She died on 8 June 1492, surrounded by her daughters and her surviving son, Dorset. At her own request to have a burial with little ceremony, her body was conveyed by water to Windsor on the Sunday, without any ringing of bells. With the exception of the queen, who was awaiting the birth of her fourth child, her other daughters attended Elizabeth's funeral at Windsor Castle.

She was buried alongside Edward IV in St George's Chapel, and their tomb inscription simply reads, 'King Edward and his Queen, Elizabeth Widville.' Henry has been criticised for not giving his mother-in-law a splendid funeral, but her will asked for a simple ceremony. The will shows that Elizabeth died with hardly any personal property, but the major holdings of the House of York were still held by the aged Cecily Neville, Duchess of York, who survived her hated daughter-in-law. Edward IV had endowed his mother as if she were a dowager queen, while his Elizabeth had been dowered on property to which Edward had possessed no real title.

Having briefly dismissed the canard that Henry ill-treated his mother-in-law, imprisoned her, and seized her non-existent estates, we must again examine why Elizabeth left her Westminster Abbey sanctuary in March 1484. Ricardians tell us that there was a *rapprochement* with Richard, and therefore she now believed that he had not killed her sons in the Tower, although he had killed her brother and another son. Her surviving son, Lord Dorset, was in exile with her brother Lionel and Henry Tudor.

In an extraordinary speech upon 1 March 1484, Richard III appeared before the summoned lords spiritual and temporal of England and the magnates of London. He publicly promised to honour the daughters of Edward IV as a condition of their leaving their sanctuary, where they had been staying with Elizabeth

Woodville, following Richard's seizure of power at Northampton and Stony Stratford on 30 April 1483. This negotiated settlement between Richard III and Elizabeth has been posited as evidence that Richard was innocent of authorising the murders of Edward V and Prince Richard of York.

Elizabeth and Margaret Beaufort had agreed that Henry should marry Edward IV and Elizabeth's oldest daughter, Elizabeth of York, who upon the death of her brothers became the Yorkist heiress. Henry agreed to this plan and in December 1483 publicly swore an oath to that effect in the cathedral in Rennes, France. A month earlier, the uprising in his favour, led by Buckingham, had been crushed. Some writers believe that Buckingham told Elizabeth that her sons had been murdered. On 1 March 1484, she and her daughters came out of sanctuary after Richard publicly swore an oath that her daughters would not be harmed or molested and that they would not be imprisoned in the Tower of London or in any other prison. Richard also promised to provide them with marriage portions and to marry them to 'gentlemen born'. The family returned to court, apparently reconciled to King Richard. Elizabeth would be given an annuity of 700 marks a year. The Ricardian defendant Kendall argued 'that she came to terms with the man who had bastardised and deposed the Princes, driven her son the Marquess into exile, and executed her other son Grey and her brother Rivers is difficult enough to understand; but that she came to terms knowing also that he had murdered the princes well-nigh passes belief, or is at least incomprehensible'. Whatever the fate of the Princes in the Tower, it was beyond question that Richard had executed without trial

Elizabeth's son Richard Grey and her brother Anthony Woodville.

Just what were Elizabeth's other options, apart from forever immuring herself and her five daughters in convents as nuns? They had stayed in heavily guarded sanctuary for ten months, in confined quarters, and the abbot must have wished to normalise his relations with the Crown. Elizabeth knew that sanctuary could be broken, as her husband Edward IV had taken out the Duke of Somerset and other Lancastrians from Tewkesbury Abbey. If she and her daughters were taken by Richard, they might never have been heard of again. Her only option was to accept Richard's offer of a pension and good marriages for the girls, with guarantees, sworn under oath in front of numerous witnesses, that Richard would not harm the women or imprison them. Elizabeth knew that Margaret Beaufort, who was deeply involved in the 1483 rebellion, had been treated leniently, and she must have also realised that Richard was simply not in a position where he could risk the consequences of harming or being suspected of harming five innocent girls of royal blood, an act which would never be tolerated.

Elizabeth had no real choices left, and negotiated with Richard for the future of her five daughters and Dorset, hopefully securing their safety. There was no longer any need for Richard to kill Dorset because he was now king, with seemingly no opposition. Dorset was living penniless abroad, like Henry and Jasper Tudor dependent upon the charity of foreign nobles. Thus Elizabeth secured an agreement, in which she made him declare publicly, 'I Richard, by grace of God, etc., in the presence of you, my lords spiritual and temporal, and you, my Lord Mayor and aldermen of London, promise and swear ... that if the daughters of Elizabeth ... will come to me out of the Sanctuary of Westminster and be guided, ruled, and demeaned after me, then I shall see that they shall be in surety of their lives ... nor any of them imprison in the Tower of London or other prison, but that I shall put them into honest places'. Richard thus promised to look after Edward IV's daughters, marry them off to lords, and importantly, not to imprison them in the Tower of London. This is fairly obviously a veiled reference by Elizabeth to the fate of her murdered royal sons.

With Edward IV's daughters, he also gained an opportunity to bind followers to him through marriage. He arranged for the marriage of one daughter, Cecily, to Ralph Scrope and now entered into negotiations with Portugal for the marriage of Elizabeth of York to the fourteen-year-old Manuel, Duke of Beja, later to be Manuel I of Portugal. It seems that Richard had originally wished to marry Elizabeth himself, and as a reward for her mother's blessing would have allowed Dorset to return in honour, but we will probably never know.

As king, Henry treated the mother of his queen with all the privileges befitting her station, and gave her dower palaces to improve her income. The Parliamentary Act by which she was deprived of her dower in Richard's reign was ordered by Henry's judges to be burnt. Elizabeth was chosen by the king, in preference to his own much-loved mother Margaret Beaufort, as sponsor to his heir, Prince Arthur. At the end of 1489 Elizabeth received the French ambassador in a splendid state occasion. In 1490 Henry VII presented her with an additional pension of £400. Only after this did she retire to the royal apartments at Bermondsey Abbey.

Richard III left illegitimate children. John Plantagenet (*c.* 1472?–99?) was an acknowledged son conceived before Richard's marriage. John Plantagenet was also known as John of Pontefract from his probable place of birth. He was also known as John of Gloucester, as Richard was Duke of Gloucester when John was born. The Great Wardrobe of the King for 1472 refers to John as 'a lord bastard'. Hicks suggests that John's mother was Alice Burgh, who was given an annuity of £20 for 'certain special causes and considerations' when Richard was at Pontefract on 1 March 1474. Rosemary Horrox posits that Katherine Haute was a mistress of Richard and possibly the mother of Katharine, and was given an annuity of £5 at this time. It is unknown whether another illegitimate child, Katherine, had the same mother as John, but both were acknowledged by Richard as his children. Another possibility is that their mother was one of the daughters of the Earl of Warwick at Pontefract Castle, where Richard was being brought up and educated. John was one of only two persons knighted on 8 September 1483 in York when his half-brother Edward of Middleham was shown as Prince of Wales.

John Plantagenet was in Calais by November 1484 and was appointed Captain of Calais by Richard upon 11 March 1485. The order referring to his appointment as Captain of Calais calls him 'John de Pountfreit [Pontefract] Bastard'. In John's letter of appointment Richard calls him 'our dear bastard son, John of Gloucester'. He was given all of the necessary powers of his appointment, except that of appointing officers, which was reserved until he turned twenty-one. John was not yet an adult so could not exercise the full authority of his position, and Robert Brackenbury was entrusted with his safety. In the Canterbury City Archives there are references to payments in November 1484 for an allowance of wine and leavened bread 'for the Lord Bastard riding to Calais', and for a pike and wine for 'Master Brakynbury Constable of the Tower of London', returned from Calais at that time 'from the Lord Bastard'. There is also a warrant dated 9 March 1485 to deliver clothing to 'the Lord Bastard'.

When Richard was killed at Bosworth, Henry VII removed John as Captain of Calais but did not further persecute him. Upon St David's Day, 1 March 1486, Henry granted John Plantagenet an annual income of 20 pounds. It is a grant to 'John de Gloucester, bastard, of an annual rent of 20 li. during the King's pleasure, issuing out of the revenues of the lordship or manor of Kyngestonlacy, parcel of the duchy of Lancaster, in co. Dorset'. To have some idea of this income, the 'labour value' of £20 today would be around £112,000, and the 'income value' around £387,000 (according to the University of Exeter 'Measuring Worth' website). Thus John Plantagenet was treated extremely generously by Henry.

In Buck's 1690 *The History of King Richard III* it is alleged that John was kept in prison for a number of years before his death. He died childless. In his confession, Warbeck stated that when he began his impersonation of Richard, Duke of York, in 1491, 'King Richard's bastard son was in the hands of the king of England'. Buck states that 'about the time these unhappie gentlemen suffered [the time of the deaths of Perkin Warbeck and the Earl of Warwick] there was a base sone of King Richard III made away, and secretly, having been kept long before in prison'. The reason for the execution was apparently the wish of some unspecified Irishmen to make him their ruler. It may be that John Plantagenet was taken to the Tower in 1491, when Perkin Warbeck arrived to try and raise an army against the king in Ireland. While Arthur Plantagenet, Edward IV's bastard, flourished, John may have died in prison in 1499. His history, after being granted £20 in 1486, is obscure. However, of major interest is the referral to John as 'the' Lord Bastard. As Edward V had been known as the lord bastard, after Richard's *Titulus Regius* had declared him illegitimate, it seems unlikely that the prince in the tower was still alive when John of Gloucester was Captain of Calais in 1484.

Nothing is known about the early lives of John and Katherine (1468/74–87?), Richard's other recognised illegitimate child, but that they could have been two of 'the children' referred to in the Regulations for the King's Household in the North in July 1484. Katherine first comes into the public record when William Herbert, Earl of Huntingdon (formerly the Earl of Pembroke), covenanted 'to take to wife Dame Katherine Plantagenet, daughter to the King, before Michaelmas of that year'. The fact that she married in 1484 is no guide to her age, as child marriages were not uncommon in the fifteenth century. She was probably not above eighteen since Richard himself was only born in 1452, and it is not thought that she was born after Richard's marriage. Katherine was probably between ten and eighteen years of age when she married Herbert.

In addition to agreeing to marry Katherine before 29 September 1484, Herbert agreed to make her a jointure in lands of £200 per annum. This is an estate settled upon the wife if the husband should die. Richard III paid for the whole cost of the marriage and undertook to settle lands and lordships to a value of 1,000 marks per annum upon them and their male heirs. On 8 March 1485 a further grant was made to the earl and Katherine. Nothing further is known about Katherine. She may have had children, but if so they did not survive, since the earl's heir was Elizabeth, his daughter by his first wife, Mary Woodville. Nor is it known when she died, but it seems very likely that she did not survive the earl and she may have been dead by 25 November 1487, the date of the coronation of Elizabeth of York. Among the lists of nobility present at that ceremony is a list of earls (including the Earl of Huntingdon), all described as 'widowers'. Upon 17 May 1488 Henry VII confirmed Herbert's charter as Earl of Huntingdon.

The following lines are found on various Yorkist internet discussion forums: 'On the orders of Henry VII, Katharine was arrested at Raglan Castle immediately after the Battle of Stoke Field in June 1487 and apparently died prior to her cousin Elizabeth of York's coronation on 25 November 1487.' However, this author can as yet find no trace of this arrest or imprisonment.

There is another possible child of Richard, Richard Plantagenet, known as Richard of Eastwell. There is an entry for 1550 in the parish register of Eastwell, 3 miles north of Ashford in Kent: 'Rychard Plantagenet was buryed the xxij daye of Desember, Anno ut supra.' The register is a 1598 copy made by the vicar, Josias Nicholls, to comply with a legal requirement that all existing paper registers would be copied into (harder-wearing) vellum books. Upon this bare record is based the possibility that this was a bastard son of Richard III. There was also a letter published by a Dr Brett in

1735. This states, with much circumstantial detail, that Richard was acknowledged by his father Richard III on the eve of Bosworth, but only privately, and that he lived in obscurity after the battle as a stonemason at Eastwell. Sir Thomas Moyle, the owner of Eastwell Place, is said to have discovered his identity and given him a cottage to live in, where he remained until his death at about the age of eighty-one.

Alison Weir in *Britain's Royal Families, the Complete Genealogy* mentions that Richard had another three unnamed illegitimate children, plus possibly Stephen Hawes (1473/77?–1523?), who has been linked with Suffolk, owning property at Aldborough. One genealogy website gives Hawes' mother as Lady Anne Beauchamp Neville, a daughter of the Earl of Warwick. The poet Stephen Hawes was educated at Oxford, travelled in Europe and became groom of the chamber in Henry VII's household. In 1502, for the funeral of Henry VII's queen, Hawes received an allowance of 4 yards of black cloth for mourning. While groom of the chamber in 1506, he wrote and dedicated apologetically to the king *The Passetyme of Pleasure*.

There was another illegitimate Plantagenet, Arthur Plantagenet, Viscount Lisle (1461/75 to 3 March 1542), a son of Edward IV, born in Calais. His mother has been speculated upon but is unknown. Arthur spent his childhood at the court of Edward IV, but it is not known where he was under Richard III. In 1501 he joined the household of his half-sister, the queen-consort Elizabeth of York, and moved to Henry VII's household after her death in 1503. After the accession of his nephew Henry VIII (1509) he was designated an Esquire of the King's Bodyguard, and was a close companion of Henry's. He acquired various positions and titles, but in 1540 several members of the Plantagenet household in Calais were arrested on suspicion of plotting to betray the town to the French. Arthur was recalled to England and arrested. The actual conspirators were executed, but there was no evidence connecting Arthur with the plot. Henry VIII decided to release him from the Tower in 1542, but upon receiving news that he was to be released Arthur suffered a heart attack and died two days later.

7

The King and Prince in the Tower

Much of all knowledge lies in the knowledge of their causes.

Select Works of Archbishop Leighton: Sermon XVIII
(Edinburgh, 1766)

Ralph Brooke wrote *Catalogue and Succession of the Kings, Princes, Dukes, Marquesses, Earles and Viscounts of this Realme of England since the Norman Conquest,* published in 1619, with a new edition in 1622. The 1619 edition does not mention the discovery of bones. In an account of the children of Edward IV, the first entry for Richard, Duke of York, reads, 'Richard, second son of King Edward the fourth ... was betrothed unto Anne [Mowbray] ... but he enjoyed neither wife nor life long, for he was [with his brother Edward] murdered in the Tower of London; which place ever since is called, The bloody Tower.' The separate entry for Richard as Duke of York states, 'This Richard ... was with his Brother, King Edward the fifth [by the command of Richard, Duke of Gloucester, their unnatural Uncle] most cruelly murdered in the Tower of London, the ninth day of the Kalends of June 1483 without issue: his place of burial was never known certainly to this day.'

In the 1622 edition, the first entry has been changed to read, 'Richard ... was [with his brother Prince Edward] murdered in the Tower of London; which place ever since hath been mured [walled] up and not known until of late, when as their dead carcasses were there found, under a heap of stones and rubbish.' Until current times, Horace Walpole has been the most famous of Richard III's defenders. His *Historic Doubts on the Life and Reign of King Richard the Third*, published in 1768, is a landmark in the defence of Richard. Walpole was outraged by the ignorance and misrepresentations of historians and, in particular, their 'partiality, absurdities, contradictions and falsehoods' towards Richard. Of Sir Thomas More's account of the murder of the Princes in the Tower he wrote, 'It is difficult to crowd more improbabilities and lies together than are comprehended in this short narrative.' Caroline Halsted's *Richard III as Duke of Gloucester and King of England* of 1844 followed Walpole's favourable assessment of Richard.

Sir Clements Markham's *Richard III: His Life & Character Reviewed in the Light of Recent Research* (1906) tells us that 'the caricature of the last Plantagenet king was too grotesque, and too grossly opposed to the character derived from official records. The stories were an outrage on commonsense ... My own conclusions are that Richard III must be acquitted on all counts of the indictment.' He somehow created a story that Henry VII killed Edward V and Prince Richard in 1486. Current pro-Richard writers lean heavily upon these three later sources of information.

The Fellowship of the White Boar was formed in 1924, and re-formed in 1956 as the Richard III Society. It has thousands of members across the globe. The followers of Richard III's rehabilitation as a 'good king' call themselves Ricardians, with an excellent and well-researched website. A detective novel by Josephine Tey, *The Daughter of Time* (1951), was based on Markham's hypothesis that Henry VII killed the king and prince. The novel has been continuously reprinted and has spawned scores of other works exculpating the king. Tey's book influenced a 'non-fiction' biography of Richard III in 1955, by the American historian, Paul Murray Kendall. Kendall tells us that Richard had actually been 'a paragon of justice and mercy and a determined friend of the poor and the oppressed'. His evidence is solely based upon Richard's record as an administrator and soldier in the north of England, under the control of his brother, Edward IV. Kendall believed that Richard was responsible for the death of 'the Princes in the Tower' because he took the kingship. However, upon no evidence whatsoever he blamed Buckingham for their actual murders. In effect most Ricardians blame Buckingham, the Norfolks or Henry for the deaths, not Richard.

In 1983 the Ricardians, under the royal patronage of the Duke of Gloucester, celebrated the 500th anniversary of Richard's accession. In 1984 the then chairman of the Richard III Society, Jeremy Potter, published *Good King Richard? An Account of Richard III and his Reputation 1483–1983*, which again portrayed the king in a favourable light. In 1984 society members appeared as defence witnesses in a television trial of Richard for the murder of the princes. *The Trial of Richard III*, a London Weekend Television production, was transmitted on Channel 4 for four hours, and the script, edited by the producers, Richard Drewett and Mark Redhead, was published as a book under the same title. The jury, representing a wide cross-section of what was referred to as the 'educated public', returned a unanimous verdict of 'not guilty', according to the *Ricardian* website. Actually the jury was unable to agree upon the basis of probabilities. Two mock trials followed in the USA with the same result. With the recent finding of Richard's bones, further interest in the king has stimulated much greater membership of the Richard III Society.

The Howards are thought by many historians to have had an involvement. It was possibly no coincidence that Thomas Howard was created Earl of Surrey and his father Duke of Norfolk (also inheriting the vast Mowbray estates) shortly after the princes vanished. John Howard was made Duke of Norfolk upon 28 June 1483, the title previously having belonged to Prince Richard of Shrewsbury, who was also Duke of York, Earl of Norfolk, Earl of Nottingham and Earl of Warenne. On the same day, the new Duke of Norfolk's son Thomas Howard was made Earl of Surrey. The Earl of Surrey and Warenne, Thomas de Mowbray, had died without heirs in 1476, with Prince Richard taking the Earldom of Warenne. Was Prince Richard therefore dead before 28 June? Would anyone not of royal blood have taken the titles of a living prince?

It is well known that rumours spread like wildfire across the nation and Europe that Richard had killed his nephews. By the standards of the times, every deposed king was killed. Edward II's queen-consort Isabella and her lover Mortimer had the king killed. As we have seen, Henry IV had Richard II killed. Edward IV and/or Richard had Henry VI killed. Any or all of

Edward IV, Clarence and Richard killed Henry VI's son and heir. Equally, rightful heirs were sometimes killed, again destroying the notion that Richard of Gloucester was of any particular royal bloodline. King John had Arthur of Brittany murdered, Richard II had Thomas of Woodstock killed, and Henry IV's son Humphrey of Gloucester was probably poisoned after being imprisoned. The people knew that Edward IV had killed his own brother Clarence. People expected, not suspected, that the princes had been done away with. Richard had deliberately refuted other rumours, such as that he wished to marry his niece Elizabeth of York, but did not respond to these allegations. He could have easily displayed the newly defined 'bastards' in public. His agents would have told him that loyal Yorkists were now beginning to support the claims of the exiled Lancastrian Henry Tudor.

Then, in autumn 1483, the former queen-consort Elizabeth Woodville gave consent for her daughter Elizabeth of York to marry Henry Tudor, and thus strengthen his claim to the crown. Richard had already illegally killed her brother Rivers and son Richard Grey. Another son, Dorset, had managed to escape from Westminster to flee from Richard and join Henry in exile. She must have known that her sons by Edward IV were now dead. Elizabeth Woodville had never been allowed to see them in the Tower, and would not leave her heavily guarded sanctuary at Westminster Cathedral, obviously fearing the worst if she did so. Regarding the 'great debate' – who killed the Princes in the Tower – *The Great Chronicle of London* describes Richard's death as justice for killing the children: 'And thus ended this man with dishonour as he that sought it, for had he continued still protector and have suffered the children to have prospered according to his allegiance and fidelity, he should have been honourably lauded over all.' The record was compiled thirty years after the event from contemporary London municipal records, but states that the rumour of the princes' death did not start circulating in London until after Easter 1484, within a year of Richard being crowned upon 6 July 1483.

However, the other main contemporary sources – John Argentine, Philippe de Commines, Dominic Mancini, Robert Ricart and the *Croyland Chronicle* – all record that the rumour of the princes' mistreatment or deaths was current by the end of 1483. Mancini's account of their reported deaths was written contemporaneously, in 1483. Commines was present at the meeting of the Estates-General of France in January 1484, and in his summary of the events of 1483 stated that Richard was responsible for the murder of the princes. Commines has no reason to blacken Richard's character. De Commines (1447–1511) was imprisoned in an iron cage in France for implication in rebellion from 1487–89, preventing him from writing his *Historical Memoirs* for some time. He records,

> Our king was presently informed of King Edward's death; but he still kept it secret, and expressed no manner of joy upon hearing the news of it. Not long after, he received letters from the Duke of Gloucester, who was made king, styled himself Richard III and had barbarously murdered his two nephews. This King Richard desired to live in the same friendship with our king as his brother had done, and I believe would have had his pension continued; but our king looked upon him as an inhuman and cruel person, and

would neither answer his letters or give audience to his ambassador; for King Richard, after his brother's death, had sworn allegiance to his nephew as his king and sovereign, and yet committed that inhuman action not long after; and in full parliament caused two of his brother's daughters, who were remaining, to be degraded, and declared illegitimate upon a pretence which he justified by the bishop of Bath, who having been formerly in great favour with King Edward, had incurred his displeasure, was cashiered, imprisoned and paid a good sum for his release.

De Commines was a writer and diplomat in the courts of Burgundy and France, and has been called 'the first truly modern writer' (Augustin Sainte-Beuve) and 'the first critical and philosophical historian since classical times' (*Oxford Companion to English Literature*). The French king who distrusted Richard was Louis XI, Louis the Prudent, who reigned from 1461 until 30 August 1483, so the princes must have been dead before the summer of 1483. The Croyland Chronicler may have been John Russell, Bishop of Lincoln, who was Richard's Chancellor until July 1485, as it was written in April 1486. We know the author was a member of the Council and a doctor in canon law. Russell's own involvement in events is never detailed, which makes him a candidate for authorship. The *Second Continuation of the Croyland Chronicle* was suppressed by Henry VII's government because it contained a copy of *Titulus Regius*, the Act of Parliament declaring Richard III's right to the throne. The *Chronicle* is usually accurate and is substantiated by other available sources.

After the death of Richard's son Edward of

Middleham at the end of March 1484, the Croyland Chronicler reported 'whisperings' that the princes were dead: 'Rumour spread that the sons of King Edward had died a violent death, but it was uncertain how.' He also quotes a contemporary poem about the kings called the 'Three Richards': 'The Third was not content therewith but must destroy his brother's progeny ... The Boar's tusks quailed and, to avenge the White, the Red Rose bloomed.' Concerning the Battle of Bosworth, the chronicler refers to 'the children of King Edward, whose cause in especial was avenged in this battle'.

John Argentine (d. 1507) was an English doctor, trained in Strasbourg, who attended Edward V and, later, Henry VII's heir, Prince Arthur. Provost of King's College, Cambridge, he was the last known attendant of the princes. He stated that Edward V, 'like a victim prepared for sacrifice, sought remission of his sins by daily confession and penance, because he believed that death was facing him'. Argentine noted that Edward suffered from a diseased jaw and perhaps a toothache, and that the pain only added to his sense of hopelessness. Argentine fled from England after Richard's coronation in July 1483 and became one of the possible sources for Dominic Mancini's report that the young King Edward V was daily in fear of his life. Argentine's evidence seems to be also the basis for French declarations that the Princes in the Tower of London had been murdered, and their assassin crowned as King Richard III.

Dominic Mancini was an Augustinian friar from Rome, a scholar who wrote moral and theological works in Latin verse. Before coming to England, he had served as an agent spying on the French. Mancini came to England to work as an intelligence agent and perhaps envoy in 1482, on instructions of his patron, Angelo Cato, Archbishop of Vienne. He stayed in England until around the time of Richard III's coronation in July 1483. He resided in Paris, where he wrote two religious books, and is believed to have died around 1514. Mancini was commissioned to report to the Archbishop of Vienne, one of the chief counsellors of Louis XI of France, upon English affairs. His *De Occupatione Regni Anglie per Riccardum Tercium* (*The Occupation of the Throne of England by Richard III*) of December 1483 seems to have had a number of informants, but the only one mentioned by name is Dr John Argentine, Edward V's physician. However, Mancini may have contacted members of the Italian community in England, including Pietro Carmeliano, court poet to Edward IV and Henry VII. Mancini had no particular reason to slander or condemn Richard.

Dr John Argentine was an Englishman who studied in Italy, spoke fluent Italian and is possibly Mancini's main source. Mancini's manuscript was only found in the Bibliothèque Nationale in Lille, France, in 1936 and notes of Edward IV's will,

> Men say that in the same will he appointed as protector of his children and realm his brother Richard duke of Gloucester, who shortly after destroyed Edward's children and then claimed for himself the throne ... Finally, the youth ... surrendered himself to the care of his uncle, which was inevitable ... Of the king's attendants, or those who had come out to meet him, nearly all were ordered home. Richard, the queen's other son, who was quite young, and but a little before had come from London to the king, was arrested with

him in the same village, and with his brother, Richard was handed over to the care of guards in the same town.

Mancini thus believed that both princes were taken at Stony Stratford, but Richard Duke of York was first taken into sanctuary by his mother.

Mancini was in England for only three months, like Argentine leaving the country immediately after Richard's coronation in July 1483. Mancini writes,

After Hastings was removed [13 June], all the attendants who had waited upon the king [Edward V] were debarred access to him. He and his brother were withdrawn into the inner apartments of the Tower proper, and day by day began to be seen more rarely behind the bars the windows, till at length they ceased to appear altogether. A Strasbourg doctor [Argentine trained there], the last of his attendants whose services the king enjoyed, reported that the young king, like a victim prepared for sacrifice, sought remission to his sins by daily confession and penance, because he believed that death was facing him ... I have seen many men burst forth into tears and lamentations when mention was made of him after his removal from men's sight; and already there was a suspicion that he had been done away with. Whether, however, he has been done away with [Mancini delivered his report in December of 1483], and by what manner of death, so far I have not at all discovered.

The merchant Casper Weinreich of Danzig mentioned the murders in his diary for 1483: 'Later this summer, Richard, the King's brother, had himself put in power and crowned King of England; and he had his brother's children killed.' Ferdinand of Aragon and Isabella of Castile received a letter written to them by Diego de Valera on 1 March 1486 which firmly convinced them of Richard's guilt. Why would Richard not defend himself against this torrent of accusations across Europe? He had two whole years in which to produce Edward V and Prince Richard, or even get a churchman to report their existence. As Hutton relates,

> If one or both had died a natural death, he would certainly have published it. If he was daring enough openly to remove those who were their known protectors, he would not scruple secretly to remove them. His strenuous endeavours to get the Duke of York into his power, after he had secured the King's person, point, as an index towards a diabolical design.

Robert Ricart, Recorder of Bristol, wrote in his Kalendar for the year ending 18 September 1483, 'In this year the two sons of King Edward were put to silence in the Tower of London.' The merchant Richard Arnold's commonplace book for 1483 also contains the item, 'Two sons of King Edward put to silence.' There is also the writing of an anonymous London citizen from 1483 to 1488: 'This year [1483] King Edward V ... and Richard ... were put to death in the Tower of London.' Guillaume de Rochefort was Lord Chancellor of France from 1483 until 1492. He reported to the Estates-General in Tours in January 1484, stating that Richard has 'massacred' the princes and had then been given the crown 'by the will of the people'. De Rochefort may have used Mancini's findings, and the intelligence was used by the French as an excuse for backing Henry Tudor's invasion. De

Rochefort stated, 'Think of his [Edward IV's] children, already grown and promising, being murdered with impunity and of the crown's passing to their assassin.' The *Croyland Chronicle*, written in the spring of 1486, states, 'A rumour was spread that the sons of King Edward had died a violent death, but it was uncertain how.'

In the collection of miscellaneous manuscripts from reigns of Edward IV through Henry VII, known as *Bodleian Ms. Ashmole* 1448, there reads, 'Richard ... removed them from the light of the world ... vilely and murderously.' In March 1486, Diego de Valera noted that Richard poisoned his nephews. Vitellus, in the *Chronicles of London*, noted, 'King Richard ... put to death the two children of King Edward, for which cause he lost the hearts of the people.' The manuscript stated that Tyrrell or an old servant of Richard murdered the boys. John Rous, the antiquarian for the earls of Warwick tells us, 'The usurper King Richard III then ascended the throne of the slaughtered children.' Henry VII's first parliament accused Richard of 'shedding infants' blood'. The princes were not mentioned by name, as Henry did not wish to remind people that he was a replacement for them, and from later actions seems to have genuinely been unaware of what had happened to them or where their bodies were.

There is also contemporary political poetry. 'The Rose of England' was written about 1486:

This Rose [Edward IV] was fair, fresh to behold;
Springing with many a royal lance;
A crowned King, with a crown of gold;
Over England, Ireland, and France.
Then came in a beast men call a Boar [Richard];

And he rooted the garden up and down;
By the seed of the Rose [Edward IV's sons and
daughters], he set no store;
But afterwards it [Elizabeth of York] wore the crown.
He took the branches of the Rose [Edward's sons] away;
And all in sunder did them tear;
And he buried them under a clod of clay
Swore they should never bloom nor bear.

'The Most Pleasant Ballad of the Lady Bessy' has
Elizabeth of York saying to Richard,

Welcome, Gentle Uncle
How like you the killing of my brothers dear?
Welcome, gentle Uncle, home!'

Having examined some of the English and Continental
sources, there is also information contained in some of
the British (Welsh) language letters and poems which
may form a useful trove for future researchers. Please
note that the 'cywyddau darogan' (vaticinatory poems)
are sometimes difficult to translate, so in the following
case the original poem in Welsh has also been included.
The poem will have been written contemporaneously –
Dafydd Llwyd met Henry Tudor on his invasion, and
died at some time between 1490 and 1500. The poem
is thought to have been written around 1486, but
judging by line 2 the cywydd could have been written
in 1485, which will not please Richard's apologists.
The small 'r' for Richard III is, in the poem, contrasted
with the capital letters 'I' (for Iorwerth, Edward IV)
and 'H' (Henry VI). We cannot find clear translations
for some words as yet, e.g. *claearchwyrn*, line 15. The
poem calls Richard little several times, and also short,

cheerless, grey, blind, not respected, etc. Ricardians for years disputed Richard's height as well as his scoliosis.

In lines 17 and 18, the murderer is derogatorily called a Jew and is accused of putting an end to Edward V in the Tower of London, without any trial. Dafydd Llwyd cannot understand why Richard has not been punished by God, so the poem must have been written before Bosworth, and even possibly upon first hearing the news of the battle. The death of Henry VI upon a Thursday night in the Tower is attributed to Richard, and the Lancastrian Henry VI at this time had almost achieved sainthood status in the eyes of the English people, a process carried on in his reign by Henry VII. Interestingly, Richard's helmet crown was said to be have been knocked off and found in a hawthorn bush, being given to Henry by Lord Stanley. According to the poem Richard may have been hampered in a hawthorn thicket in the marshes. Wherever Richard fell, it is certain that his crown, which would have been merely a circlet of gold that fitted over his battle helmet, either fell from his head or was removed after his death.

The battered coronet was said to be found in a hawthorn bush by Sir Reginald Bray, who hastened to what is now called Crown Hill in Stoke Golding, where Henry and his army were gathering. Lord Thomas Stanley placed the battered circlet on his stepson's head and proclaimed him king. The field became known as Halloa Meadow in consequence of the cheering of the new king. A field in the vicinity of the crowning was styled 'Le Gulden' (The Golden) shortly afterwards and some claim that the addition of the word Golding after the name of the village was derived from this great event. Some historians state that there was no evidence for the thorns, but the hawthorn was added to Henry's arms after the battle. Indeed Henry's tomb in Westminster Abbey shows the device of the crown and the hawthorn branches, with the crown tangled in the branches of two hawthorns.

Cywydd i'r Brenin Richard a Ddistrywiodd ei Ddau Nai, Meibion Brenin Edward – Prophetic Poem to King Richard upon the Destruction of his Two Nephews, the Sons of King Edward

1	Mae'r goron ym mrig eryr,	The crown is on the head of the eagle [an allusion to Henry Tudor],
2	Os gwir lladd y wadd a'i wŷr.	If it is true that the mole [a derogatory term for little grey Richard] and his men are killed.
3	Cnwcwerio mae'r cing Harri,	King Harri [Henry Tudor] is conquering,
4	Coron aur, a'n caru ni.	A golden crown, and loving us.
5	Llyna feirdd yn llawenach	Behold the bards are more happy
6	Llwyddo'r byd a lladd R. bach,	- The world goes easier after killing little Richard, -
7	Llythyren aflawen lwyd,	A cheerless grey letter [message, cipher?]
8	Fforchog, yn Lloegr ni pharchwydd.	Who divided, and in England was not respected.
9	Ni allau'r R. yn lle'r I	Richard could not, in the place of Edward IV
10	Na rhywlio Lloegr na'i rholi.	Either govern England or control her.

11 Nid âi, ni reportiai'r part,
He would not go, he did not represent the part played

12 I'r adwy lle'r âi Edwart.
Into the breach [crisis?] where Edward IV would stand.

13 Cas yw gweled, coeg heusawr,
It is hateful to see a good for nothing herdsman

14 Coes lwyd yn lle morddwydd mawr,
An unhealthy limb [leg] instead of a great thigh [an allusion to Edward IV being a big man, and small Richard somehow deformed – he may have slightly dragged a leg owing to his scoliosis].

15 Yn ceisio'r cyrn, claerchwyrn, clau,
Seeking the horns, clearly stern [or purely violent?], noisy [or swift? The horns may refer to the horns of the bull, Henry Tudor, known as the 'bull of Anglesey'. Again they may refer to the 'horns' of an altar, which men held while praying deeply.]

16 Collai'r clowstr, colli'r clustiau.
He lost [or missed] the church, he lost the hearing [of the people?]

17 Iddew oedd a ddiweddwyd,
He was a Jew who put an end

18 Corn Brydain, caer Lundain lwyd;
To the horn of Britain [Corn Brydain is the horn of Britain, representing the Duke of Cornwall, Prince Edward of Wales], London's grey castle [the Tower];

19 Baedd caeth a wnaeth yn ei wart
An enslaved boar [Richard] who, in his charge [wardship]

20 Benydio meibion Edwart.
Tormented the sons of Edward IV.

21	O lladdodd, heb fodd y fainc,	Yes he killed them, without the means of the bench [judiciary],
22	Ei ddau nai oeddyn' ieuainc	His two nephews who were young,
23	Rhyfeddu bûm, rhyw fodd bar,	I was amazed, in some sort of anger,
24	Ar Dduw nas llyncai'r ddaear.	That God did not swallow him into the ground.
25	Mefl i'r Sarasin gwefldrist	A curse on the hang-lipped [sad-lipped, dejected] Saracen
26	Am ladd angylion gradd Grist.	For slaying angels of the orders of Christ.
27	Gwarth a wnaeth, myn gwrthiau Non,	He was disgraced, by Non's miracles, [this is a well-known medieval oath, using the mother of the patron saint David],
28	Gwroliaeth Herod greulon.	A homage of Herod's cruelty. [Herod ordered the first-born sons killed]
29	Duw o'r nef, ein creawdr ni,	God from Heaven, our Creator,
30	A sorres pan las Harri.	Was displeased when he [Richard] killed Henry VI.
31	Os ef a laddodd nos Iau	If it was he who killed [Henry VI on] Thursday night
32	Y Sant, ef a'i llas yntau.	The Saint [Henry VI] would kill him also. [a cult of sainthood grew up almost immediately after Henry's murder].
33	Nid byw y trymyniad bach,	The little raider [Richard] is not alive,
34	Ni las un elusenach.	No one more charitable has been killed;

35	Llunio a wnaeth dwyll anial,	He hatched an unsuccessful [barren] plot,
36	Llyna ei dwyll yn ei dâl	There was deceit in his tribute [or there was deceit in his head].
37	Os Risiart, fal Sarasin,	If Richard, as a Saracen
38	A wnaeth y farfolaeth flin,	Caused the grievous death,
39	Di-frys y denfyn Duw fry	It is without haste that God above will send
40	Y dialedd lle dyly	Vengeance where it is deserved.
41	Dialedd Duw a'i olwg	God's vengeance and his countenance
42	A ddaw yn drwm i ddyn drwg.	Will descend heavily on a bad man.
43	Cael yndroi mewn cwlwm drain	Having to linger in a knot of thorns [Richard's crown was found in a hawthorn bush]
44	Bu'r lindys byr o Lundain.	Was the short caterpillar [a derogatory term] from London.
45	Torres, o ddrwg naturiaeth,	He cut, because of an evil nature,
46	Pennau ieirll; pwy a wnâi waith?	The heads of earls; who could do worst?
47	Pennau'r arglwyddi penna',	The heads of the chief lords,
48	Pen dug heb un piniwn da.	The head of a duke without one good idea. [Buckingham or Clarence – both were thought to be a little stupid]

49	Rhaid oedd i'r ceiliog rhedyn	The locust [or grasshopper, a derogatory term] had to
50	Dalm hir gael dial am hyn.	Wait a long time to get revenge for this.
51	F'ewyllys fu, fo'i las fo,	My will was, he killed him.
52	A'i lladdodd Duw a'i llwyddo.	He killed him, with the will of God.
53	Y ci a las yn y clawdd	The dog [Richard] was killed in the hedge [or ditch]
54	Llwyddiant i'r neb a'i lladdawdd.	Good luck to the person that killed him.
55	Drwg a wnaeth a drig yn wall	He did evil deeds, they will always remain a wrong,
56	Draw, ac aros drwg arall.	Over there, and wait for another wrong.
57	Ceisio dringo drwy angen,	Trying to climb through need,
58	Cael cwymp adlam ceiliog hen,	-And having a rebound fall [bouncing up and down?] of an ancient cockerel, –
59	Cwymp ni'm dawr yn fawr o'i fod	A fall that will not concern me greatly for its being
60	Megis cwymp Simon Magus.	Like the fall of Simon Magus [the Biblical magician who claimed that he could fly].
61	Gwir anap oedd goroni	It was a true mishap crowning
62	Gwrab bach a garai pi.	A little ape [derogatory term for Richard, who could have hunched a little like a monkey] that loved magpies [i.e. thieves].

63	Orn am gam goron arnaw,	Terror on him for a crooked crown [a twin reference to a crown he did not deserve, and to his stature],
64	Gafar drwg gyfarfu draw.	He met with an evil goat [Satan] over there.
65	Rhyfedd oedd fod I'w feddiant	It was strange that it accorded to his possession [Henry VI was imprisoned by Richard]
66	Roi Sais yn ôl Harri Sant, –	To give an Englishman Saint Henry [VI] –
67	Y Sant ni adewis ŵr	The saint did allow know a man [Richard]
68	Dan goron, ond yn garwr.	Under a crown, but a believer [Henry VII].
69	Harri fu, Harri a fo,	[Saint] Henry was, Henry will be,
70	Harri sydd, hiroes iddo.	Henry is, long life to him

Polydore Vergil, writing in 1510, but drawing upon eyewitness reports of courtiers, noted that Richard continually bit his lower lip while thinking, while toying with a dagger. Others noted that Richard was always twisting his rings. Dafydd Llwyd calls Richard 'hang-lipped', knowing of this habit. He is also named a Saracen twice, as being an enemy of Christianity – at the time of the Crusades Muslim armies were called Saracens. The 'homage to Herod's cruelty' reminds us that Herod ordered the killing of first-born sons. It is out of the remit of this book to research Irish, Scottish and Welsh sources for this time, but it would be a rewarding research project. A rhyming translation of lines 3–24 has been given by a Mr Justice Bosanquet,

here taken from the 1847 edition of the works of Lewis
Glyn Cothi. It reads,

> King Harry had fought, and bravely done,
> Our friend the golden crown hath won.
> The bards resume a cheerful strain;
> For the good of the world little R. was slain.
> That straddling letter, pale and sad,
> In England's realm no honour had:
> For ne'er could R., in place of I,
> Rule England's people royally;
> Not stem the foe with puissant hand,
> Nor in the breach like Edward stand.
> How odious the vile cur to spy,
> With withered shank for brawny thigh,
> Partake the banquet's circling cheer,
> Where Gloucester's cunning cheats the ear!
> Old London saw, in an evil hour,
> A Jew usurp the British power;
> The boar, on murder foul intent,
> Brave Edward's sons in durance pent;
> His tender wards, his nephews two,
> By lawless, ruthless force he slew.
> Out on his savage Saracen's face!
> Who angels killed of Christian race,
> And brought (by holy Non) the shame
> Of Herod on a manly name!
> I marvel that the wrath of Heaven
> Had not the earth beneath him riven.

Lewis Glyn Cothi, in an ode to Jasper Tudor, told him
that the nation was impatiently awaiting the landing
of Jasper and his nephew. In *Cywydd i Siasbar ab
Owain Tudur*, he asks what has become of Jasper,

'the bull of the conflict', and tells him that he has been expected since May 1485. The month is now August, and he urges him upon his arrival to admit the 'Raven', the powerful Rhys ap Thomas, into his counsels. By alliance with Rhys and the North Walians, Jasper and Henry will be able to put an end to the claims of 'Edward's family' to the throne of England.

> Bron tarw a dyrbraint Iorwerth,
> Brev ar Dduw nev yn dy nerth!

Lewis has several poems in praise of Henry, Jasper, Rhys ap Thomas and Welsh supporters at Bosworth. One poem written while Jasper was in exile just before the invasion, reads partially,

> I is beyond the sea,
> I traverses the three seas
> And nine havens dread his approach.
> I's guiding star blazes over the two glaives [Daugleddau
> – Milford Haven]
> I will land,
> I will give battle,
> I will revenge his wrongs.
> After his victory
> I will offer gold
> Upon two altars to his guardian saint
> The North can read I
> And the North men will declare for him
> There is not a Saxon from hence to Windsor
> But trembles at the thought of the transmarine I ...

There is no J in Welsh, so it is represented by what the bard calls 'the Capital I' of Irish Ogham.

Detailed examination of the surviving poems of several Welsh bards of this period can probably inform us more about events, for instance those of Dafydd Llwyd of Mathafarn (c. 1420–c. 1500), Guto'r Glyn (c. 1412–93), Tudur Penllyn (c.1420–90), his son Ieaun ap Tudur Penllyn (fl. 1480), Lewis Glyn Cothi (c. 1420–90), Ieuan Brydidd Hir (fl. 1450–85), Tudur Aled (1465–1525), Huw Cae Llwyd (fl. 1431–1504), and his son Ieuan ap Huw Cae Llwyd (fl. 1475–1500). These were among the bards known as 'Beirdd yr Uchelwyr' (Poets of the Nobility), who travelled between the stately homes of Welsh nobles, and were probably the main forms of communication in these times.

Contemporary sources are unanimous in recording that Edward V and his brother Richard of York were dead, or believed to be dead, in 1483 or early 1484. Their cousin John de la Pole, and the others who spearheaded the Lambert Simnel rising in 1487, never claimed that the princes were alive in Richard III's time and murdered in Henry's. These allies would have replaced Lambert Simnel with someone pretending to be one of the princes, rather than offering an impostor of Edward of Warwick, who was alive and Henry's prisoner. Henry was easily able to confound the conspirators by displaying Edward of Warwick alive. This is in contrast to Richard III, who never displayed Edward V or Richard of York alive in order to dispel rumours of their deaths. The much later Perkin Warbeck imposture was also not believable, as the supporters of Richard of York would have advanced his candidacy early in Henry VII's reign, when Henry was still insecure and vulnerable. There has never been a scrap of evidence to support the

Richard of York Society's speculation that Edward V and Richard survived Richard III.

It is almost impossible for the princes to have been alive in 1485, when Henry took the throne, but he has often been posited by Ricardians such as the novelist Philippa Gregory as the killer of the princes. Henry was overseas, impoverished, and possibly only visited England once or twice briefly until he passed through Shrewsbury on his way to Bosworth Field. The main Tudor sources are John Rous, Polydore Vergil and Sir Thomas More. Thomas More wrote that on the day Richard ascended the throne, Prince Edward sighed and said, 'Alas, I would my uncle would let me have my life yet, though I lose my kingdom.' According to More's account, the prince was so sunk in misery and fear that he could not perform even basic tasks, such as dressing himself properly. The earliest Tudor chroniclers, admittedly, give us a picture of Richard as a 'black' king, biding his time during his brother's reign, who would stop at nothing – including the murder of his nephews – to gain the crown, and whose life and reign were steeped in blood.

Hume closely followed More's account and recorded what the actual events in the Tower were thought to be:

This ridiculous farce was soon after followed by a scene truly tragical: The murder of the two infant princes. Richard sent orders to sir Robert Brakenbury, constable of the Tower, to put his nephews to death; but this gentleman, who had sentiments of honour, refused to have any hand in the infamous office. The tyrant then sent sir James Tyrrel, who promised obedience; and he ordered Brakenbury to resign to this gentleman the keys of the Tower for one night. Tyrrel, choosing three associates, Slater, Dighton and Forrest, came in the night time to the door of the chamber where the princes were lodged; and sending in the assassins, he bid them execute their commission; while he himself stayed without. They found the young princes in bed, and fallen into a sound sleep. After suffocating them with the bolster and pillows, they showed their naked bodies to Tyrrel, who ordered them to be buried at the stair foot, deep in the ground, under a heap of stones. These circumstances were all confessed by the actors in the following reign; and they were never punished for the crime: Probably, because Henry, whose maxims of government were extremely arbitrary, desired to establish it as a principle, that the commands of the reigning sovereign ought to justify every enormity in those who paid obedience to them.

Sir Robert Brackenbury had been treasurer of Richard's household when he was Duke of Gloucester. Under Richard III, Brackenbury received a number of appointments. After the collapse of the Buckingham Rebellion, he was rewarded with large grants of land forfeited by Rivers and the Cheney family. Also Sheriff of Kent, upon 17 July 1483 he was appointed Constable of the Tower for life. Brackenbury was also given the financially rewarding posts of Master of the King's Moneys and Keeper of the Exchange (i.e. Master of the Mint), after the murder of Hastings. In March 1485 Brackenbury was entrusted with Richard's illegitimate son, John of Gloucester, whom he took to Calais to become its captain. Brackenbury's income now exceeded that of many important barons, and he died fighting for Richard at Bosworth.

Buckingham has been suggested as the murderer of the princes between their joint confinement in June 1483 and his rebellion in October. Buckingham rebelled in favour of Henry Tudor's claim to the throne, rather than that of Edward V, so Buckingham probably knew the princes were already dead. Commines stated that Buckingham 'had put the children to death'. In the 1980s, within the archives of the College of Arms in London, further documentation was discovered which states that the murder was conducted 'be [by] the vise of the Duke of Buckingham'. Another reference, surfacing this time in the Portuguese archives, states that 'after the passing away of king Edward in the year of 83, another one of his brothers, the Duke of Gloucester, had in his power the Prince of Wales and the Duke of York, the young sons of the said king his brother, and turned them to the Duke of Buckingham, under whose custody the said Princes were starved to death'. However neither document states whether Buckingham acted for himself, on Richard's orders, or in collusion with Tudor supporters.

There are reports of a great argument between Richard and Buckingham at Gloucester, during the new king's progress. Richard had already granted Buckingham the disputed de Bohun lands and titles, so this was not the reason. It may be that Buckingham had murdered the sons of Edward IV without Richard's permission and that, upon discovering the crime, Richard had sent Buckingham away from court and the progress to Brecon. Equally, it may have been that Buckingham had learned of the killing, and after seeing Hastings so easily disposed of, feared for his own safety. To be brutally honest, if Buckingham had killed the princes without Richard's authority, why did Richard not announce this upon Buckingham's death?

The October 1483 rebellion, which involved Buckingham, Lady Margaret Beaufort, her son Henry Tudor and the boys' mother, Queen Elizabeth Woodville, initially wanted the restitution of the princes only to switch in Henry Tudor's favour, following rumours of their deaths. Several sources claim that Buckingham told her that her sons were dead. Would Elizabeth Woodville have sided with someone expected of killing her sons? Buckingham joined the conspiracy when it had been developing for some time – he was not an instigator, but something triggered him to rise against the new king. Plans for the rebellion were well advanced before Buckingham joined the conspiracy, so few of Buckingham's Welsh retainers ever joined it.

Henry VII's actions indicate that he simply no idea of what had happened to the heirs to the throne. He made most strenuous investigations to prove that the impostor Perkin Warbeck was not Richard, Duke of York. Sir Thomas More was only five at the time of Bosworth but had access to many important people who had been involved in public affairs during Richard's short rule. More states that the order to kill his nephews was given by Richard, while on progress to Gloucester following his coronation. John Green was given a letter for Sir Robert Brackenbury, Constable of the Tower, but Brackenbury refused to kill them. Richard then approached Sir James Tyrrell, and sent him to the Tower with an order to Brackenbury that the keys be surrendered to Tyrrell for one night.

More says that Tyrrell employed two men to carry out the murder. Miles Forest, 'a Fellow fleshed in murder before time', and John Dighton, 'a big broad square knave', smothered the boys under the feather bed and pillows. The bodies were buried 'at the stair foot meetly deep in the ground, under a great heap of stones'. Dighton was released after 'confessing'. Forest has been discovered to be a Keeper of the Wardrobe at Barnard Castle, the home of Richard's mother, Cecily, Duchess of York. Thomas More reports that due to Richard's uneasy conscience, the children's bodies were later disinterred and buried elsewhere. James Tyrrell was appointed Master of the King's Henchmen. Tyrrell was in London early in September 1483, collecting clothing from the Tower for the investiture at York of Richard's son, Edward, as Prince of Wales. He was appointed as High Sheriff of Cornwall in 1484 but then went to France, returning only after Bosworth. Tyrrell was supposed to have confessed to the murders in 1501 prior to being hanged for another offence, in 1502.

In November 1483, Tyrrell played a role in securing the Duke of Buckingham and conducting him to Salisbury for execution. Three days later, he was made commissioner of array for Wales, and was appointed Steward of the Duchy of Cornwall for life. When Anne Tyrrell's half-brother Thomas Arundell was attainted after Buckingham's rebellion, Richard's parliament awarded his property to the Tyrrells. In February 1484, Sir James was granted the stewardship of Buelt in South Wales, also for life, and in September he was made one of the Chamberlains of the Exchequer. Near the end of 1484, according to the docket book of Richard's Privy Seal, this 'right trusty knight for our body and counsaillour' was sent 'over the See into the parties of Flaundres for diverse maters concernying gretely oure wele'.

In January 1485, Tyrrell assumed command of the garrison at Guisnes Castle, one of two fortresses guarding Calais, replacing the ailing and unreliable Lord Mountjoy. In June, he was made Constable of Tintagel Castle. In spite of the anticipated invasion of Henry Tudor, and the fact that Tyrrell was commissioner of array for Wales, Richard did not feel it necessary to recall him to England in the spring and summer of that year. Despite being so close to Richard, Tyrrell suffered very little under Henry. As he was not at Bosworth, he was not attainted by Henry's first parliament, but he lost the post of Sheriff of Glamorgan and Morgannok, as well as many of his other offices in Wales. Henry allowed him to continue his command at Guisnes. In January 1486, he returned to England when summoned as a witness in a dispute concerning the Countess of Oxford's lands, coerced from her by Richard. In February, he was restored as Sheriff of Glamorgan and appointed Constable of Cardiff Castle.

Henry granted Sir James a pardon for unspecified offences on 16 June 1486, and then issued a second one on 16 July 1486. Sir Clements Markham thus theorised that Tyrrell was responsible for the murders of the princes, and that he did it within that month-long period. This still does not explain two pardons, and Audrey Williamson (*The Mystery of the Princes*) considers it trifling, as repetition often occurred, and that the pardon was possibly just 'wiping the slate clean' for all association with Richard. The documents do not specify the reasons for the pardons. Probably the second pardon was an administrative error, or issued because the original paperwork had been misplaced. Bertram Fields points out in *Royal Blood* that the second pardon could have been 'for some entirely different and unrelated act'.

Tyrrell rose in Henry's favour, as he favoured competence over placements, and had been officially restored to his post as Lieutenant of Guisnes in December 1486. In that month, he was sent from Guisnes on an embassy on behalf of Henry to Maximilian, King of the Romans. He attended the coronation of Elizabeth of York in November 1487. He fought at the Battle of Dixmude in 1489 and, as Captain of Guisnes, took part in the negotiations leading to the Peace of Étaples in June 1492. Tyrrell took part in the tournament celebrating the creation of Prince Henry as Duke of York in 1494, and during the festivities marking the arrival of Katherine of Aragon in England in 1501. Tyrrell had become an accepted and respected figure in the Tudor administration.

However, in 1501, he harboured the Yorkist heir, Edmund de la Pole, Earl of Suffolk. Suffolk had fled to Guisnes to escape criminal charges and stir opposition to Henry. Henry demanded that Tyrrell returned to England to answer charges of assisting Suffolk. Tyrrell refused and Henry's troops besieged the castle. Tyrrell was promised safe passage, guaranteed by the Privy Seal, but was arrested and his eldest son Thomas was forced to surrender the castle. Sir James Tyrrell, Thomas Tyrrell, a Tyrrell retainer named Christopher Wellesbourne, Sir John Wyndham and 'an unnamed sailor' were then charged with treason in London. Under torture, Tyrrell is said to have confessed to the murder of the princes.

Tyrrell and Wyndham were tried at the Guildhall, convicted and beheaded upon 6 May 1502. For treason, Henry could have had them hanged, drawn and quartered, or even just hanged, so the sentence was lenient for the times. It appears that Tyrrell was either not allowed, or declined, to make the customary final speech from the scaffold. Thomas Tyrrell and Wellesbourne were imprisoned, and the poor unnamed sailor was hanged, drawn and quartered. Tyrrell's body was taken from Tower Hill and interred in the church of the Austin Friars in London, which was also the final resting place of Perkin Warbeck. His son Thomas Tyrrell received a king's pardon in April 1504. Sir James was officially attainted by the parliament of 1504 of treason on account of his connection with Edmund de la Pole, Earl of Suffolk, and his lands were forfeit to the king. Three years later, Thomas successfully appealed the attainder, and was restored his estates at Gipping. Again, Henry is shown to be a non-vindictive and merciful king for his times.

Tyrrell's role in the murder is first mentioned around 1512 in *The Great Chronicle of London*. Polydore Vergil, writing *Anglica Historia* around 1516, notes that Tyrrell was an unwilling killer, riding 'sorrowfully' into London to carry our the murders. However, Vergil states, 'With what kind of death these sely [innocent] children were executed, it is not certainly known.' Vergil later comments that it was thought 'that the sons of Edward IV were still alive, having been conveyed secretly away, and obscurely concealed in some distant region'. Sir Francis Bacon repeated the rumour, which may have come about because Henry, once king, seemingly made no attempt to investigate or refer to the disappearance of the princes. To be fair, Henry would not have wanted to find them. He had enough problems to deal with in bedding down his new dynasty after decades of bloodshed across the land. And to discover the real heirs would have been problematic, to say the least.

In *Harleian MSS 433*, there is recounted a journey to Flanders by Sir James Tyrrell upon King Richard's behalf late in 1484. Williamson speculates that Sir James visited Margaret of Burgundy (Richard's sister) to prepare the way for, or even escort, one or both of the princes out of the country. But why would Richard allow such a thing to happen? It is far more likely that Tyrrell wished to promise Dorset a safe return to England, further isolating the Lancastrian Henry Tudor from any potential Yorkist support. The same manuscript records that a sum of £3,000, almost the equivalent of the annual royal budget, was paid out to Tyrrell at Calais upon assuming his post as commander of Guisnes Castle, in January 1485. It seems possible that Tyrrell was delivering the money to France or Burgundy to pay for the capture and return of Henry Tudor. Henry had escaped to France from Brittany by September 1484. The Harleian manuscript also mentions a document authorising entry permits for messengers from the Duchess of Burgundy, one of them being allowed to enter England without any search of his belongings or person. In 1486, after Henry took the crown, Margaret, Duchess of Burgundy, was the main driving force behind the attempt to place Lambert Simnel in Henry's place.

A month before the alleged confession, Henry's heir Prince Arthur had died at Ludlow. Ferdinand and Isabella of Spain needed to be assured, before they betrothed their daughter Katherine of Aragon (Arthur's widow) to Prince Henry, that the Tudor dynasty was secure. Henry had no knowledge of the princes' whereabouts, dead or alive, and Tyrrell had been arrested and executed for treason. To be brutally honest, if he had confessed to killing the princes, he could have suffered the worst excesses of public hanging, drawing, quartering and the display of his head in London and his quarters across the kingdom. James Tyrrell would have been guilty of the most heinous crime – regicide – but was simply beheaded, the quickest form of the death penalty, reserved for gentlemen. He was a known associate of Richard and had been a prominent Yorkist. Henry and/or his advisors could have easily manufactured a confession to implicate Tyrrell and Richard. It may well be that Henry told Ferdinand and Isabella that Tyrrell had confessed to their deaths, thus satisfying them as to the security of Henry VIII on the throne.

At this time, bodies were needed as proof of murder, so Tyrrell could not have been convicted. Most of those who had known the princes, and could possibly dispute any confession, were dead. Their mother Elizabeth Woodville had died in 1492. Henry's main advisor, Cardinal Morton of Ely, had become Archbishop of Canterbury, dying in 1500. Richard III's mother, Cecily Neville, Duchess of York, had died in 1495. Thomas Rotherham, Archbishop of York, died in 1500. Edward V's tutor, John Alcock, Bishop of Worcester and twice Lord Chancellor, died in 1500. Alcock had been arrested at Stony Stratford when Edward V was taken by Richard. He was, however, soon reinstated upon Richard's council, and was one of the clergymen who actively canvassed for Henry Tudor to marry Elizabeth of York.

Sir James Tyrrell was not executed for regicide, but merely attainted in 1504 for the crime of associating with Edmund de la Pole, when Suffolk fled to France.

It seems more and more likely that Thomas More fabricated the Tyrrell confession to lend veracity to his imaginative description of the murders of the princes. Richard Marius, in his biography of More, theorises that Tyrrell was Henry's agent, murdering the princes to clear the way for Henry's claim, but there is not a shred of proof for this supposition.

It is somewhat strange that Henry VII did not publish Tyrrell's 'confession', if indeed there was one, to clarify the matter and take advantage of the opportunity presented to blacken the reputation of his hated rival. It may be that Thomas More was just tying up loose ends to ensure that Henry VIII's father was never blamed for the murders. Undertaking research upon Richard's reign, Amy Licence unearthed records of his activities in Canterbury, six months after the boys' disappearance, which could offer evidence that the king wished to offer penance for his sins. Richard may have been in the North during the summer of 1483 when the deaths are thought to have occurred.

In 1674, workmen employed in demolishing a staircase within the Tower of London, leading to the chapel of the White Tower, made the discovery of the bones of two children in an elm chest, at around a depth of 10 feet. They were originally thrown aside with some rubble, until their significance as the possible bones of the two princes was recognised. Charles II asked Sir Christopher Wren to design a white marble container and they were reverently placed in the Henry VII chapel at Westminster Abbey, close to the tomb of the princes' sister, Elizabeth of York. George V gave permission for the exhumation of the bones in 1933. An examination was conducted concluding that these were the bones of two children, the eldest aged twelve to thirteen and the younger nine to eleven. The heights of the two children were calculated to be 4 feet 9½ inches and 4 feet 6½ inches respectively, somewhat taller than their age estimates suggested. (The princes' father, Edward IV, stood at 6 feet 4 inches tall.) They further stated that a large red stain on the skull of the elder child reaching from below the orbits to the angles of the lower jaw was consistent with death by suffocation, and that congenital missing teeth and certain bilateral Wormian bones (islands of bone) of unusual size and similar shape on both crania were evidence of consanguinity. The lacrimal bone, the smallest and most fragile of the face, of one of the boys was abnormal, which suggested that he had 'cried his eyes out'.

There is consensus of opinion among modern experts that Wright's determination of the ages of the skeletons and the age differential between the two sets of bones is approximately correct. In the absence of modern carbon dating or DNA analysis on the forensic evidence of the bones, it is still not possible to say that these are the bones of Edward V and his brother Richard.

8

The Strange Case of the Bones in the Car Park

Thomas More relates that Richard was 'slain in the field, hacked and hewed of his enemies, carried on horseback dead, his hair in despite torn and togged [clothed] like a cur dog'. According to the Burgundian chronicler Jean Molinet, writing in 1490,

> His horse leapt into a marsh from which it could not retrieve itself. One of the Welshmen then came after him, and struck him dead with a halberd, and another took his body and put it before him on his horse and carried it, hair hanging as one would bear a sheep. And so he who miserably killed numerous people, ended his days iniquitously and filthily in the dirt and mire, and he who had despoiled churches was displayed to the people naked and without any clothing, and without any royal solemnity was buried at the entrance to a village church.

Robert Fabyan's *Great Chronicle*, compiled around 1500, tells us, 'Then was the Corpse of Rychard late king Spoiled & naked as he was borne caste behind a man and so carried unreverently athwart ye horse back unto the Friars at Leicester where after a season he had lain that all men might behold him he was there with little reverence buried.' The Tudor chronicler Edward Hall (1497–1547) stated in 1542 that the body was carried to Greyfriars: 'naked and despoiled to the skin, and nothing left above him not so much as a cloth to cover his privy members ... trussed ... like a hog or calf, the head and arms hanging on the one side of the horse, and the legs on the other side, and all by sprinkled with mire and blood.' We know that bodies were stripped on the battlefield of anything of worth, and that his washed body, presumably wrapped in a cloth, was displayed as was the custom for people to see that Richard was dead. Richard suffered two 'humiliation injuries' after his death, probably inflicted by troops filled with adrenaline and joy after having survived a battle they looked like losing. It was not in Henry's interests at all to despoil the corpse, as his intention always was to unite the Yorkists with Lancastrians. He wanted no bitterness, and his behaviour to Yorkists after the battle and during his reign was indeed exemplary.

There was no point in arranging a wonderful funeral cortège to take the corpse back to Westminster – Henry wanted no symbolism, or pilgrims to his enemy's grave, until he had properly grasped the kingship. Henry had seen the way that Henry VI was still revered, almost as a saint, with miracles being attributed to him. We seem to disparage Henry's motives, but Hitler's remains will never be found, deliberately, and after

Mussolini was killed, a decision was made to obscure his grave site. In more recent times, military officials in the Transitional National Council of Libya chose to bury Muammar el-Qaddafi in a secret location and American commandos buried Osama bin Laden at sea, to avoid creating a shrine for their supporters. Richard had a quick burial, but his grave site was widely known, and Henry headed to London.

The home page of the website of the Richard III Society, accessed upon 2 February 2013, reads,

Philippa [Langley] is a screenwriter with a passion to tell stories that challenge our perception of established truths. Currently writing a film script about the real Richard III, she inaugurated the quest for King Richard's lost grave as part of her ongoing research into history's most controversial monarch. Philippa is the secretary of the Scottish Branch of the Richard III Society ... Philippa Langley knew King Richard III had been 'piteously slain' at Bosworth Field ... King Richard was waiting to be found, and in 2009 Philippa decided to find him.

'I never saw it like that. My passion for the search was based on personal intuition, which only became stronger and stronger. The moment I walked into that car park in Leicester the hairs on the back of my neck stood up, and something told me this was where we must look. A year later I revisited the same place, not believing what I had first felt. And this time I saw a roughly painted letter "R" on the ground (for "reserved parking space", obviously!). Believe it or not, it was almost directly under that "R" that King Richard was found. This was the first area we excavated in fact, and it proved to be the choir of the church, the very place where we knew he was buried. And it was on the very first day, the anniversary of Richard's burial, that we came across his remains. We couldn't know it then, of course. We simply stared in disbelief and wondered just how lucky you could get on the first day of a dig! By the time he had been freed from his surroundings, and we saw his curved spine and battle wounds, I needed no further proof. We had to wait for the scientific tests, of course ... but for me, my quest was over.'

To be frank, everyone who dies in battle is 'piteously slain'.

In 2012, Langley had been walking over a particular spot in a municipal parking lot when in her words she had 'goosebumps' and 'absolutely knew I was walking on his grave'. This 'screenwriter' with no previous evidence of any screenplays, has been a foundation of the current interest in Richard. Like most of those involved, she is a sympathiser of Richard, along with the novelist Philippa Gregory. Gregory has yet another new book out, *The White Princess*, this time about Elizabeth of York, Henry's wife, whose 'lover' and true love was her little uncle Richard III, the man whom she knew had imprisoned and probably killed her brothers. The problem is that audiences enjoy historical romances and then treat and remember their fanciful and memorable hypotheses as fact. 'Dour' Henry VII even rapes his bride before the marriage in this unfortunately bestselling novel.

Richard's body was taken to Leicester to be displayed as proof of death before his burial. His head was not spiked and sent to London for display, as his predecessor Plantagenets were wont to do, but his body lay in state for at least two days, probably at the church of St Mary de Castro, next to Leicester Castle. It was then carried along Friar Lane to the Grey Friars (Franciscan) house, where he was buried. The priest John Rous (*c.* 1411–91) wrote that Richard 'at last was buried in the choir of the Friars Minor at Leicester'. Despite much evidence, some Ricardians persisted for years in the belief that Richard had been thrown into the River Soar and that his body would never be found, but he had a known Christian burial inside a known church. In 1495, secure upon the throne, Henry VII disbursed £10 1*s* for an alabaster tomb erected marking Richard's burial site at Greyfriars, which was later destroyed during the Dissolution of the Monasteries.

In 1612, Christopher Wren, father of the famous architect, visited Robert Herrick, Mayor of Leicester, and recorded seeing a handsome 3-foot-high stone pillar in Herrick's garden. Inscribed on the pillar was, 'Here lies the body of Richard III sometime King of England.' Herrick's mansion was demolished in the 1870s and municipal buildings erected. Herrick's garden seems to have remained a garden, or wasteland, up until the 1930s or 40s, when it became a council car park.

The project initiated by Langley to search for the body of Richard was backed by several key partners – Leicester City Council, Leicester Promotions (responsible for tourist marketing), the University of Leicester Archaeological Unit (ULAS), Leicestershire Archaeological and Historical Society (LAHS), Leicester Cathedral, Darlow Smithson Productions (responsible for the planned TV show) and the Richard III Society. The excavation was announced on 24 August 2012 at a press conference in Leicester. Philippa Langley of the Richard III Society announced, 'So much dirt has been thrown at Richard; his burial represents one of the worst injustices of all time. The history of the time was written by the Tudors, who could say whatever they wanted. Whatever we find, it will tell us a huge amount about his true nature.' To be candid, a deposed usurper being hastily buried is not 'one of the worst injustices of all time'. Hyperbole is not a substitute for historical fact.

On the first day of the archaeological dig, 25 August 2012, with the first trench being carefully excavated down to medieval levels, a skeleton was found. Until an exhumation licence was obtained, no further action could be taken except to protect the finds. After a fortnight two other trenches revealed that Greyfriars church had been found. The human remains from the first trench had been placed in a grave in the centre of the choir. The back of the skull of the skeleton had been cut open by a bladed weapon. The skeleton also had severe scoliosis, a form of spinal curvature in which the back bone is twisted sideways, which would have made the right shoulder noticeably higher than the left.

Buckley *et al.* of Leicester University record,

According to contemporary accounts, Richard III was buried without any pomp or solemn funeral. The archaeology of the grave, and the position of the body in it, reflect this. The body appears to have been placed in the grave with minimal reverence. Although the lower limbs are fully extended and the hands lay on the pelvis, the torso is twisted to the north and the head, abnormally, is propped up against the north-west corner of the grave. Irregular in construction, the grave is noticeably too short for the body ... The significance of the choir as the chosen burial place is ambiguous. It is one of the more important areas of the church (though not as high in status as the presbytery), commonly reserved for the burial of important individuals and highly visible to the friars attending divine office. The choir of a friary church was not generally accessibly to the laity, however, thereby hindering public veneration of the tomb. Friaries typically 'attracted' burials of affluent townsfolk and their specific patrons, which could include both royalty and nobility.

It is true that Richard III is the only king to remain buried in a friary; although the deposed and murdered Richard II (d. 1400) was initially laid to rest at the Plantagenet Dominican foundation at Kings Langley, his body was translated to Westminster in 1419 by Henry V. Perhaps significantly, friaries frequently seem to have served as resting places for the executed dead, where these were of high standing ... There was no evidence for a shroud or coffin ... That no effort was made to rearrange the corpse once again implies haste. Even moving the body to the centre of the grave would have allowed the torso and head to be straightened and the body to be arranged more carefully. The haste may partially be explained by the fact that Richard's damaged body had already been on public display for several days in the height of summer, and was thus in poor condition...

Guto'r Glyn composed a eulogy in 1485, crediting Richard's death to Sir Rhys ap Thomas, and the head wound that killed him:

Cwmcweriodd y King Harri	King Henry won the day
Y mae, drwy nerth ein meitr ni.	Through the strength of our master.
Lladd engyll, llaw ddiangen,	[Sir Rhys] killed Englishmen, capable hand,
Lladd y baedd, eilliodd ei ben.	He killed the boar [Richard], he shaved his head.

Guto's description seems to be a literal account of the injuries that Richard suffered, as the blows sustained to the head would have sliced away much of his scalp and hair as well as slivers of bone. The skull shows signs of two lethal injuries: the base of the back of the skull had been completely cut away by a bladed weapon, exposing the brain, and another bladed weapon had been thrust through the right side of the skull to impact the inside of the left side through the brain. Elsewhere on the skull, a blow from a pointed weapon had penetrated the crown of the head. Bladed weapons had clipped the skull and sheared off layers of bone, without penetrating it. The chin and cheek show injuries consistent with dagger wounds. The body bears marks of violence. One of the right ribs had been cut by a sharp implement, as had the pelvis. Taken together, the injuries appear to be a combination of battle wounds, which were the cause of death, followed by post-mortem 'humiliation wounds' inflicted on the corpse.

Buckley *et al.* noted,

The individual is male, with a gracile [slender] build, in his late 20s to late 30s, compatible with Richard's known age at death of 32. He had severe idiopathic adolescent-onset scoliosis. This may have been progressive and would have put additional strain on the heart and lungs, possibly causing shortness of breath and pain, although not all scoliosis sufferers experience pain from their condition. Unaffected by scoliosis, he would have stood around 5ft 8in (1.73m) tall, above average height for a medieval man, though his apparent height might have decreased as he grew older and his disability may have lifted his right shoulder higher than his left. This is consistent with the few contemporary reports of Richard III's physical appearance ... Ten peri-mortem [at or near the time of death] wounds have been identified on the remains, eight on the skull and two on the post-cranial skeleton. Two large wounds underneath the back of the skull, consistent with a halberd and a sword blow, are likely to have been fatal. A third, smaller, penetrating wound to the top of the skull is more enigmatic, but may have been caused by a sharp blow from a pointed weapon, such as a dagger, on the crown of the head. Other wounds were more superficial and none of the skull injuries could have been inflicted on someone wearing a helmet of the type favoured in the late fifteenth century. Two wounds, a cut on a right rib and a cut to the right pelvis typical of a thrust through the right buttock, are again unlikely to have been inflicted on someone wearing armour. These, along with two wounds to the face, may be 'humiliation injuries' delivered after death.

The skull wounds would have been prevented if the person had been wearing a helmet, so it must have been knocked off by the time the king received his head injuries. The post-mortem body wounds indicate the corpse had been stripped of its armour, as the stabbed torso would have been protected by a backplate while the pelvis would have been protected by armour. The wounds were made from behind on the back and buttocks while they were exposed to the elements, consistent with the contemporary descriptions of Richard's naked body being tied across a horse with the legs and arms dangling down on either side. There were possibly further flesh wounds but these are not apparent from the bones.

By 12 September 2012 a preliminary examination had been made, and the discovery of Richard's remains was announced to a massive press conference. George Buck (1560–1622) in his history of Richard III (begun in 1619, printed in a shortened version in 1646) used a heading, 'King Richard not deformed'. Partially because of this, the Richard III Society had always disputed that Richard had a crookbacked appearance, as usual blaming 'Tudor propaganda', but the skeleton is the same as the body depicted by Richard's contemporaries and later writers. Before his death in 1491, John Rous described the king's 'unequal' shoulders, the right higher and the left lower. Thomas More's unfinished history of Richard III, written around 1513–18, states, 'And his other shoulder more upright.' Thomas More called him 'croke backed' in the English version but the Latin version has 'extanti dorso', with a projecting (or prominent) back. Richard's contemporary Polydore Vergil also pointed out that one of Richard's shoulders was higher than the other, as did the later Elizabethan chronicler Raphael Holinshed.

Richard came to be known as 'Richard Crookback' and 'Richard the Usurper'. Shakespeare's Richard is called 'crookback' in *Henry VI, Part 3*. In the play, Prince Edward calls Gloucester a 'scolding crookback' and 'mis-shapen Dick', Edward IV 'lascivious' and Clarence 'perjured'. The prince calls all three usurpers, before being killed by them. Unhappily for Ricardians, Edward IV was known for his carnality, Clarence for his treason and lies, and Richard of Gloucester as a 'crookback' in Shakespeare's day, so it seems that the 'Tudor spin doctor' had no little knowledge of these Plantagenets. The *OED*'s first recorded use of 'hunchbacked' is the second quarto of Shakespeare's *Richard III* (1598). Queen Elizabeth Woodville in *Richard III* calls Richard 'that foule hunch-backt toade' and also 'bunch-backt' – it may well be that hunch is a printer's error for bunch. Hutton says, 'Richard was about five feet four, rather runted, but only made crooked by his enemies; and wanted six weeks of thirty-three. Henry was twenty-seven, slender, and near five feet nine, with a saturnine countenance, yellow hair, and grey eyes.' From the latter description, Penn and others wrongly use the term 'sallow' to describe Henry, but few blondes have a sallow complexion. Saturnine relates to the 'doctrine of humours' and means gloomy, not dark.

University of Leicester archaeologists took four small bone samples for radio-carbon dating and analysis from one of the ribs of the Greyfriars skeleton and sent them to two specialist units with the facilities to analyse them: the Scottish Universities Environmental Research Centre (SUERC) at the University of Glasgow, and the Oxford Radiocarbon Accelerator Unit, part of the University of Oxford's Research Laboratory for Archaeology and the History of Art. The SUERC results showed a 95 per cent probability that the bone samples dated from around 1430–1460, and in Oxford the results both came out at around 1412–1449, again with a 95 per cent confidence.

These findings seemed to disprove that it was Richard's skeleton. However, the proportion of C-14 in the atmosphere, and hence in living things, is not constant but varies over the centuries, and it also varies between the atmosphere and the oceans. Radiocarbon dating of marine organisms can be out by up to several hundred years, and this effect can occur to a lesser degree in terrestrial life where seafood forms part of the diet.

The mass spectrometry of the Greyfriars bone samples revealed that the individual in question had a high-protein diet, including a significant proportion of seafood, which would seem reasonable for a member of the royal family. Bearing in mind that the results could therefore not be later than the 1538 dissolution of the friary, a Bayesian statistic modelling technique gives the approximate date as 1475–1530 (with a 69 per cent confidence). This does not prove that the bones are those of the king, but removes one possibility which could have proved that these are not Richard's remains. Obviously 69 per cent is not a high level of confidence, and whether the reanalysis is scientifically sound is outside this author's sphere of knowledge, but one assumes that this is the case.

The skeleton is of a small male, and early Latin accounts note Richard's small frame and narrow face. Rous says that Richard was both 'corpore parvus', small in body, and 'viribus debilis', weak in terms of physical strength. Vergil also states that the king's stature was very small ('statura fuit pusilla'), and More also calls him 'habitu corporis exiguo', and 'little of stature' in the English version. Vergil presents Richard as using his size to help his claim to the throne, asking the clergyman Ralph Shaa to give a sermon on how the strapping Edward IV was not Richard of York's son because Edward was 'great in stature', while his father Duke Richard of York was very small. Edward was 6 feet 4 inches, the tallest English monarch. Also, Edward had a 'generous-sized face', while Richard of York's was 'small and compact', and 'no man could doubt that Richard was the true son of the Duke'.

At a press conference upon 4 February 2013, the University of Leicester confirmed that the human remains of King Richard III had been positively identified. They revealed a range of supporting evidence, including DNA analysis, radiocarbon dating and skeletal examination – proving the identity of the skeleton. DNA from the skeleton matched two of Richard III's maternal line relatives. A genealogist had verified these living relatives of Richard III's family. 'Surface loss on a number of back teeth and upper-right teeth suggest he also suffered from stress-related bruxism, or teeth grinding.' Richard was known to tug his lower lip when stressed, and this may be related.

The Leicester team is investigating the paternal DNA of the remains. Kevin Schürer, a historian at the university, found four descendants of John of Gaunt, Richard III's great-great-grandfather. Dr Turi King checked that the Y chromosome, which is carried only by men, matched, establishing that they were all true descendants of John of Gaunt. Although the Y-DNA from the skeleton is somewhat degraded, Dr King hopes that there can be a match to the men. As yet, however, there is better DNA evidence upon the maternal side, mtDNA. John Ashdown-Hill used genealogical research to identify an all-female-line descendant of Cecily Neville, Richard's mother. Ashdown-Hill discovered that a British-born woman who had migrated to Canada, Joy Ibsen (*née* Brown), was a sixteenth-generation great-niece of the king in the same direct maternal line.

From Ashdown-Hill's account on the website plantagenetdna.webs.com we read,

> When I first made contact with her [2005], Joy had no idea that she was descended from the house of York, but fortunately she was fascinated by the idea. Even more fortunately she agreed to provide a DNA sample, the analysis of which led to a DNA sequence, which is the sequence not only of Joy herself, but also of Edward IV, Richard III and Margaret of York. It was very fortunate that I found Joy in time to record her mtDNA sequence. Joy died in 2008. She has living children, but it seems probable that her all-female line of descent from Anne of York – an unbroken line, preserved for us through a total of 17 generations – is now coming to an end, and I don't currently know of any other. Nevertheless, her DNA sequence is now on record. It belongs to one of the rarer European groups, and is believed to indicate descent from a population which migrated to Europe from the near east in comparatively recent times (in the order of 10,000 years or so ago).

However, scientifically speaking, the reality is that such analysis did not lead to a 'DNA sequence', but to the inheritance of a single nucleotide variation.

There is some real confusion about whether Joy Ibsen's mtDNA sequence has been used throughout the research process. It is said that the now deceased Joy Ibsen's mitochondrial DNA was tested and belongs to mtDNA haplogroup J, which by deduction should be the mitochondrial DNA haplogroup of Richard III. Her son is Michael Ibsen, a cabinetmaker in Canada, who agreed to have his DNA tested. The genetic work also led to 'another individual in the maternal line' who wanted to remain anonymous. Michael Ibsen's mitochondrial DNA and that of the anonymous donor matched the DNA extracted from the skeleton. Unlike nuclear DNA, mitochondrial DNA is not usually unique to individuals, but it is far more prevalent in the body and more likely to be found when remains are very old, or not much is left, hence its frequent use in forensic investigations. The DNA signature shared by the skeleton, Michael Ibsen and the third individual, called haplotype J1c2c, is quite rare, says King, making the match a strong argument for relatedness.

Buckley *et al.* record,

The genealogical link between the two modern-day descendants and Richard III has also been verified. Initial analysis of the mitochondrial DNA has revealed a match between sequences in the control region of the mtDNA from the skeleton and two direct descendants of Richard III's sister, Anne of York, through the female line. All three also share a type of mtDNA that is relatively rare in the population of Europe, so it is highly unlikely that the match is coincidental. Further genetic research will not change these conclusions, and full results will be published when the analysis is completed by Turi King.

The researchers stated that they have used the two

living descendants to 'triangulate' the DNA results, misusing the word 'descendants', as Richard III has no living descendants. They were descendants of his mother Cecily, via Richard's eldest sister Anne of York. The evidence rests upon whether Michael Ibsen and the anonymous DNA donor have sufficiently rare mtDNA to make it unlikely that they both match the dead king by chance. However, they must also not be too closely related. If Richard III's living descendants shared a common female ancestor even 150 years ago, their DNA could still be too close for the pair to count as distinct samples, states Mark Thomas, Professor of Evolutionary Genetics at UCL.

There is now a problem. Many scientists believe that the 'anonymous donor' is Joy Ibsen, the deceased mother of Michael Ibsen, whom the historical researcher John Ashdown-Hill met in 2005. If this is the case, or if the anonymous donor is Michael Ibsen's sister, we possibly cannot trust the DNA evidence. The team may not have had the proper informed consent of Joy Ibsen, who died in 2008 in London, Ontario. It is not at all clear. If the team had access to Joy's sample and did not use it, they should so state this and the reasons it could not be used. Was her DNA sampled prior to her death or after her death? Ashdown-Hill is quoted as saying, 'Eventually I traced one line to Joy Ibsen in Canada, and I contacted her and she gave a DNA sample.' This certainly implies Joy Ibsen's consent was gained. Besides the DNA sample from the skeleton and that from Michael Ibsen, they sought a third sample (and perhaps a fourth one) for mtDNA triangulation purposes and indeed one of the DNA samples may have been from Joy. Mitochondrial DNA is transmitted along the line of mothers, the matrilineage.

Further evidence that Joy had her DNA tested is here:

> They will also be subjected to DNA analysis. The remains will be matched against the DNA of Joy Ibsen, a 16th generation descendant of Anne of York, the sister of Richard III. Mrs Ibsen died four years ago, aged 82. At the site yesterday, Mrs Ibsen's son Michael, 55, watched as the search began. The furniture-maker, who was born in Canada but now lives in London, said his mother would have been thrilled by the project ... 'The family were entertained when she got the call several years ago from a historian claiming she was a descendant,' he added.
>
> *Daily Mail*, 24 August 2012

However, Dr Turi King, the geneticist who performed the analysis, has identified the anonymous second person tested as both male and a second cousin of Ibsen's.

MtDNA degrades over time. A 500-year-old skeleton may only provide 50–150 usable fragments (from out of 15,000 original base pairs). What if the fragments contained a previous mutation (in the living individual) that skews the results? Also mtDNA is not appropriate in pinpointing identity, just broad population identification. Anyone could have the same mtDNA as in those 50-150 fragments, and not be related to Richard III directly, though that person could be related to the same population as the king. Mark Thomas of University College London says, 'It is right that they used mitochondrial DNA based on the maternal line ... since genealogical evidence for the paternal lineage cannot be trusted ... I could have the same mitochondrial DNA as Richard III and not be related to him.' In other words, 'people can have matching mitochondrial DNA by chance and not be related'.

The skeleton's haplogroup J is one of the less common haplogroups, and once one reduces the type to J1c2c, one is greatly reducing the number of possible matches. What was missing from the announcement was any indication of how common such mtDNA sequences might be in Western European populations. Any presence of amplified DNA (e.g. of the distant cousin) can easily create cross-over contamination, and since the exhumation, Dr King has taken appropriate steps to avoid such contamination, using the most specialised laboratories in the field.

The research team said that 'only a few percent of Europeans' carry the same mtDNA as Ibsen, but geneticists state that '1 percent of the English population carries this type'. Chris Tyler-Smith, a geneticist at the Wellcome Trust Sanger Institute near Cambridge, said the mitochondrial DNA type identified by Dr Turi King at Leicester was 'rare enough to be interesting, but not rare enough to be conclusive'. At best mtDNA is corroborative *versus* definitive proof of an individual's identity. Mitochondrial DNA thus has limitations. It does reflect the deepest ancestry, but is also prone to contamination, especially concerning skeletons interred improperly for centuries in damp soil. Timothy Bestor, Professor of Genetics and Development at Columbia University Medical Centre, is quoted in the NY *Academy of Sciences* article, 'Skeletal Remains of King Richard III Reportedly Discovered', as saying that the possible quality of the mitochondrial DNA, under the given circumstances, was one of his key reasons for scepticism: 'After 500 years or more in a wet environment like England's, the microbes are going to degrade the DNA. It's just food to them.'

Dr Bestor argues that beyond the high risk of sample contamination, there are other 'particularly complicating factors'. It is often an overlooked fact that 'the English aristocracy reproduced within a closed gene pool in order to preserve lineages. This inbreeding results in consanguinity ... You may have the same mitochondrial haplotype, but that does not guarantee a lineal descent from a given individual.' Mitochondrial DNA analysis is not the same as Y haplotype DNA analysis because it focuses on deeper ancestry whereas male haplotype DNA analysis is linked to more recent male lines. Bestor also points out the possibility of adoption. A confounding factor is that, in the seventeen to twenty-five generations separating Richard III's sister from her extant relatives, there is a fair chance that children of deceased parents may have been adopted by their parents' siblings somewhere along the way. Medieval lives were short, and such adoptions may have been kept private and excluded from historical or genealogical records. The possibility of an adoption or any type of non-paternity event increases as one delves back into the distant past of any family tree.

Some scientists have raised concerns upon the internet that there has been a lack of control and no co-publication of data on the sensitivity and selectivity of the genetic probes used. Where was the contemporaneous data (e.g. parallel comparative data on other known Bosworth Field victims) to give context to the selectivity of the seventeenth successive generation linkage found? Because of due process of research, we will have to wait until 2014 for a peer review, a scientific paper and experimental data.

Maria Avila, a computational biologist at the Center for GeoGenetics at the American Natural History Museum tells us, 'The DNA results presented today are too weak, as they stand, to support the claim that [the] DNA [sample] is actually from Richard III ... more in-depth DNA analysis summed to the archaeological and osteological [bone analysis] results would make a round story.' She is requesting autosomal DNA analysis and wonders about contamination with the type of DNA testing that was done. Mitochondrial DNA is contained in the part of the cell that transforms nutrients to energy; and ancient DNA is very susceptible to contamination. Avila agrees with Thomas, and warned in an email to the website LiveScience that people could share mtDNA even if they did not share a family tree. To be confident that Michael Ibsen is related to the owner of the disinterred skeleton, the researchers must present statistics showing how common the DNA profile is in the United Kingdom, otherwise, the similarities between Ibsen's mtDNA and the skeleton's could be coincidental.

Avila noted that she does not necessarily disbelieve the team's conclusion that the skeleton is Richard III's, only that the DNA evidence isn't the strongest piece of the puzzle: 'It seems to me that osteological as well as archaeological evidence is stronger, however "DNA evidence" sounds fancier so it looks like they used it as the hook to capture the attention of media.'

Charles Brunner, seventeenth great-nephew of Richard, says that York would be the only appropriate resting place for the last monarch of the House of York. The Duke of Gloucester, patron of the

Richard III Society, says that it made him 'emotional' when he saw the remains. He said he could see why Leicester and York wanted him 'for business and tourist reasons'. Fifteen living relatives of Richard III are threatening to launch a legal challenge seeking Richard III's reburial in York Minster, rather than the proposed Leicester Cathedral. They have somehow managed to launch their campaign under the banner of the catch-all Article 8 of the European Convention, which guarantees the right to a private and family life.

The Plantagenet Alliance, which claims the fifteen descendants of relatives of the king as members, insists York is the most appropriate place, pointing out that although he was born in Fotheringhay, Northamptonshire, he grew up in Middleham in Yorkshire and visited York several times during his reign. A University of Leicester spokesman said, 'As the [archaeology excavation] licence holder, the university is responsible for the location of reinterment. Our decision was, and remains, that Richard III should be reinterred at Leicester Cathedral. Reinterment on the nearest consecrated ground is in keeping with good archaeological practice. Richard has lain in the shadow of St Martin's Cathedral, Leicester, for over 500 years. Richard III is believed to have no living descendants. Any distant relations are therefore descended from his siblings. Statistically speaking, many tens of thousands of individuals alive today are descended in this way. There is no obligation to consult living relatives where remains are older than 100 years.'

Leicester City Council is planning a permanent exhibition centre overlooking the car park that covers the foundations of the medieval Greyfriars church. Tourists will replace worshippers, as they head like pilgrims to seek the holy relics of a warrior king, bringing extra alms to the cathedral and its environment. Sir Peter Soulsby, Mayor of Leicester, announced the king's skeleton would be reinterred at Leicester Cathedral in early 2014 in a 'Christian-led but ecumenical service'. The Conservative MP Chris Skidmore proposed a state funeral for the king, while the Labour MP for Bassetlaw asked for Worksop in his constituency, halfway between York and Leicester. Sir Peter Soulsby (not a native of Leicester) stated, 'Those bones leave Leicester over my dead body.' A High Court judge ruled in August 2013 that the Plantagenet Alliance had a case for the king to be buried in York. Leicester was only given cathedral status in 1927, and as of 19 August, 27,713 people had signed a Government e-petition for him to be interred in York Minster as against 8,268 for Leicester. There seems no real precedent for burying someone in a particular area, with which they have no connection, other than that they were killed there.

There is also growing lobby in the UK advocating a Catholic reinterment with a requiem Mass of the pre-Reformation monarch. The design commissioned for the society is for a free-standing table tomb and features Richard's boar, the white rose for the House of York and the cross of St Cuthbert, this being a symbol of Richard's 'piety'. Piety could be achieved by purchasing pardons in the Middle Ages. Devout believers in the Roman Church could literally get away with anything and still go to Heaven if they confessed and paid enough to the Church. In Richard's case his gifts to the Church, in exchange for forgiveness for his sins, came from illegal confiscations of properties and fees.

In February 2013 Leicester Cathedral announced their procedure and preliminary timetable for the interment. On 12 February they announced that Richard III will be buried inside the cathedral, in a 'place of honour'. He will be in a £1 million raised tomb. Leicester City Council has spent £850,000 to buy the freehold of St Martin's Place, formerly part of Leicester Grammar School, across the road from the cathedral. The site adjoins the car park where the body was found, and overlies the chancel of the Greyfriars Friary church. The council intends to convert the building into a Richard III museum. Richard's bones will become the latest in Christian relics to attract pilgrims, aka today's tourists, with income to spend.

The process of rewriting history is ongoing, as cathedrals and churches squabble for the relics. In this context, Philippa Langley's full speech at the 4 February 2013 'Looking For Richard' project press conference is reported here:

Today marks the culmination of an extraordinary journey of discovery. When I embarked on the Looking For Richard project 4 years ago – the quest to find a king in a car park – almost everyone thought I was mad. Let's face it, it's not the easiest pitch in the world – to look for a king under a council car park – but luckily the R3 Soc, LCC, and the University, as well as C4 and DSP – partners with vision, came on board. But, as we got ready to look for Richard, at the 11th hour one of our funding bodies pulled. The dig was to be cancelled so, together with writer Annette Carson we launched an international appeal. The search for Richard was saved by donations from around the world, but they also gave the project its mandate when they said – search for him – find him – honour him.

Richard III *gave us the system of bail and opened up the printing industry, giving us books and the freedom of information. He also initiated – and applied – the legal principles of the Presumption of Innocence and Blind Justice.* [Author's emphasis] It is ironic then that Richard is still presumed guilty of the murder of his nephews, until proven innocent, even though there is no evidence that points to him having killed them. The Richard III Society is founded on a simple principle – that truth is more powerful than lies. It also considers that when investigating someone you have two sources – those that knew them, and those that didn't. They believe that your primary source must always be those that knew them.

After Richard's death at Bosworth the men of the north who had known Richard – man and boy – described him thus: The most famous Prince of blessed memory. In the intervening centuries since King Richard's death many have told his story, not least Shakespeare and the Tudor writers. But now, here today, it is Richard who has finally been able to reveal himself. When Richard's body was stripped naked at Bosworth his physical condition, his scoliosis, became known, and it was used to insult and degrade him. Today we know that a physical abnormality is not a sign of evil. We find this idea abhorrent. We are no longer in the Tudor mind-set.

On Channel 4 this evening, and tomorrow morning at the R3 Soc conference, you will see Richard's face for the very first time through the facial reconstruction by Prof. Caroline Wilkinson of the University of Dundee. The 2-dimensional caricature promoted by the Tudors will be no more. In September 2010, the

Looking For Richard project commissioned the design of a tomb based upon Richard's life and what was important and meaningful to him. Undertaken by a team of Ricardians, it has been welcomed by the cathedral, council and R3 Soc and will be revealed in the next few weeks. The first donation of £10,000 has already been received.

The discovery of King Richard is an historic moment when the history books will be rewritten ... a wind of change is blowing ... one that will now seek out the truth about the real Richard III. And as regards our mandate from those around the world: We have searched for Richard, and we have found him – it is now time to honour him.

The text on the screen is the Act of Parliament that settled the crown upon King Richard and his heirs – all copies of which Henry Tudor tried to destroy. Be it pronounced, decreed, and declared, that our said Sovereign Lord, the King was, and is, very and undoubted King of England.

One could deconstruct the whole of the above speech, but the elements in the process of Richard's hagiography are fairly absurd, as demonstrated in the sentences I have italicised above. The system of bail existed in Saxon times, and from Norman times onward, sheriffs (and the Marcher Lords) possessed sovereign authority to hold or release suspected criminals. However, some sheriffs might exploit the bail for their own gain. In 1275 the Statute of Westminster limited the discretion of sheriffs with respect to the bail. Sheriffs still had the authority to fix the amount of bail required, but the statute stipulated which crimes were bailable and which were not.

Upon 23 January 1484, Richard's only parliament assembled. It passed eighteen private statutes and fifteen public ones. The eighteen private statutes consisted of *Titulus Regius* claiming title to the throne, various attainders, inheritance claims and benefits for individuals. The fifteen public statutes were involved with ending benevolences, protecting land purchase rights ('clear title'), reforming the justice system, preventing commercial dishonesty in the cloth trade, protecting the English merchant, preventing fraudulent collection practices and an Act against the former queen Elizabeth Woodville. Professor Harold Hanbury assessed Richard's new laws in 1962, and only the third private statute seems to have any application to the claims above: 'every Justice of the Peace may let a prisoner to mainprize. [This is the taking or receiving of a person into friendly custody who might otherwise be committed to prison, upon security given that he shall be forthcoming at a time and place assigned.] No officer shall seize the goods of a prisoner until he be attainted.' The statute allowed 'bail to those suspected of felony, protected them from imprisonment before trial, and at the same time prevented their goods being forfeited before conviction.' The law simply gave more protection to those deemed to be on bail, rather than 'gave us the system of bail', as Langley states.

Again, it is not discoverable where Richard gave us the 'presumption of innocence and blind justice'. The representation of justice as 'blind' did not occur in the fifteenth century, and equality of treatment for different classes did not feature in his laws. Also, the maxim 'innocent until proven guilty' is well-known, and was incorporated into the United Nations Declaration of Human Rights in 1948. However, it cannot be found in Magna Carta, the English Bill of Rights of 1689, the Declaration of Independence, or in the Constitution of the United States; nor in the works of the greatest English legal writers in history: Bracton, Coke, and Blackstone. The maxim 'innocent until proven guilty' cannot be found in any English court case or any jurisprudential treatise before around 1800. The origin seems to be in the French Declaration of the Rights of Man and Citizen of 1789, which stated that 'every man is presumed innocent until declared guilty'.

However, Langley's main piece of disinformation seems to be that Richard 'opened up the printing industry, giving us books and the [sic] freedom of information'. This is quite a claim, as in a previous work (*Breverton's Encyclopedia of Inventions*) I gave Johannes Gutenberg the credit for printing and printed books between 1436 and 1440, and also freedom of information is still a tenuous concept for many authorities. The mercer (merchant) William Caxton (1420s–1492) was based in the trading centre of Bruges. In the early 1470s he also spent time in Cologne, where he first engaged with the new process of printing books. Around 1473, probably in Bruges, Caxton was responsible for the first book to be printed in English. Late in 1475 or early in 1476 he came to Westminster and set up the first English press. The first substantial book produced by him in England was probably Chaucer's *Canterbury Tales* in 1478. To make money, Caxton needed to sell books to the wealthy public, but also needed patronage and sponsorship from the highest levels of society. He seems to have written extensive prefaces to maintain political connections in the rapidly shifting situation during the reigns of Edward IV, Richard III, and Henry

VII. Like most mercers, he supported the Yorkist side of the Wars of the Roses.

Caxton was close to Margaret of York, Duchess of Burgundy, the sister of Edward IV, and later allied himself to the family of Elizabeth Woodville, Edward IV's wife. Margaret gave Caxton an annual fee. One surviving copy of 1473–74 *The Recuyell of the Histories of Troy*, the first book in English, has a specially made engraving showing Caxton presenting the book to Margaret. Caxton dedicated his English edition of the history of Jason to Elizabeth's eldest son, Edward V, who was to be murdered in the Tower of London. Queen-consort Elizabeth's brother Anthony Woodville, Earl Rivers, was an extremely important patron of Caxton, until his murder by Richard III in 1483. Three French works translated by Earl Rivers were published by Caxton, one of them appearing in three editions.

With the death of Edward IV in April 1483, the murder of that king's two sons in the Tower of London and the fall of the Woodville family, Caxton lost his powerful friends at court. However, Caxton remained loyal to Elizabeth Woodville after Edward's death, while she lived in refuge from Richard III in sanctuary at Westminster Abbey. Around April 1484 Caxton dedicated to Richard III his translation of the *Ordre of Chyvalry or Knyghthode*. This is his only known connection with Richard III, and it was a diplomatic act as he was a friend of the ousted Woodvilles. With the new Tudor dynasty, in 1489 Caxton was commissioned by Margaret Beaufort, Henry VII's mother, to translate and print the romance *Blanchardyn and Eglantine*. Through John de Vere, the Earl of Oxford, he obtained a commission from Henry

VII for an English translation of Christine de Pisan's *Faits d'armes et de Chevalerie*, completed in 1489.

The Earl of Oxford also commissioned the translation and printing of the *Four Sons of Aymon*, and in 1490 Caxton dedicated to Arthur, Prince of Wales, his English translation of a French romance, *Eneydos*. In 1491, towards the end of his life, he printed the *Fifteen Oes*, a collection of prayers, by the commandments of Margaret Beaufort and Elizabeth of York, respectively Henry VII's mother and wife. In 1490 his new connections with the court also gave him the job of printing the statutes enacted by the first three parliaments of Henry VII, the first time statutes of England were printed in English rather than legal French. How, from this history of Caxton's work, Richard III in his short reign 'opened up the printing industry' is beyond this researcher. However, Lord Rivers is spoken of by Commines as 'un très gentil chevalier', and by Sir Thomas More as 'a right honourable man, as valiant of hand as politic in counsel'. His protection and encouragement of Caxton were of inestimable value to English literature, and in the preface to the *Dictes* Caxton gives an account of his relations with the statesman which illustrates the dignity and modesty of Lord Rivers in a very agreeable way. Rivers was one of the purest writers of English prose of his time, and far more important in the history of printing than the man who had ordered his murder.

One further note upon the rewriting of history: in her recent non-fiction book, *Anne Neville: Richard's Tragic Queen*, Amy Licence fondly describes the 2013 facial reconstruction of Richard from his skull.

The face of Richard III had a strong nose and jaw but

the reconstruction captured a pleasantness, a softness about the mouth and eyes, even a half smile. Dressed in a dark wig and soft velvet cap with a dangling jewel, after the style of the portraits, it exudes a certain unexpected charisma. It was not difficult to see the man whom Anne Neville may have fallen in love with...

We might compare this to another Ricardian-leaning writer's description of Henry VII's effigy in the next chapter.

9

The Evidence: a Black, Grey or White King?

Each 22 August, an obituary is inserted into major newspapers including the *New York Times*: 'PLANTAGENET – Richard, great king and true friend of the rights of man, died at Bosworth Field on August 22, 1485. Murdered by traitors and, dead, maligned by knaves ...'

The beginning of the rehabilitation of Richard 'Crookback' was the research of Sir George Buck (1560–1622), Master of the Revels, who died insane. His major work, *The History of the Life and Reigne of Richard III*, was not published until 1646. Buck discovered the only known copy of the Act of Parliament, *Titulus Regius*, which brought Richard III to the throne. Buck found it in the *Croyland Chronicle*. Buck also claimed to have seen a letter written to John Howard, 1st Duke of Norfolk, by Elizabeth of York, dated shortly before the death of Richard's Queen Anne. In it Elizabeth declares her love for Richard

III and her hope of becoming his wife. Buck wrote that the letter asks Norfolk 'to be a mediator for her to the King, in behalf of the marriage propounded between them', who was her 'onely joy and maker in this world', and that she was his in heart and thought: 'withall insinuating that the better part of February was past, and that she feared the Queen would never die'. The original letter, if it ever existed, is now lost. The corrupted text can be interpreted as suggesting that Elizabeth was asking Norfolk to arrange her marriage to someone else, not Richard. That such sentiments should have been expressed about a man responsible for the murder of her infant brothers seems so improbable that most historians have chosen to doubt the letter's existence.

Buck may have begun his history in 1619, the date of its dedication. Buck continued to revise it into 1620, but gradually abandoned the effort as his mind failed. He died in October 1622. A much-corrupted version of his history was published eventually by his great-nephew in 1646. Loyalty is emphasised by Buck as his rationale for writing his work: the loyalty of Richard to his brother King Edward IV (1442–83), and the loyalty of the Buck family to the Yorkist cause. Buck's great-grandfather, Sir John Buck of Harthill, fought for Richard at Bosworth, and Buck believes that he was beheaded with Catesby at Leicester. This author can as yet find no evidence of this, and John Buck may instead have been killed in battle at Bosworth, being among those attainted by Henry VII.

George Buck had been educated at Cambridge and subsequently went on to the Inns of Court. In 1588 he was appointed esquire of the body and on James I's accession he became a gentleman of the privy chamber and was knighted. Appointed Master of the Revels in 1603, Buck was responsible for censoring plays and arranging court entertainments, including a number of Shakespeare's plays. The timing of Buck's *History of the Life and Reigne,* during the reign of James I, is not surprising as it attempts to undermine what is now called 'the Tudor propaganda campaign' against Richard III. It was in the interests of the new Scottish Stuart dynasty not to glorify their English predecessors, the Tudors. We see parallels with political parties when they exchange power – Republicans blame Democrats and vice versa for the state of the USA and promise better when in or out of power, as do Labour and the Conservatives in Britain. Buck later fell out of favour in court, and died insane, overwhelmed by debts.

Buck makes a strong emphasis on the legality of Richard's claim to the throne. He notes the arguments set out in *Titulus Regius,* which had been ratified by Parliament and which established the illegitimacy of the children of Edward IV and Richard III's subsequent legal right to succeed him. While not denying the murder of Hastings, Buck set out to demolish More's account of the murders of Edward V and his brother Prince Richard in the Tower. Buck points out that Richard did not have a motive for killing the princes, since he had already declared them illegitimate. It could be also argued that the daughters of Edward IV and Elizabeth Woodville survived, and would have inherited their brother's claims to the throne had the boys predeceased them. Buck argued that no murder took place under Richard. The main suspects apart from Richard are Henry VII, Buckingham and, somehow, Henry VII's mother, Lady Margaret Beaufort. Buck strongly argues that Edward V died naturally (but why no public announcement or funeral?), and that his brother Richard, Duke of York, escaped and became known as the pretender Perkin Warbeck.

Both Buck and his grand-nephew had reasons to reassess Richard in a favourable light, gaining favour by blackening the previous dynasty's claims to the throne. There was an identical circumstance under the new German Hanover dynasty. In both England and America Bishop William Stubbs (1825–1901) became universally acknowledged as the head of all English historical scholars, and no English historian of his time was held in equal honour in European countries. In 1866, Stubbs began writing *The Constitutional History of England* (1873–78), revolutionising the teaching of British history from the time of the 'noble' and civilising influence of the Romans, up to 1485. His Germanophile book was written to be the official curriculum for all schools and colleges – the history of Romans, Anglo-Saxons and Normans – not the history of the British people.

Bishop Stubbs wrote, in his *Select Charters from the beginning to 1307* (Oxford ninth edition, 1951), the following piece of pre-Hitlerian dogma. The Welsh, i.e. the original British people, were a

> tolerated remnant ... The English nation is of distinctly Teutonic or German origin. The Angles, Jutes and Saxons ... Entered upon a land ... whose inhabitants were enervated and demoralised by long dependence, wasted by successive pestilences, worn-out by the attacks of half-savage neighbours and by their own suicidal wars ... This new race was the prime stock of our forefathers, sharing the primaeval German pride of purity of extraction ... and strictly careful of

the distinction between themselves and the tolerated remnant of their predecessors ... It is unnecessary to suppose that any general intermixture either of Roman or British blood has affected this national identity ... from the Briton and the Roman of the fifth century we have received nothing... The first traces, then, of our national history must be sought not in Britain but in Germany.

Stubbs' work is still the basis of what is taught (and unfortunately believed) today. The pagan Anglo-Saxons practised genocide across England, forcing the Christian British, speaking the British language, westward into Wales, the West Country and Cumbria. Another population was pushed into Strathclyde by the Picts and Scots. Children are not taught that the Venerable Bede praised the barbarian Germans for victory against the Christian Welsh at Bangor-upon-Dee around 606.

Brian Davies has written that our understanding of British history is still subject to the prejudices of nineteenth-century 'Saxon nationalism':

The Times in a reply to a polite letter from Matthew Arnold asserted that: 'An Eisteddfod is one of the most mischievous pieces of sentimentalism which could possibly be perpetrated ... Not only the energy and power, but the intelligence and music of Europe have mainly come from Teutonic sources ... The sooner all Welsh specialities disappear from the face of the Earth the better.' This is a clear enough agenda, which will be familiar to many. What may not be fully appreciated is that, although most of the Welsh were Nonconformist by the 19th century, the early history of the Church in Wales was still a prime target for these Teutonic racists. For them it was an uncomfortable problem that the foundation of the Church of England can only be pushed back to 597 AD when Augustine landed in Kent, while the major figures of the Welsh 'Age of the Saints' were active between half a century and a century earlier.

Christian civilisation in Britain had to be presented as an achievement of the English. The Welsh Church could only be allowed some vitality after the time of Alfred, the celebrated founder of the Saxon state. In order to create the 'Dark Ages' required by Saxon triumphalism, the evidence of the continuous history of the Welsh Church back to Roman times, preceding the foundation of the 'national' Church of England by several centuries, had to be pushed to the margins of consciousness and if possible be literally buried ... It is unfortunate that present day mediaevalists do not normally study nineteenth-century history. If they did they would realise that the basic framework of interpretation of early British history which they still innocently use is not the product of calm, objective collection and assessment of data. It is a politically motivated construct; a falsification of history for the purposes of English nationalism ... We need to write post-Imperialist history free of this Victorian master race theory.

As was stated in the preface to this book, history is not exact. Every political party and dynasty has a different version. In Britain today our history glorifies Germanic and then Franco-Danish invaders at the expense of the native British people. As regards the Tudor dynasty, it was disparaged by those who have a preference for the previous Plantagenets and those who favour the succeeding Stuarts, and all of British history has been affected by pro-Germanic Hanoverian propaganda.

In an article in *The Guardian*, 2 March 2012, upon how Henry VII 'branded' the Tudors, Thomas Penn called Henry 'the most flagrant usurper of them all, the half-blooded Lancastrian exile who, with a meagre claim to the throne, won the battle of Bosworth and founded England's most notorious dynasty, the Tudors'. The most flagrant usurper? As in his recent pejoratively titled book upon Henry, *The Winter King*, this author is demonstrating his writing abilities with the type of florid prose used by romantic novelists to sell books. This 'half-blooded' exile sounds like one of J. K. Rowling's characters. Unfortunately, research abilities are required by historians – they need to balance facts and evidence. Historical researchers will find that Richard's claims to the throne rested upon centuries of violence and bloodshed, not upon what he would call a royal bloodline – no such thing exists in Britain. The present English royal family changed its name to Windsor, and Prince Philip changed his name to Mountbatten. Indeed, without these name changes, Charles Prince of Wales, who is a quarter Scottish and three-quarters Germanic, would not be named Charles Windsor but officially Charles of Schleswig-Holstein-Sonderburg-Glücksburg, Battenburg, Wettin and Saxe-Coburg and Gotha. This is hardly an English royal bloodline.

Let us, for argument's sake, assume Edward III was a 'rightful king'. In fact his great-great-grandfather, John, had usurped the throne and killed the rightful king, but let that pass. Edward III had five sons: the eldest was Edward the Black Prince, whose son Richard II was murdered by Henry IV; the next son was William of Hatfield, who died in infancy; the next was Lionel of Antwerp; the third-oldest surviving son was John of Gaunt; the fourth was Edmund of Langley; and the fifth Thomas of Woodstock. The fourth son, Edmund of Langley, Duke of York, had two sons, the eldest being Edward, 2nd Duke of York, and the youngest being Richard, 3rd Earl of Cambridge. The second son, Cambridge, received no lands from his father Edmund, was not mentioned in either his father's or his brother's wills, and may have been the child of an illicit liaison between his mother Isabella of Castille and the Duke of Exeter.

Cambridge had two sons: Henry of York, who probably died young, and Richard of York, who fortunately inherited his dukedom from an uncle. Richard III was the fourth and youngest son of Richard of York (his third-eldest brother, Clarence, was executed by his oldest brother, Edward IV, and his second-oldest brother, Edmund of Rutland, was killed aged seventeen at Wakefield). Thus Richard was the fourth son of a second son of a possibly illegitimate second son of a fourth son. This is hardly a straightforward succession of a full-blooded royal bloodline, which Penn would seem to require. Also, speaking of the 'purity' of a royal line, Richard of Cambridge was the grandson of Pedro the Cruel of Castille and his favourite mistress. Again, the required purity seems to be missing. Finally, Richard III's claim to the throne came from Richard of Cambridge's wife, Anne Mortimer. Her father, the Earl of March, was heir presumptive to Richard II via his mother Philippa Plantagenet, the daughter of Lionel, 1st Duke of Clarence. Again, Richard III's mother, the wife of Richard of York, was Cecily Neville. Her mother was Joan Beaufort, the daughter of John of Gaunt and Katherine Swynford. Ricardians claim that this line had been bastardised by Parliament, so Henry, the son of Margaret Beaufort, had no claim to the throne. The same could be claimed against Richard – no recent books seem to mention this. Anti-Henry writers decry the fact that Henry's real claim came via his mother, whereas in fact Richard's real right also came via his mother. Both inherited through the female line, and if Henry was bastardised, so was Richard.

Hutton made the point in 1788 that out of the leading seventy-four nobles of the House of Anjou/Plantagenets, which became extinct in the male line in 1499, twenty-one males died young, twenty-four in middle age, twenty-one by violence and only eight saw old age:

> If a Plantagenet was destroyed, it was generally by the hand of a Plantagenet; in name always honourable, but frequently dangerous. No family was better acquainted with the axe; and if they shewed no mercy to each other, the stranger could not expect it. They dealt out destruction with a savage hand; hence the nobility and gentry fell by multitudes in the tempests of their wrath.

We can now briefly summarise Richard's involvement in just some of the main events in his short life in the fourteen years from the age of eighteen to his death:

	Person	Event	Richard's involvement
1471	Somerset and other nobles	Killed after battle	Guilty

1471	Prince Edward, crown prince	Killed after battle	Possibly guilty with his brothers
1471	Henry VI	According to *Chronicles of London* 'slaine as it was said by Gloucester'	Possibly guilty
1471	'Bastard of Fauconberg'	Beheaded without trial	Guilty
1473	Anne Beauchamp	Illegally takes lands	Guilty
1473	Clarence, Richard's brother	Richard 'in arms against' Clarence over Beauchamp's property	Guilty
1473	Countess of Oxford, mother-in-law	Illegally takes lands after threats	Guilty
1475	George Neville	Takes Neville lands after special Act of Parliament	Guilty
1476	Isabel Neville, sister-in-law	Poisoned?	Unknown
1478	Clarence, Richard's brother	Implicated in Clarence's guilt and death	Probably guilty, Richard gained the most

1478	Clarence's son Warwick	Takes lands, and other illegal land seizures	Guilty
1478	George Neville	Main beneficiary of degrading George from Dukedom of Bedford	Guilty
1483	George Neville	Dies in unknown circumstances aged 21 at Middleham	Possibly guilty of killing his ward
1483	Edward IV, brother	Poisoned?	Possibly guilty
1483	Essex	Killed	Unknown
1483	Edward V's bodyguard	Wrongly arrested	Guilty
1483	Rivers, queen's brother	Killed without trial	Guilty
1483	Grey, queen's son	Killed without trial	Guilty
1483	Vaughan, Edward V's chamberlain	Killed without trial	Guilty
1483	King Edward V, nephew	Captured and imprisoned	Guilty
1483	Prince Richard, nephew	Captured and imprisoned	Guilty

1483– 1484	Queen (sister-in-law) and her five daughters	Forced into sanctuary	Guilty
1483	Woodvilles (queen's family)	Falsely claims that they had gathered arms to attack him	Guilty
1483	Edward Woodville, queen's brother	Falsely accuses of taking crown treasure	Guilty
1483	Rivers, Grey, Dorset and Woodvilles	Illegally takes estates, as if attainted	Guilty
1483	Hastings, Stanley, Bishop Morton, Bishop Rotherham and others	Wrongly arrested, Stanley injured	Guilty
1483	Lord Hastings	Killed without trial	Guilty
1483	Jane Shore, Queen Elizabeth and queen's mother Jacquetta	Accused of treachery and/or witchcraft	Guilty
1483	Queen-consort Elizabeth	Accused of adultery	Guilty

Year	Person	Action	Verdict
1483	Edward V and brother, nephews	Made illegitimate	Guilty
1483	Cecily Neville, Richard's own mother	Accused of adultery – she denied it in her will	Guilty
1483	Edward V, Richard's nephew	Murdered	Almost definitely guilty
1483	Prince Richard of York, Richard's nephew	Murdered	Almost definitely guilty
1483	Richard of Gloucester	Usurps crown as Richard III	Guilty
1483	Buckingham	Executed without trial	Guilty
1483	Buckingham's heir	Takes his estates (restored by Henry VII)	Guilty
1483	Thomas St Leger, Richard's brother-in-law	Executed despite promising vast monies, confiscated estates	Guilty
1485	Queen Anne	Poisoned?	Possibly guilty
1485	Lord Strange, Stanley's son	Ordered death, but not carried out	Guilty

Colin Richmond has estimated that only six peers turned out for Richard at Bosworth, several for Henry, and the rest stayed home. Richmond points out that many of those present at the battle did not fight, and that many of Richard's Northerners may have been in Northumberland's inactive ranks. In his opinion, what principally happened at Bosworth was the desertion of Richard. This was unsurprising. This author is a Fellow of the Institute of Consulting, a Certified Management Consultant and a Fellow of the Chartered Institute of Marketing, with a career in research and fact-finding. It is a fact that very, very few people in his time trusted Richard. Not surprisingly, few supported him. There was not a well-heeled Southern conspiracy against the impoverished North. A history book will rarely change people's formed opinions, but it is as well to have at least one on record at this time of renewed interest in Richard, which represents a more independent view of that king.

The Winter King is Thomas Penn's first book, and he presented a recent BBC documentary in 2013 with that title. It was announced as 'the dark and chilling world of the winter king', who, after a 'furtive and anxious invasion', used 'ruthless methods' to control England. Penn calls Henry a 'usurper' with 'barely a claim to the throne of England', 'manipulative', paranoid', a 'dark prince' with a 'hunger for power'. His reign was 'one of the strangest in history', a 'bleak wintry landscape', 'oppressive' and 'terrifying'. His effigy portrays 'the face of a man who's never known a moment's peace'. The 'true king' Richard III was 'viciously battered to death' and Lincoln 'slaughtered'. Perhaps someone should inform the writer that both died in battle and medieval battlefields were like slaughterhouses. Henry's 'claim to the throne was precarious', with his grandfather Owen Tudor being a 'chamber servant', 'a fast-talking

Welsh servant, not exactly the best pedigree for a king'. He was 'not of right King of England' – Henry's claim did not come from his paternal grandfather, however.

'Henry VII rewrote history' and 'the Commons was shocked' when he dated his reign to the day before Bosworth. Penn does not repeat the new premarital rape story but merely states that Prince Arthur was born early, and that Henry was devoted to his wife. For some reason Penn seems to resent the fact that Henry minted a new gold coin called the sovereign, with the Tudor rose on the reverse. Henry was distraught when Prince Arthur died, shortly after marrying Katherine of Aragon, and 'beside himself' when Elizabeth died. Penn admits that his 'marriage was one of genuine love and Henry was shattered by her loss ... her death threatened to tear the country apart'. Henry had a 'complete physical collapse' and came 'close to death', grieving for six weeks for Elizabeth. 'Money was dearest to his heart', however. 'He spun a web of surveillance'; he was 'remorseless' and 'obsessed with control, especially when it came to money'. 'To Henry money meant security and control'. Is there anything wrong with this? Richard left an empty Treasury, and Henry was focussed upon passing on the crown peacefully.

Henry had 'a remorseless drive for control', he was 'suspicious and unable to trust people', and 'if his subjects did not love him, he would make them fear him'. He was 'remote', with 'little claim to the throne', a 'wintry, miserly king'. There was very little justifiable content in the programme, filled with adjectives as it was. Moreover, the 'Winter King' title came from a poem by Thomas More, celebrating the new 'spring' of his friend Henry VIII's reign when he came to the throne. More was more than anything a political animal – it proved to be in his interests to celebrate the new king, for which he was richly rewarded until the split with Rome. Penn sagely informs us that spring follows winter, so obviously Henry was a 'Winter King', but this writer knows in which reign, out of Richard III, Henry VII and Henry VIII, he would have preferred to live out his life in relative safety.

A blog was recently set up called 'The Henry VII Appreciation Society'. Unlike the Richard III Society, with its royal patronage, it is a one-man band. It came to the attention of the Richard III Society Yahoo discussion group, and one person said that the site was 'like running an Adolf Hitler appreciation society'. This is one person facing the members of twenty-two national groups of the Richard III Society, plus their American, Continental, Australian, Canadian and New Zealand branches. The writer of this book will face similar virulent criticism. It will be savaged in the book reviews on Amazon, mainly by non-readers, to take its rating and thus popularity down. Truth seems to be an ever-shifting target. Independent readers can decide for themselves whether Richard was 'noble' and whether he deserves an honourable cathedral burial.

Tourists will flock to the king's new cathedral tomb and visitor centre, and receive the truth that the Church and tourist board wish them to hear. Thus our understanding of history slowly changes. By a mixture of information, misinformation, disinformation and selective information, we can make any case we wish.

We can now return to the dedication at the beginning of this book: 'I have always thought the actions of men the best interpreters of their thoughts' (John Locke, *An*

Essay Concerning Human Understanding, 1689). We must also repeat, from the same source: 'It is one thing to show a man that he is in error, and another to put him in possession of the truth.'

Partial List of
Sources

Adams, M., *Echoes of War: A Thousand Years of Military History in Popular Culture* (University Press of Kentucky, 2002)

Arthurson, I., *The Perkin Warbeck Conspiracy, 1491–1499* (The History Press, 2009)

Ashdown-Hill, John, *Eleanor, the Secret Queen: The Woman Who Put Richard III on the Throne* (The History Press, 2010)

Bacon, Sir Francis, *The Historie of the Reigne of King Henry the Seventh*, ed. J. R. Lumby (1622; Cambridge, 1876)

Baldwin, D., *Elizabeth Woodville: Mother of the Princes in the Tower* (Stroud: Sutton, 2002)

Baldwin, D., *Richard III* (Amberley, 2012)

Barnard, E., *New, Comprehensive, and Complete History of England* (London: Alexander Hogg, *c.* 1783)

Barnfield, M., 'Diriment Impediments, Dispensations and Divorce: Richard III and Matrimony', *The Ricardian*, XVII (2007)

Bennett, M. J., *The Battle of Bosworth* (Gloucester: Alan Sutton, 2000)

Brooke, Ralph, *Catalogue and Succession of the Kings, Princes, Dukes, Marquesses, Earles and Viscounts of this Realme of England since the Norman Conquest* (London, 1619 and 1622)

Bruce, J. (ed.), *The Historie of the arrival of Edward IV in England and the Finall Recouerye of His Kingdomes from Henry VI. A.D. M.CCCC.LXXI* (Camden Society, 1838)

Buck, Sir George, *The History of King Richard the Third* (1619; reprint Alan Sutton, 1982)

Buckley, Richard, Mathew Morris, Jo Appleby, Turi King, Deirdre O'Sullivan and Lin Fox, 'The King in the Car Park: New Light on the Death and Burial of Richard III in the Grey Friars Church, Leicester, in 1485', *Antiquity: A Quarterly Review of World Archaeology* 87(336) (2013), pp. 519–38

Carson, A., *Richard III – The Maligned King* (History Press, 2009)

Chrimes, S. B., *Henry VII* (1972; reprinted Yale University Press, 1999)

Clive, M., *This Sun of York* (London: Cardinal, 1973)

Collection of Ordinances and Regulations of the Royal Household, Society of Antiquaries (1790)

Commines, Philipe de, *The Memoirs of Philip de Commines, Lord of Argenton, Volume 1* (H. G. Bohn, 1855)

Cox, J. and N. Pronay (eds), *The Croyland Chronicle Continuations* (1459–86; Gloucester: Sutton, 1986)

Crawford, Anne, *The Yorkists: The History of a Dynasty* (London: Hambledon Continuum, 2007)

Cunningham S., *Richard III: A Royal Enigma* (National Archives, 2003)

Dockray, K., *Richard III: A Source Book* (Sutton, 1997)

Driver, John T., 'Sir Thomas St Leger, *c.* 1439–83: the

Rise and Fall of a Royal Servant During the Reigns of Edward IV and Richard III', *Surrey Archaeological Collections* 94 (2008)

Evans, H. T., *Wales and the Wars of the Roses* (Hardpress reprint, 2013)

Fabyan, Robert, *The New Chronicles of England and France*, ed. Henry Ellis (London: Rivington, 1811)

Fields, Bertram, *Royal Blood: Richard II and the Mystery of the Princes* (New York: Harper Collins, 1998)

Gainsford, Thomas, *The True and Wonderfull History of Perkin Warbeck, Proclaiming Himselfe Richard the Fourth* (London, 1618)

Gairdner, J., 'Did Henry VII Murder the Princes?', *The English Historical Review*, VI(XXIII) (July 1891)

Gairdner, J. (ed.), *Letters and Papers Illustrative of the Reigns of Richard III and Henry VII* (Rolls Series)

Gairdner, J., *Life of Richard III* (2nd ed., 1898)

Gillingham, J. (ed.), *Richard III: A Medieval Kingship* (Collins and Brown, 1993)

Given-Wilson, Christopher (ed.), *Parliament rolls of Medieval England 1275–1504* (Boydell and Brewer, 2005)

Goodman, A., *The Wars of the Roses. The Soldier's Experience* (Gloucester, 2005)

Gristwood, S., *Blood Sisters: The Women Behind the Wars of the Roses* (Harper Press, 2013)

Hall, Edward, *Hall's Chronicle, Containing the History of England During the Reign of Henry IV and the Succeeding Monarchs to the End of the Reign of Henry VIII*, ed. Henry Ellis (1809)

Halsted, C. A., *Richard III as Duke of Gloucester and King of England* (London: Longmans, 1844)

Hammond, P. W., *Edward of Middleham, Prince of Wales* (Kent: Gloucester Group, 1973)

Hammond P. W. and A. F. Sutton (eds), *The Coronation of Richard III: The Extant Documents* (Alan Sutton, 1983)

Hanbury, H. G., 'The Legislation of Richard III', *American Journal of Legal History* (1962)

Hancock, Peter A., *Richard III and the Murder in the Tower* (The History Press, 2011 reprint)

Hanham, Alison, *Richard III and His Early Historians* (Oxford, 1975)

Hicks, Michael, *Anne Neville, Queen to Richard III* (Stroud: Tempus, 2006)

Hicks, Michael, *False, Fleeting, Perjur'd Clarence: George Duke of Clarence 1449–78* (Alan Sutton, 1980)

Hicks, Michael, *Edward IV* (London: Bloomsbury, 2004)

Hicks, Michael, *Edward V: The Prince in the Tower* (Stroud: Tempus, 2003)

Hicks, Michael, *Richard III* (Stroud: History Press, 2001)

Hicks, Michael, *Richard III and His Rivals, Magnates and their Motives in the Wars of the Roses* (London: Hambledon Press, 1981)

Hicks, Michael, 'The Changing Role of the Woodvilles in Yorkist Politics to 1483' in Hipshon, David, *Richard III and the Death of Chivalry* (History Press, 2009)

Hicks, Michael, *Warwick the Kingmaker* (Oxford: Blackwell, 1998)

Horrox, Rosemary, *Richard III: A Study in Service* (Cambridge, 1989)

Hume, David, *The History of England: from the*

Invasion of Julius Caesar to the Accession of Henry VII (1754–61)

Hutton, William, *The Battle of Bosworth Field, Between Richard the Third and Henry Earl of Richmond, August 22, 1485: Wherein is Described the Approach of Both Armies: with a Plan of the Battle, Its Consequences, the Fall, Treatment, and Character of Richard: to which is Prefixed, by Way of Introduction, a History of His Life Till He Assumed the Regal Power* (1788)

Jenkins, Elizabeth, *The Princes in the Tower* (Phoenix Press, 2002)

Jones, Evan D. (ed.), *Gwaith Lewis Glyn Cothi* (Gwasg Prifysgol Cymru, 1953)

Jones, Michael and Philippa Langley, *The King's Grave: The Search for Richard III* (John Murray 2013)

Jones, W. Garmon, 'Welsh Nationalism and Henry Tudor', *Transactions of the Honourable Society of Cymmrodorion*, Session 1917–18

Kendall, Paul Murray, *Richard III* (London: George Allen and Unwin, 1965)

Kendall, Paul Murray (ed.), *Richard III: The Great Debate* (New York: W. W. Norton & Company Inc., 1965)

Kimber, Isaac, *The History of England from the Earliest Accounts of Time, to the Death of the Late Queen Anne Vol. 1* (London,1722)

Kingsford, C. L. (ed.), *Chronicle of London* (1905)

Laynesmith, J. L., *The Last Medieval Queens: English Queenship 1445–1503* (Oxford UP, 2004)

Licence, Amy, *Anne Neville: Richard III's Tragic Queen* (Amberley, 2013)

Licence, Amy, *Elizabeth of York: The Forgotten Tudor Queen* (Amberley, 2013)

MacGibbon, David, *Elizabeth Woodville: A Life* (Amberley, 2013)

Mancini, Dominic, *The Usurpation of Richard III*, ed. C. A. J. Armstrong, (Oxford, 1969)

Marius, Richard, 'The History of King Richard III' in *Thomas More* (New York: Knopf, 1984)

Markham, Sir Clements, *Richard III: His Life & Character Reviewed in the Light of Recent Research* (1906)

Miller, Michael D., *Wars of the Roses: An Analysis of the Causes of the Wars and the Course Which They Took* (Online: http://warsoftheroses.co.uk, 2003)

More, Thomas, *History of King Richard III*, ed. R. Sylvester (New Haven, Conn., 1963)

Norton, Elizabeth, *Margaret Beaufort: Mother of the Tudor Dynasty* (Amberley, 2011)

Okerlund, Arlene, *Elizabeth Wydeville: The Slandered Queen* (Stroud, 2005)

Penn, Thomas, *The Winter King* (Penguin, 2012)

Pollard, Anthony J., *Richard III and the Princes in the Tower* (New York: St Martin's Press, 1991)

Potter, Jeremy, *Good King Richard? An Account of Richard III and his Reputation* (Bury St Edmunds, 1998)

Richards, W. Leslie (ed.), *Gwaith Dafydd Llwyd o Fathafarn* (Gwasg Prifysgol Cymru, 1964)

Richmond, Colin, '1485 and All That, or What Was Really Going on at the Battle of Bosworth' in Hammond (ed.), *Richard III: Loyalty, Lordship, and Law* (Michigan: Richard III and Yorkist History Trust, 1986)

Richmond Colin, *Richard III – A Medieval Kingship* (Collins & Brown, 1993)

Ross, Charles, *Edward IV* (Yale University Press, 1997)

Ross, Charles, *Richard III* (Eyre and Methuen, 1981)

Rous, John, *The Rous Roll* (Alan Sutton, 1980)

Rymer, Thomas, *Foedera Vol. 12* (London, 1704–13)

Scofield, C. L., *The Life and Reign of Edward the Fourth* (Routledge, 2005)

Seward, Desmond, *A Brief History of The Wars of the Roses* (Robinson, 2007)

Seward, Desmond, *Richard III: England's Black Legend* (New York: Franklin Watts, 1984)

Seward, Desmond, *The Last White Rose: Dynasty, Rebellion and Treason – The Secret Wars Against the Tudors* (Constable, 2010)

Skidmore, Chris, *Bosworth, The Birth of the Tudors* (W&N, 2013)

Thomas, Roger S. and Ralph A. Griffiths, *The Making of the Tudor Dynasty* (The History Press, 2002)

Tudor-Craig, Pamela, *Richard III* (The Boydell Press, 1977)

Vergil, Polydore, *Anglica Historia* (London: J. B. Nichols, 1846)

Walpole, Horace, *Historic Doubts on the Life and Reign of Richard III*, ed. P. W. Hammond (1768; Gloucester, 1987)

Weir, Alison, *Lancaster and York: The Wars of the Roses* (Vintage, 2009)

Weir, Alison, *The Princes in the Tower* (Vintage, 2008)

Wilkinson, Josephine, *Richard: The Young King To Be* (Amberley, 2009)

Williamson, Audrey, *The Mystery of the Princes* (Alan Sutton, 1978)

Wood, C. T., 'Richard III, William, Lord Hastings and Friday the Thirteenth' in Griffiths, R. A. and J. Sherborne (eds), *Kings and Nobles in the Later Middle Ages* (Gloucester, 1986)

Wroe, Ann, *Perkin: A Story of Deception* (Vintage, 2004)

List of Illustrations

his accomplices, which assassination was ordered by the Duke of Gloucester, their Uncle afterwards Richard III.' (From Barnard's *New, Comprehensive, and Complete History of England*, 1783). Author's collection.

14. The White Tower. This late fifteenth-century manuscript illumination shows the Tower of London much as it would have looked in 1483. Courtesy of Jonathan Reeve JR992b4p640 14501550.

15. The north-west tower staircase. Courtesy of Stephen Porter.

16. Edward V (1470–1483). Courtesy of David Baldwin.

17. Elizabeth Woodville, mother of the Princes in the Tower and Richard III's sister-in-law. Courtesy of the Amberley Archive.

18. *The Princes in the Tower* (1832) by J. E. Millais. Courtesy of Jonathan Reeve JR1588b61p620 14501500.

19. Richard III carved in a misericord as a hunchback. Courtesy of Jonathan Reeve JR1559folio5p640 14501500.

20. On 12 October 1483 Richard wrote to the Chancellor, John Russell, ordering him to bring the Great Seal to him at Grantham. The postscript referring to 'the malice of him that had best cause to be true, the Duke of Buckingham, the most untrue creature living' is in his own hand. Courtesy of Jonathan Reeve JR1572b13p721 14501500.

21. Middleham Castle, Richard III's principal residence in the North. Courtesy of David Baldwin.

22. Skull of Richard III. Courtesy of University of Leicester.

About the Author

Terry Breverton is a former businessman, consultant and academic and now a full-time writer. He has presented documentaries on the Discovery Channel and the History Channel. Terry is the author of *Jasper Tudor: Dynasty Maker, Everything You Ever Wanted to Know About the Tudors but Were Afraid to Ask, Owain Glyndwr: The Story of the Last Prince of Wales, Wales: A Historical Companion, The Welsh: The Biography, Wales' 1000 Best Heritage Sites* and *Breverton's First World War Curiosities*, all published by Amberley. He has also written *Immortal Words, Immortal Last Words, I Have a Dream, Breverton's Nautical Curiosities: A Book of the Sea, Breverton's Encyclopedia of Inventions, Breverton's Phantasmagoria* and *Breverton's Complete Herbal*, all published by Quercus. He lives near Maesycrugiau in Carmarthenshire.

Also available from Amberley Publishing

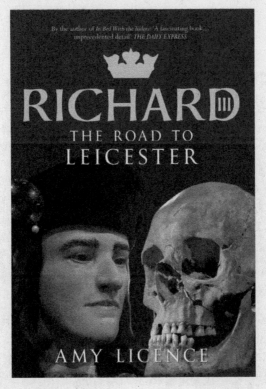

Following the dramatic announcement that Richard III's body had been discovered, past controversies have been matched by fresh disputes. Why is Richard III England's most controversial king? The question of his reburial has provoked national debate and protest, taking levels of interest in the medieval king to an unprecedented level. While Richard's life remains able to polarise opinion, the truth probably lies somewhere between the maligned saint and the evil hunchback stereotypes. Why did he seize the throne? Did he murder the Princes in the Tower? Why have the location and details of his reburial sparked a parliamentary debate? This book will act as both an introduction to his life and reign and a commemoration to tie in with his reburial.

£9.99 Paperback
75 illustrations
96 pages
978-1-4456-2175-3

Available from all good bookshops or to order direct
Please call **01453-847-800**
www.amberleybooks.com

Also available from Amberley Publishing

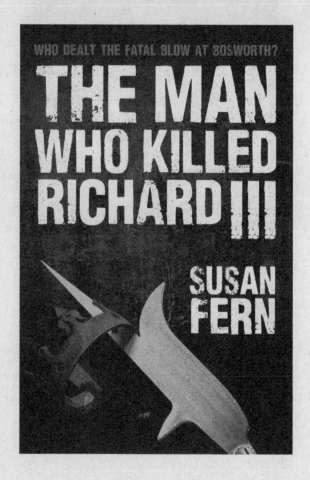

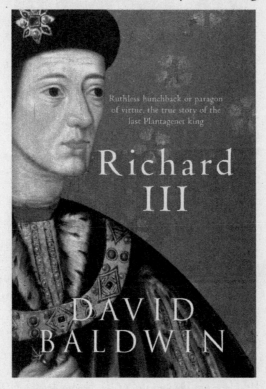

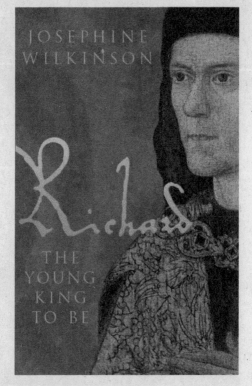